RUSSIAN IMPERIALISM

RUSSIAN IMPERIALISM

Development and Crisis

Ariel Cohen

Westport, Connecticut
London

Library of Congress Cataloging-in-Publication Data

Cohen, Ariel.
    Russian imperialism : development and crisis / Ariel Cohen.
        p.   cm.
    Includes bibliographical references and index.
    ISBN 0–275–95337–8 (alk. paper)
    1. Russia—Historiography   2. Soviet Union—Historiography.
    3. Former Soviet republics—Historiography.   4. Imperialisms.
    I.   Title.
    DK38.C64   1996
    947′.0072—dc20   95–43730

British Library Cataloguing in Publication Data is available.

Library of Congress Catalog Card Number: 95–43730
ISBN: 0–275–96481–7 (pbk.)

First published in 1996

Praeger Publishers, 88 Post Road West, Westport, CT 06881
An imprint of Greenwood Publishing Group, Inc.

Printed in the United States of America

The paper used in this book complies with the
Permanent Paper Standard issued by the National
Information Standards Organization (Z39.48–1984).

10 9 8 7 6 5 4 3 2 1

To Rena

Contents

Acknowledgments   ix

Introduction   xi

1. Definitions, Theories, and Methodology   1

2. Historical Development of the Russian Empire   29

3. The Soviet Empire: 1917-1985   67

4. *Perestroika* and the End of Empire   117

5. Conclusions   151

Selected Bibliography   169

Index   177

Acknowledgments

Many people contributed to this effort, both directly and indirectly. I would like to express my gratitude to Professor Richard Schultz, director of the International Security Studies Program at the Fletcher School of Law and Diplomacy, Professor Hannes Adomeit, also of Fletcher, and Professor G. Paul Holman of the Naval War College, whose encouragement and advice were so vital to the preparation and completion of this work. I will always be indebted to R. Eugene Parta, former director of the Media and Opinion Research office of Radio Free Europe-Radio Liberty, with whom I had the privilege of working for several years, and who consistently encouraged my involvement in Russian area studies. I am also grateful to Dan Eades, senior editor at Praeger Publishers, for having faith in this project. Some of the research conducted for this work would not have been possible without the help of friends in Russia who shall remain anonymous, but whom I would like to thank nonetheless. Finally, without the steadfast patience and help of my wife, Rena, this entire project might have remained only a dream.

Introduction

The collapse of the Soviet Union was one of the most dramatic events of this century. It was also one of the most important ones, not only for our time, but for the century to come. Yet despite the work of a battery of Sovietologists, Kremlin-watchers, and area experts, it was also one of the least expected analyzed developments of modern history.

When this work was first conceived in the spring of 1990, the question that seemed relevant was, "Is the Soviet Union going to collapse?" It was with this query in mind that the next one arose: "What kind of state is the Soviet Union?" Was it an empire, as its multinational character and the domination of non-Russians by the Russians suggested? How had its Bolshevik founders dealt with the fact that after 1917 they had come to rule the old Romanov empire, known as the "prison of peoples?" What could one learn by looking at other multiethnic empires and their development and decline? Finally, what historic linkages between the Soviet state and its Russian imperial predecessor were relevant to predicting the future of the Soviet Union?

While this book was in its early stages, it became clear that the Soviet Union was indeed collapsing. It was now a question of time frame and the extent of collateral damage, not whether the event would take place. However, many in the Sovietological profession "kept the faith" in the ability of the Communist party, the Central Committee, and Mikhail Sergeyevich Gorbachev personally to remain in power, even though their political capital in Moscow and elsewhere in the USSR had been wasted.

Most area specialists spent little time examining available comparative history or political science theories, hardly looked at the historical experience of the Romanov empire, and disregarded the surge toward independence in the union republics of the USSR, including Russia. Instead, the profession continued to debate the question of whether the Soviet Union would disintegrate right up until the failed coup of August 1991. This despite the fact that a close comparison with Ottoman Turkey, Austria-Hungary, and Romanov Russia would have disclosed that the USSR was at the end of its imperial life cycle.

The imperial nature of the former Soviet Union also has great implications today. Conflicts in the former USSR are the result of the collapse of a great empire, of the vanishing of state authority, and of an immense power vacuum in which old and new elites compete for control. Similar to the wars following the disappearance of the British and French colonial empires, the Ottoman Porte, and others, some conflicts in the former Soviet Union are "defrosted" ethnic animosities that were stringently suppressed by the Soviet regime. Others are struggles to control vital resources, such as oil, or strategic ports or coastlines.

Parts of the former Soviet Union, such as the North Caucasus, Transcaucasus, and Central Asia, can be seen as historically gravitating toward the Middle East and South Asia. They are located at the "great rift" between Islam and Christianity, in a friction zone between Europe and Asia. To see them as only parts of Russia, to expect a harmonious succession from the USSR to the Commonwealth of Independent States (CIS), or to anticipate that Moscow will install order in areas of local conflicts is naive at best.

Between 1985 and 1991, the USSR's leadership under Gorbachev embarked upon a broadening social and political reform and rethinking of its foreign and domestic policies. This attempt followed the Brezhnev years, characterized by malaise, corruption, increasingly costly involvement abroad, and ever-growing military spending. However, cutting the bonds of the Stalinist "command-administrative system" generated a failure of political power rarely seen in Russian history.

For an observer of empires, these phenomena indicated not just another case of Soviet reforms going awry, but rather a change of a different nature and proportions—a dissolution of the multiethnic Russian/Soviet empire which had been evolving since the fifteenth century. Only twice before, in the Time of Troubles (*smutnoe vremia*) of the early seventeenth century and in the period from 1917 to 1920, did Russia experience similar political turbulence. Both of these past upheavals were followed by a reconsolidation of central authority after a period of foreign intervention, internal strife, and civil war.

This book will demonstrate that a phenomenon of similar magnitude has occurred. The Russian/Soviet empire has collapsed. It is still too early to predict the geopolitical results of such a planetary political earthquake.

Under Gorbachev, the Soviet Union, in less than one year (1989), lost its informal imperial domination of Eastern Europe, as the communist regimes of East Germany, Poland, Hungary, Czechoslovakia, Bulgaria, and Rumania were swept out of power. In addition, for the first time since the creation of the USSR, the republics had an opportunity to secede from the union, and they duly proceeded to avail themselves of it.

This was an extremely rapid disengagement. The Soviet retreat was reminiscent of the collapse of the Ottoman, Romanov, and Habsburg empires in the aftermath of World War I, although the USSR did not suffer a comparable military disaster. Was this a revival of the liberation process that began in 1917 with the collapse of the House of Romanov, only to be forcibly reversed by Lenin and Stalin?

Was the quest for independence of these nations, and especially on the part of their elites, suppressed for awhile, but not eliminated from their national consciousness? Ukraine attempted independence in 1917–1918 and again during World War II. The Balts treasured the memory of their brief independence in the 1920s and 1930s. Even the short period of sovereignty of the Transcaucasian states in 1918-1921 appears to have contributed to the popular will to leave the Soviet Union.

Pre-1991 Sovietology often treated the USSR as a state characterized by unusual ethnic harmony. A number of questions needed to be asked. Did the structure of the regime after the Bolshevik revolution answer to the definitions of empire used in current political science literature? This structure was indeed created by a force emanating from an imperial center. It was built by a bureaucratic and military imperial elite. The system utilized the internal rifts and deprivations of the peripheral nationalities to enhance its own control mechanisms. As was the case with other empire builders, the Soviet leadership worked to further the geopolitical interests of the nascent Soviet state within the limitations of the international system of the time.

If the USSR *was* an empire, as posited here, how can analysis of the "life cycle" of empires (i.e., their development and decline, as these appear in modern political science literature) be applied to the Soviet experience? There were enough characteristics of a decaying empire, such as stagnating elites, falling living standards, and foreign policy fiascos, to suggest that this body politic was in agony. By 1990 there was no longer a consensus among the political elites of the USSR (as there was in 1917) to the effect that Russia must "keep the empire." If the termination of empire was only *one* of the political options being explored by Soviet politicians, scholars, and the informed public, what were the other options? Could the Soviet regime maintain the empire indefinitely? An analysis of previously secret Central Committee and Politburo materials (offered here in Chapter Four) indicates that while such an outcome seemed most desirable in the eyes of the Communist party leaders, it could not be accomplished in reality. An alternative scenario, confederation of some of the Soviet republics, was rendered infeasible by the August 1991 coup and the internal political developments that led to it.

The purpose of this book, therefore, will be to analyze the development of the Russian/Soviet empire and its decline during Gorbachev's regime, from both political science and comparative history perspectives. Eastern Europe will be outside the scope of this work.

In Chapter One an outline of the major theoretical frameworks for understanding imperial development and decline will be presented.

Chapters Two and Three will examine how Russia and the USSR developed as a classic, contiguous, multiethnic empire which underwent several stages (Muscovy, the Westernized empire of Peter the Great and his heirs, and Stalinist/post-Stalinist) before entering its systemic crisis under Gorbachev.

Chapter Four will concentrate on Gorbachev's Soviet Union as an empire in decay and will address the inability of the *nomenklatura* to deal effectively with the collapse of the state system. It will also examine the attitudes toward the question of empire among various segments of the Russian and non-Russian elites and the general population.

The conclusion will synthesize the approaches elaborated in Chapter One and will discuss their application to the Russian and Soviet cases. It will also focus on the centrifugal processes that led to the disintegration of the USSR as a multinational empire.

This book is intended for both area specialists and the interested general reader. Chapters Two and Three provide an overview of Russian and Soviet history that analysts of Russia and of the Newly Independent States (NIS) are no doubt largely familiar with, but which will be of greatest benefit to the student or lay reader. For area experts, Chapters One, Four, and Five will be most interesting.

The end of 1991 was a time of great hope. It seemed that the only rational alternative open to the USSR's leaders was the creation of several nation-states in its stead. Such a solution would have meant, for the first time in Russian history since the fifteenth century, the abandonment of attempts to become a "universal empire" or a "dominant state"—one that, in various ideological guises, incessantly strives for imperial control of a known political universe. Independence had been proclaimed by all members of the union. Thus, a new page in East-Central European, Central Asian, and world history appeared to have been opening, a page that would include the participation of Russia in a multipolar, more democratic, and hopefully more cooperative international political system. Unfortunately, post-1991 developments in Russia and the NIS have raised the specters of reemerging Russian imperialism and aggressive nationalism, which would bring with them immeasurable suffering for the peoples of Russia and the former empire.

It is hoped that an increased understanding of the historical and political processes addressed in this book on the part of Eurasian and Western policy makers will contribute to peace, stability, and prosperity in Russia, Ukraine and the former Soviet empire.

RUSSIAN IMPERIALISM

1

Definitions, Theories, and Methodology

DEFINITIONS

The word "empire" stems from the Latin *imperium* which means "command." This was the meaning of the word before it came to define the realm commanded.[1] Empire can be understood to be an age-old form of government between the subjects and the objects of political power, involving two or more national entities and territorial units in an unequal political relationship.

John Starchey defined empire as "any successful attempt to conquer and subjugate a people with the intention of ruling them for an indefinite period" with the accompanying purpose of exploitation.[2] Michael W. Doyle maintains that empires are "relationships of political control imposed by some political societies over the effective sovereignty of other political societies."[3] According to Maxime Rodinson, empires are "state units within which one ethnic group dominates others."[4]

B.J. Cohen writes that the word "imperialism," a highly emotionally charged term, first appeared in nineteenth century France to denote the ideas of partisans of the one-time Napoleonic empire, and later became a pejorative for the grandiose pretensions of Napoleon III. In the 1870s the word "imperialistic" was used in Britain by supporters and opponents of Prime Minister Benjamin Disraeli to denote the policy of British imperial expansion.[5]

It is ironic that in most cases neither the Soviet effort to sustain the Romanov realm nor the American expansion westward during the nineteenth century were labeled "imperialistic" but were rather seen as "nation-building."[6] Imperialism at the end of the nineteenth century denoted mostly the colonialism of maritime powers, from the Spanish and the Portuguese, to the British, the French and other Europeans, to the Japanese and Americans.[7]

While the definition of imperialism was hotly contested, there appears to be a consensus in most current political science, political economy, and comparative history literature that empires include more than formally annexed lands but do not necessarily encompass all forms of international inequality, despite the contrary views of surviving Marxist-Leninists and neo-Marxists.

METROCENTRIC APPROACHES

The first critics of imperialism came from two camps: the radical-liberals (John A. Hobson) and the Marxists (Rosa Luxemburg, Rudolf Hilferding, and primarily Vladimir Ilyich Lenin). Such authors as Christopher R.W. Nevinson, Henry N. Brailsford, and later John Starchey, Harold Laski, and Victor G. Kiernan, writing in the Marxist or socialist tradition, managed not only to dominate the debate but to define its basically anti-Western, anticapitalist terms. The main thrust of this critique concentrated on issues of financial penetration, domination of markets and sources of raw materials, and securing investment outlets.

Austrian political economist Joseph Schumpeter attacked imperialism from a different angle, criticizing the expansionist inclinations of military elites. For Hobson and Lenin, as well as for Schumpeter, empire *is* imperialism. It is a product of internal, metropolitan drives to external expansion. It is a *metropolitan disposition* toward satisfying the lust for profit of financiers (Hobson), the necessities of growth of monopoly capital (Lenin), or the objectless drive of militaristic elites (Schumpeter). Approaches that stem from these three schools rely heavily on an observation of metropolis (as opposed to periphery), arguing that imperialism is necessary to sustain industrialization or to solve the problem of domestic instability.[8]

Hobson was the first to treat imperialism as the disposition of metropolitan society to extend its rule. He was also the first to connect imperialism and capitalism, disregarding all available evidence that empires have existed based on slave and feudal social organization, and that presumably there could be empires under societal formations other than capitalism. Hobson portrayed British imperialism as the result of forces emanating from metropolitan Britain. Special interests, led by financiers, encouraged an expansionist foreign policy designed to promote the needs of capitalist investors for investment outlets. These interests succeeded in manipulating the metropolitan politics of parliamentary Britain through their influence over the press and educational institutions.[9]

Lenin, as well as Schumpeter, offered dispositional, metrocentric approaches to imperialism, although both differed from Hobson in a number of respects. Lenin defined modern imperialism as the monopoly stage of capitalism which, he argued, "converted this work of construction into an instrument for oppressing *a thousand million people* [in the colonies and semi-colonies], that is, more than half the population of the globe, which inhabits the subject countries, as well as the wage slaves of capitalism in the lands of civilization."[10]

Lenin's "territorial division of the world" broadened Hobson's concept of formal territorial annexation to include the exercise of controlling influence by economic means—one of the modes of so-called informal imperialism. For Lenin, imperialism was not only the product of high finance, it was capitalism in its final, monopolistic stage driven to search for overseas profits, raw materials, and markets. According to Lenin, the connection between capitalism and imperialism was neither marginal nor mistaken. It was vital to capitalism as a whole, and not amenable, as Hobson thought, to democratic reform. For Lenin, the concept of the export of capital was central to his theoretical construct.

In the international sphere, Lenin assumed that alliance building by the capitalist countries for the purpose of protecting their spheres of interest is motivated by financial considerations. The relative power of states in alliance change; the alliances are nothing but a truce in periods between wars.

Lenin ends with a total condemnation of capitalist imperialism, arguing that it is beyond repair. To the numerous "old" motives of colonial policy, finance capital has added the struggle for the sources of raw materials, for export of capital, for "spheres of influence," i.e., "spheres for profitable deals, concessions, monopolist profits and so on."[11]

One could argue that Lenin's polemic was directed against Kautsky and the Austrian social democrats rather than against the imperial powers of the time. History has proven the ability of capitalism (and social democracy) to reform itself and to improve the living standards of the working class. It has also proven the skills of Western governments in handling decolonization. Thus, Lenin's critique, especially in view of Western investment failures in the Third World in the 1960s and 1970s (Nigeria, Brazil, Peru, Mexico, etc.) and the reliance of developed countries on trade primarily between themselves, was rendered obsolete by the actual course of events.

Schumpeter, in striking opposition to Lenin, stated that pure capitalism and imperialism not only were unrelated, but were antithetical to each other. He defined imperialism as the objectless disposition of a state to unlimited forcible expansion (formal imperialism or territorial conquest). This phenomenon originated in atavistic, militaristic institutions, such as the "war machine" of ancient Egypt. Modern capitalism's only link to these aggressive forces of imperialism lay in the historical residue of the corruption of true capitalism by the war machines of the absolutist monarchies of seventeenth- and eighteenth-century Europe. When warped by the tariffs that mercantilistic considerations imposed on free market capitalism, it became "export monopolism"—an economic system such as that of turn-of-the-century Germany, which produced incentives for military conquest to expand closed national markets.[12]

Schumpeterian influence can be discerned in the writings of E.M. Winslow which, unlike those of the Marxists, distinguished between earlier liberal, philosophically radical, laissez-faire capitalism, pacifistic and anti-imperialist in nature, and latter-day militaristic imperialism.[13] Winslow concludes that war cannot be blamed on the existence of economic power.

The Schumpeterian, Marxist-Leninist, and Hobsonian approaches influenced numerous liberal and socialist writers who analyzed imperialism from the (metrocentric) perspective of national pride and honor, including the "aggressive altruism" of the "white man's burden," and the control of vital strategic areas, markets, and sources of raw materials.

Some contend that even after decolonization the basis of relations between former colonial powers and what became known as the Third World did not change: "Westerners do not now sit behind the desks in government offices, but everyone of importance there knows how to reach them. The territorial empires disappeared—but not the impulses that helped to build them and not the system of power and its relationships in which they played their part."[14]

A.P. Thornton defines imperialism as a product of the white man, American or Western European, although he occasionally mentions the imperialism of Japan, "accepted" by other great powers of the period, without elaborating on its non-Western character. He also mentions the necessity for cooperation of Europeanized local elites for the successful administration of colonies.[15]

Thornton's definition of the phenomenon is a narrow one; he notes, for instance, that communists do not see themselves as empire builders. But he does concede that in 1920

the dreaded Bolsheviks in the same year were busy with the policy of destroying the ambitions and the resistance of all the peoples of Russia who were not and never had been Russian. To the men with their eyes on the correct shape of the future, empire, direct rule, and modernity were all aspects of the same issue. Devolution of power was mere weakness, not to be thought of, traitorous even to consider.[16]

Neo-Marxist analysis of imperialism was popular especially after World War II, when decolonization was under way and traditional political control was disappearing. It seemed to some that the end of colonial empires meant the end of capitalism. History itself seemed to have vindicated Lenin. As one writer commented, "Economic imperialism is a political rather than an historical label: and political polemicists know what they want to say long before they find evidence to support it."[17]

A rebuttal to the economic (Marxist) interpretation of imperialism was put forward by W.W. Rostow, who maintained that imperialist expansion is in principle of only marginal importance to the development of modern industrial societies and that the principal elements responsible for the development of imperialism are noncapitalist. He pointed out that parallel to the decline of Western imperialism, capitalism thrived in Western Europe, Japan, and the Americas.[18]

George Lichtheim offers an incisive analysis of imperialism devoid of the usual Marxist classifications. He traces the transition from nationalism to imperialism in the second half of the nineteenth century among the European ruling elites that abandoned any notion of national self-interest and democracy.

The theorists and practitioners of empire building saw the future in terms of economic clashes between *continental*, not national units. Even socialists became converted to the new creed after World War I. The Germans from the 1890s onward convinced themselves of the inevitable showdown with the Russians that came into being in 1914–1918 and again in 1941–1945.[19] Lichtheim shows how the doctrines of imperialism, initially the exclusive realm of royalty and courts, filtered through the middle classes all the way down.[20] This transformation allowed the ruling elites to harness imperialism in support of traditional institutions.

German historian Wolfgang J. Mommsen contends that "national enthusiasm and jingoism were certainly an important driving force" for imperialist ventures abroad.[21] David K. Fieldhouse cites "national hysteria" as the source, or breeding ground, first of imperialism and later, fascism.[22] Many writers argue that one of the primary weaknesses of the Marxist interpretation of imperialism is its identification of dependence with imperial control. Dependence can be identified as the constraint or unequal degree of influence that occurs as a result of the international division of labor. However, not all raw material producers suffer from dependency, at least not all the time. For example, members of the Organization of Petroleum Exporting Countries (OPEC), especially in the 1970s, did not suffer from either low income or impediments to social change emanating from the (former) metropole.

Metrocentric approaches, despite their limitation of monocausality, deserve our attention when studying the dispositions of the ruling elites of an empire. In the cases of Russia and later the USSR, attention should be paid to the justification of empire building and retention based on prevailing concepts of security and insecurity, as well as to the dominating ideologies and to the sense of religious mission and cultural superiority of the rulers, the bureaucratic "imperial mind," and the "war machine." Equally important will be the examination of the *economic* modus operandi of the empire toward the periphery.

To achieve these goals, this book will examine, among other questions, whether we witnessed a change of attitude among the political elites of the former USSR to the question of imperial domination of the Russians over other nationalities during the late 1980s. Did the Soviet elite change its attitude toward the perceived need and cost of maintaining an empire. A change of attitude, if present, would indicate a transition from the mind-set of the imperialistic elite of a "dominant state" or a "universal empire" to that of a status quo state preoccupied, as are many others, with domestic politics and economics and with a foreign policy of compromise, balance of power, and multipolarity.

COMPARATIVE APPROACHES

The Creation of Imperial Order

A successful analysis of the imperial experience was undertaken by, among others, Robert Wesson. The cases he examined included ancient India, China, Egypt, the Inca empire, Persia, Rome, Byzantium, the Ottoman empire, and Russia.

The "universal empire" is a political world unto itself, a single and essentially contained entity, usually sprawling for thousands of square miles. It is a seemingly unchallengeable power, dominating its subjects and enhancing its masters. It rests upon conquest and can be established whenever geography permits such a state to be built and held together.

When an empire disintegrates, a new one may arise after a period of turmoil in the same geographical area. The quest for order is stronger than the quest for freedom.[23]

In building an empire, power outgrows its rational use and fails to be checked by contrary power, that is, it fails to be divided.[24] Empire building requires that the defeated in war are incorporated into the victors' political structure.[25]

As a rule, the empire-building states came from the peripheries of older civilizations. They were geographically close enough to learn the arts of war and administration, but far away enough not to fully share their values. Most often, they were bigger than the civilization centers that they subjected to their power. Such a state steps into local conflicts as an outsider with slogans of pacification, making it more acceptable for its future subjects to bow to the imperial *diktat*.

Such were the cases of the Macedonians and Romans conquering the feuding Greeks, and of the Ch'in unifying central China. Some would argue that even the United States in establishing its domination in Western Europe after World War II utilized such a Hobbesian slogan.[26] It is clear that some in postcommunist Russia might utilize the quest for peace in the "near abroad" in order to rebuild its realm.

Generally, according to Wesson, peripheral states were more warlike because of their contact with still less civilized peoples. "The will to dominion rises stronger in those who sense their own crudity but are confident of their strength. The outer state, less advanced in the ways of business and production, sees military power as the easiest way to riches."[27]

The ideology of the universal empire is as a rule amoral and well suited to ruthless leaders. Makers of empire, espousing at once untempered violence and peaceful order, have no use for internationalist dreams or balance-of-power politics and would put an end to both by conquest.[28]

However, from the point of view of a government's self-preservation, the best army is the one that is pacific, with a military of low status and a society that is demilitarized. After years of imperial glory, "creeping conservatism and lethargy want only calm. Despite the wish to remove examples of independence and freedom from the borders, they may shrink, in a growing lassitude, from acquiring new territories and responsibilities."[29]

Universal empires more often than not become isolationist, building a semblance of the Great Wall of China (or the Iron or Bamboo curtain) around themselves. Even nonpolitical trade is potentially subversive. Little trade was conducted by Rome outside the empire, and the frontiers of Egypt were closed, except for persons with special permits. Muscovy strictly controlled the movement of foreigners and travel of her subjects abroad. In the days of Ivan IV (the Terrible) foreign merchants were admitted only to border towns, and those who came to Moscow were restricted, from the mid-seventeenth century, to a special quarter *(Nemetskaya Sloboda)*.[30] The USSR under Stalin, Khrushchev, and Brezhnev allowed a much lower level of economic intercourse and exchanges even with the countries of the socialist bloc than anything acceptable in the West.

Empires borrow from each other the arts and techniques of political domination as easily as they borrow weapons and the techniques of warfare. The empire itself is an artifact to be copied, and the imperial idea is tremendously attractive to the power seeker.[31]

The political evolution of universal empires usually is attempted in one direction—elevation of the autocrat. All Soviet leaders, however debilitated (Brezhnev) or murderous (Stalin), were depicted by their propagandists as pivotal to the state.   In this vein, Gorbachev, too, attempted to cast himself as unexpendable—and he succeeded, at least for awhile, as far as the Moscow intelligentsia and the Western political elites were concerned.[32]

It is usually the *founders* of empires who are in most effective control; but after the apparatus is set up, it acquires momentum and a purpose of its own. Their successors are more often carried by the apparatus than able to control it. Moreover, those who choose emperors are likely to elect those whom they consider to be docile nonentities. As a result, the emperor is often part and parcel of a huge machine.[33]

The military is usually a force which the holder of absolute power both depends upon and fears. The role of the Praetorian Guard and of the Janissaries in the making and breaking of emperors is well known. Armies have often forced the removal of disagreeable ministers and determined outcomes in palace coups. The Soviet General Staff, for example, was involved in the execution of Beria, the support of Khrushchev against the Politburo in 1956, and his removal in 1964. Marshals and generals were pivotal in the resignation of Edward Shevardnadze, the dismissal of Interior Minister Vladimir Bakatin in December 1990, and the failed coup of August 1991.[34] The role of the military in Boris Yeltsin's dispersal of the Supreme Soviet in September-October 1993 is worthy of a separate study. However, while the Soviet military played an important political role as the empire grew weaker, it has limited itself, as other military machines in other empires, to *taking* or *giving* power, rather than exercising it.[35]

Unlike the army, the bureaucracy, as long as it presents a united front, is more effective in staying the course of the government rather then raising or casting away rulers. The chief means of exercising power over the bureaucracy for the sovereign is to divide it so that he can better exercise his role of supreme judge.

The leader is dependent on the security apparatus for personal protection, and fear of a coup or assassination breeds "precautionary terror" which in turn brings about fear and isolation of the instigator. The emperor comes to rely on informers and elimination by suspicion—hardly a sure way to win friends and influence subordinates. The scores of Roman, Persian, Byzantine, and Ottoman rulers poisoned, stabbed, and strangled by their intimates prove the case in point.

Stalin's terror is a classic example of such a tendency. First, he exterminated his colleagues. Next, he proceeded to eliminate his subordinates. And to this day, the circumstances of his own death remain unclear. It is open to question whether Beria, Malenkov, and Molotov eliminated their master when they became possible candidates for execution.

With ruler, bureaucracy, and coterie representing an imperial system of checks and balances, very little is usually known by the outside world as to the real locus of power. Stalin elevated favorites such as Kirov, Yezhov, and Zhdanov only to discard or execute them later, as did Tiberius, Constantine, Selim I of the Sublime Porte, and Ivan IV. But the very irregularity and lack of orderly structure necessitates the need for a final arbiter between the competing cliques and factions. An imperial system requires an arbitrary ruler almost automatically.

Russia lacked an orderly and representative political structure and separation of powers. Based on a geographical and political history spanning 800 years, Russian empire and the Soviet Union developed an imperial power structure with all the drawbacks described above.

The use and abuse of force, while almost certain to occur while an empire is built, are not sufficient in the long run to hold it together. As Wesson writes, "If empire can be made by force, it cannot be governed by force alone, not even by repression of dissent, control of information, and propaganda. To remain strong it must appeal by virtue of the blessings it confers."[36]

Many empires have tried to obtain these "blessings" by building extensive road networks, pyramids, monuments, and temples. The USSR attempted to achieve its glory through monumental architecture, primarily in Moscow (in the style known as pseudo-classicism), colossal projects (including giant canals, typical of imperial China and Mesopotamia), and breakthroughs in the area of science and technology (the H-bomb, Sputnik). The USSR also was anxious to bolster its image through sports and culture.

Throughout history, empires have justified the use of force in the name of establishing universal peace and creating a new society that will forever eliminate the scourge of war. The "struggle for peace" (*bor'ba za mir*) was a universal topic of Soviet propaganda, with serious attention given to the promotion and leadership of the international peace movement and Soviet front organizations advocating causes advantageous to the USSR.[37] The slogan "better Red than dead," which seemed appealing in its simplicity, was useful to the USSR in the years of its imperial ascendancy.

Empires are distinctly leveling societies, with the ethnic and social origins of their servants often deemed insignificant, as long as they serve the supreme ruler. In imperial Rome, in the Mogul empire and at times in tsarist Russia, ethnic origin was not an overwhelming consideration for a successful career. In the Soviet Union, Russians (Lenin, Bukharin, Molotov, Zhdanov, and Gorbachev), Georgians (Stalin, Ordzhonikidze, and Beria), Armenians (Mikoyan), and Jews (Trotsky and Kaganovich) were equally dedicated to the empire. It was during the decline of the last decades that the Politburo and the Central Committee of the Communist Party of the Soviet Union (CPSU), as well as top positions in the Central Committee (CC) apparatus, the General Staff, and the Committee on State Security (Komitet Gosudarstvennoi Bezopasnosti, or KGB) became almost exclusively staffed by Great Russians, with the implicit exclusion of members of other nationalities from the national body politic and the pinnacle of political power.

Empires require that the population, and especially (multiethnic) elites, acquire adequate knowledge of the imperial lingua franca and common culture. The Chinese, the Persians, the Inca, the Ottomans, and the Russians utilized their respective languages, religion, and service in the military and the bureaucracy to mold the "new imperial man."

Similarly to ethnicity, humble social origins were not an impediment to the successful career of many a servant: imperial China, Ottoman Turkey (where Janissaries rose to be viziers), and tsarist Russia, with a great number of its generals being grandsons of serfs, prove the point. In the USSR, the humble origins of general secretaries, beginning with Stalin, are no secret.

Empires, as a rule, cast themselves as egalitarian, with the broad masses indoctrinated to prefer equality (more imagined than real) over freedom. As Wang An-shih, the great Chinese reformer of the Sung dynasty stated, "the state should enforce obedience by wise and inflexible laws. In order to prevent oppression of man by man, the state should take possession of all resources of the empire and become the sole master and employer."[38] Universal empires often assume equality in submission. And in hierarchical organizations equality quickly becomes ephemeral, as the old inequality of wealth is replaced by the new, more arbitrary one of power.

Universal empires are fearful of and inimical to any and all organizations that are or might one day become a channel of independent political expression. Absolute rulers from Trajan to Richelieu were suspicious of innocuous professional guilds, fire brigades, and reading clubs. In imperial Rome only burial societies were free for all to join. In decaying Ch'ing China (1810), any gathering of more than five people was proclaimed seditious. The concern of political monopolists is that any group of people not under government control will become a political association before long, and that economic power will be translated into political power. The Stalinist USSR took this principle one step further, not only banning, but also arresting and killing the members of such "threatening" associations as philatelist and Esperanto clubs, hunger relief leagues, and charitable societies.

Empires that improved their road and communications infrastructures almost never used them for the purpose of private business. Roads, postal, and courier services were employed almost exclusively for the business of ruling, whereas communications and the freedom of movement of citizens were severely curtailed.[39]

Internal passports were the invention of great empires; and in the ancient Indian Maurya empire they were required for internal travel. They were necessary in Russia for in-state travel and registration with the police from the days of Peter I until Gorbachev. Although able to maintain a network of military communications and reconnaissance satellites similar to that of the United States, the Soviet government was unwilling to allow its citizens to communicate freely with the West.[40] The USSR was a superpower with a civilian communications infrastructure comparable to that of Burma.

Empires forcibly relocate their subjects for political reasons, to preempt opposition, to punish rebellions, and to weaken real or potential enemies. The Accadians, Assyrians, Persians, and Ottomans often displaced (and in the process decimated) scores of peoples. The Romans used individual and mass exile as a common form of punishment, and so did Muscovy, starting with the fifteenth century "punishment" of the free city of Novgorod. Stalin's USSR performed similarly in the cases of the Crimean Tatars, Volga Germans, Chechens, and others. Many empires took regional chiefs or governors' families hostage to indoctrinate and ensure compliance. Stalin often jailed or executed the families of "counter-revolutionaries" (KRs). Thus, limitations on freedom of movement, the punishment of family members of real or imagined opponents, and even of entire ethnic groups were as widespread as the imperial form of government itself.

Universal empires that appeared in both hemispheres in different historical periods have a great number of characteristics in common. One phenomenon is the prevalence of institutionalized informers and the preponderance of internal surveillance and espionage.

Empires, including rulers personally, engage in control of literature and the arts, as well as the rewriting of history. The burning of prerevolutionary philosophic and religious writings in communist Russia is an illustration of this principle. Almost universally, these are highly ideologized societies with a flourishing censorship.

Imperial order is sometimes the antithesis of the rule of law—the autocrat stands above and beyond the law, which has to be adjusted to the supreme will (and whim), becoming, like the Russian tsars, holy ex officio. Thus, when temporal power and religion become closely intertwined, the church (ideology) suffers a decline together with the ruling apparatus and sometimes shares the fate of the state.

Empires come to overwhelm their citizens by the sheer size and mass of their organization. Many lose their hope of changing life for the better because the empire seems so enormous and the task so gigantic. There seems to be no other means of personal fulfillment or improvement toward the general good but through the state.[41]

The larger the state, and the more powerful, the more difficult is outside interference. Even when the real power is long since gone, as in the decaying Mogul and Chinese empires, the masses—but especially the bureaucracy—remain submissive and reverent. Any critique of the supreme authority is viewed as sedition, and most of the rulers, including the liberal Gorbachev (in the cases of the Valeria Novodvorskaya trial and the *Argumenty i fakti* magazine incident, for example)[42] express their belief that those who voice negative opinions of the supreme authority should be punished as criminals.

The beginning of Gorbachev's reforms, coming from above and supported by the liberal wing of the establishment, indicated that the imperial crisis had become clear to some at the top echelons of the Soviet hierarchy. A faction of the imperial elite was trying to preserve itself via reformist measures. However, as the process went out of control, a wave of popular participation and elite fragmentation destroyed the very state it had been trying to save.

Stagnation and Decline of Imperial Order

The time comes (rather quickly) when political power projection and diplomacy replace military conquest, whatever inclination to world domination universal empires may demonstrate. Even mighty Rome at its peak under Augustus accepted defeats by the Germanic tribes and the Parthians, reverting to appeasement of the barbarians. War requires active armies that represent a threat not only to external enemies but also to the domestic political authority.

Empires often boast cultural achievements, but these usually are a continuation of previous cultures. Rome subsumed the Greek culture; the communist Russians claimed prerevolutionary culture as their own. The development of technology was also stifled and eventually retrogressive; agricultural methods were not advanced. It seemed that time stood still in the Middle Eastern and Indian empires. Cities were built and rebuilt based on the same blueprints several times over. The Byzantine, Ottoman, Mogul, and Chinese empires showed outstanding resistance to change and innovation that could have affected their survival. Muscovy and even Peter's Russian empire resisted such "seditious" innovations as geometry, printing, and the theories of Copernicus and Galileo (in the eighteenth century), as well as changes in religious theory or practice.

Stalin rejected the "bourgeois pseudo-sciences" of genetics, cybernetics, the theory of relativity in physics, and even supersonic flight. Similarly to the stagnating Chinese empire, the Soviet Union, with no profit to motivate entrepreneurs or engineers, became a land of unapplied inventions. Soviet products, such as antiquated cars and drab clothing, became the laughingstock of Europe. The Soviet rejection of Western advanced economic and business methods enlarged the Soviet gap vis-à-vis the developed West and Newly Industrialized Countries (NICs).

Universal empires crush internal diversity and concentrate all authority, wealth, art, and education in the imperial capital to a tremendous degree. The *diktat* of the "center" in the USSR was a direct result of this development, epitomizing the concentration of all economic, political, and scientific levers of power in a Moscow-based, Kremlin-controlled apparatus.

Empires become smug, believing the finality of their self-proclaimed truths, the effects of their own propaganda.

The universal empire prefers autosuggestion to inquiry, policing to improvement. Such attitudes have again and again made the greatest polities into magnificent collective idiocies, unable to absorb even childishly obvious lessons most vitally needed for their own survival.[43]

The incapacity to examine and address its own ills is such that the empire has to borrow ideologies that might suit its needs from freer societies. Thus, the Chinese repeatedly imported foreign ideas, from Buddhism to Marxism, to address the ills of the (Confucian) state, while the Russians adopted a Western European brand of socialism.

Those who run empires rise by loyalty, usefulness, and the favor of superiors, "The official wants those below him to be cooperative and obedient rather than brilliant and creative, much less self-willed. If the subordinate would progress, he seeks to please by thinking in the same way as his superior; he should even be discreet in his achievements lest he annoy by showing up his betters."[44]

Empires, ever preoccupied with enhancing the finances of a perpetually growing state apparatus, impoverish themselves with growing taxation. This process becomes increasingly pronounced as they deteriorate. Taxation becomes a means of redistribution of wealth from producers to nonproducers. Forced labor appears as a usual practice, no matter how inefficient its results. The consequences are the abandonment of land and the desertion of villages, a phenomenon all too familiar to students of Soviet agriculture.

Exaction also leads to the deterioration of industry and commerce; moneys received are not returned to the productive sector but rather are channeled to support the court, the bureaucracy, and the army. As Nikolay Kluchevsky put it, "The state swells and the people shrink."[45] All empires begin with relatively low taxes and then proceed to increase them, sometimes up to twentyfold.

As the population becomes more impoverished and degraded, the ruling elite despises it more and more. Alexander Solzhenitsyn wrote that the more heartily they loved the people (*narod*), the more they hated the populace (*naseleniye*). The empire will keep the appearance of power and grandeur almost until its deathbed, and efforts will be made to support the apparatus of suppression until its eleventh hour—but the defenses crumble, and there is less and less money to pay the military. With Soviet Army officers and their families bitterly complaining about deteriorating living standards, and with conscription evasion at an all-time high, one definitely was led to wonder about the reliability of the Soviet Army as a tool for the defense of the existing order. In the end, "Revolt, unthinkable while the great empire was in health, becomes inevitable in its sickness. With or without invasion, the end of the grand order is at hand."[46] After the downfall of a dynasty and its replacement, the cycle repeats itself; in the case of China, it has happened over twenty times.

Succession is always a problem, as autocratic power lapses at the point of succession. The institution of elections does not play the role it usually does in democracies.

Empires also fail bureaucratically. The bureaucracy becomes extremely conservative and inflexible, and the criteria for promotion ensure that stagnation will reign supreme. Eventually, through overpopulation, corruption, and inflexibility, the apparatus paralyzes itself. The Russian imperial bureaucracy, and even more its communist counterpart, are two examples: "When power at the top is arbitrary, irregular and self-justified, the delegates of power cannot be impartial and self-restrained."[47] The officials, including those of tsarist, Soviet, or postcommunist Russia, often view their service as little more than a cornucopia of wealth, the surest way to personal enrichment in the shortest possible time. As abuses multiply, the sternest edicts are issued against them with no effects whatsoever.

Not that empires are incapable of rebounding: Egypt, Persia, Rome, many Chinese dynasties, all had an Indian summer during which demoralization nevertheless continued. Revival is usually an outcome of disorder. The system needs to be badly shaken in order to be resolidified. However, a reformer can be successful only in an area as large as he can personally oversee; and there is only so far a reformer can go against his own stratum.

As in the case of Peter the Great, a reformer may implement strong rule—but even intelligent reformers fail to alter the *basis* of the old order. Reformers tend to appear after an empire loses a war. This was the case with Russia both after the Crimean and Russo-Japanese wars, and the USSR after the failure in Afghanistan. But these reforms were abandoned by the authorities after they ran into too much bureaucratic resistance. They also turned out to be "too little too late." Ruling elites almost universally are struck by the impotence and inactivity facing the collapsing imperial house. It took a military catastrophe and the loss of imperial possessions for the Ottoman empire finally to transform itself into the Turkish nation-state. In the Soviet case, as in the case of the late Han, war proved to be unnecessary. The empire collapsed under its own weight. However, without a clear military defeat, the temptation to rebuild an empire is ever greater.

To conclude, the list of political characteristics common to the ancient (and not so ancient) universal empires—both in their development and decline—is quite extensive. Such common characteristics, almost all of which are applicable to the Soviet case, indicate that a contiguous empire existing as a closed political world is a type of state structure commonly reoccurring throughout history. The Soviet Union underwent a deep imperial crisis similar to other empires before it. Such disintegration brings with it either geopolitical breakdown and the eventual creation of new states in place of the old multinational entity, or imperial rebirth. "The empire lacks unifying principle. The great would-be universal order turns into disorder, and union brings disunion."[48]

Geopolitics as Imperial Raison d'Etat

A comparative investigation of several empires prompted Geoffrey Parker to formulate his concept of the geopolitical mode of dominance. This British scholar analyzed the growth and decline of imperial Spain, Austria, France, and Germany, as well as the Ottoman empire. His model, among others, is applicable to Russian/Soviet imperial development, and, in fact, Russia underwent expansion and consolidation in ways that fit Parker's theory.

According to Parker, the initial geopolitical characteristics of the state bidding for regional or "ecumenal"[49] domination is that its original core area is located at the junction between the territory of its parent culture and that of a different, usually alien culture. These were the cases of Castile and Austria, situated on the border between Christendom and Islam; the Ottoman Empire, between Islam and Byzantium; and Germany, between the Holy Roman Empire and the Slavs.

These states usually are founded at the periphery of a parent culture for the dual purpose of providing a basis for protection and further territorial expansion. They then expand into the territory of an alien culture.[50]

The expansion of the historic core is followed by the formation of a nation with a high level of linguistic and cultural homogeneity. This nation occupies both the core and conquered territories, and homogeneity between the two sections is reinforced both by migration of the population from the old metropolis into newly acquired territories, and by the centralizing policies of the state. This results in concentration on the pivotal role of the imperial (core) nation and its world view. A dominant empire would be heavily ideological and would try to impose its ideology in the ecumene it is attempting to conquer.

After the initial consolidation, expansion into contiguous lowlands and/or maritime expansion takes place. This expansion in many cases continues until "natural frontiers" of some kind are achieved, after which the empire stabilizes for a long time and proves to be quite durable.[51]

As the diverse population of the newly acquired ecumene may not "convert" automatically to the new creed, uniformity must be imposed by the central government with a great degree of coercion. The uniformity of the internal political structure is designed to make the parts fit more readily into the wider whole. The parts are then grouped around the core nation, which remains central to the working of the system. The world-view of the dominant nation becomes increasingly dogmatic. The process is completed when state and cultural uniformity finally triumph. This, then, constitutes the geopolitical "substance" of the dominant state.[52]

Retreat from Dominance

Dominant states are an intimidating political phenomenon to their own citizens and to those smaller nation-states which have the misfortune to exist in the same ecumene with the empire. But even dominant states eventually dissolve, to be replaced by new ones. The process of dissolution is programmed into the blueprint of the dominant state. The actual scenario of the end of the period of domination of a particular state involves the buildup of a countervailing power, usually in the form of a coalition of states, which challenges and defeats the dominant state.

Parker emphasizes the *geopolitics* of decline. Similar to the rise, the decline results from the change in geopolitical factors—this time an adverse change. The processes of expansion eventually take the dominant state into an unfamiliar and hostile physical environment. This was the nature of the defeat of the Ottomans and the Austrians in the Balkans, the Spaniards in the seas of Northern Europe, and the French and Germans in the frozen Russian steppes. The dominant powers were confronted with physical conditions with which they were unable to cope; native populations that were accustomed to the local environment had an easier time resisting their foreign invaders. Dominant states often expend vast resources trying to defeat a faraway nation and refuse to face the reality of overextension.

As the going gets rough, the rulers of the dominant states increase the centralization of control and attempt to render the population more homogeneous. Elements of the population considered subversive and dangerous to the cohesion of the state—Moors, Jews, Protestants, aristocrats, Armenians—are removed, expelled, or discriminated against. The results of such actions are inevitably the opposite of what was intended—repression leads to widespread dissatisfaction and to resistance to the ruling elite.

Another characteristic of decline is the state's failure to win the final bid for domination or to hold onto its vanishing position of supremacy. As a rule, a combination of opposing powers and internal weakness prove to be overwhelming for the declining empire:

As the outlying parts of empire then begin to break away, a resurgence of nationalism takes place within the core nation itself. There is a nostalgic turning away from the declining empire towards the nation's heroic and semi-mythical past. In both the Ottoman and the Austro-Hungarian empires strong Turkish and German-Austrian nationalism emerged during the period of advanced decline. The most important overall effect of these changes is to undermine the degree of unity which was created during the period of ascendancy. They exacerbate the central geopolitical problem of dominance and the ultimate source of its weakness—the seemingly endless appetite for territory.[53]

One can only admire the accuracy of this description of the upset equilibrium that dissolved and destroyed the USSR.

PERICENTRIC VIEWS

The Pericentrism of Gallagher and Robinson

As a reaction to the prevailing views of the metrocentrists, British historian John A. Gallagher, along with a number of pupils and collaborators (including Ronald Robinson and Anil Seal) developed a theory of imperialism that is concerned primarily with events in the imperial periphery. The first step in this direction was Gallagher and Robinson's "The Imperialism of Free Trade."[54]

Prior to their theories, empire had been analyzed as if rulers had no subjects and as if Europe's pursuit of profit and power was carried out in a world in which external forces did not exist.[55] Therefore the scope of research had to be shifted from the metropole to the colonies, and beyond, to what came to be known as the "informal empire of influence." Local circumstances in colonial societies, whether successful collaboration or crisis-ridden resistance, were the previously neglected factors Gallagher and Robinson excelled in examining.[56]

Gallagher and Robinson defined expansion as a set of "unequal bargains" between metropolitan agents, sometimes with little support from the center, and their indigenous allies and opponents, who are primarily concerned with defending or improving their positions inside their own societies. Such a view made it impossible to regard imperialism as a unified process. Gallagher and Robinson also developed such important tools as analysis of the "official mind," local crises, and protonationalism.

Eventually, especially in his examination of British behavior in India, Gallagher turned to provincial and local studies, from which he concluded that "what looked like the national movement of a people struggling rightfully and unitedly to be free appeared more like a ramshackle coalition, its power throughout its long career as hollow as that of the imperial authority it was supposedly challenging."[57]

Gallagher eventually synthesized from his studies an overall view of empire as a composite entity guided by national interests:

The Imperial Grand Master played simultaneous chess games on innumerable boards, running into stalemates on many of them. Since many of the factors inside the empires were interdependent, it was an integrated game and had to be studied as such. It was a question of examining the interactions between the expansive propensities of advanced states and the local circumstances in the regions into which they were expanding.

Since these regions contained people riddled and etiolated by internal rivalries, Europe was able to profit from their divisions. Hence the importance of the notion of collaboration.[58]

The paradigm of imperial domination was developed from "informal control if possible, formal rule if necessary" to "indirect rule if necessary, direct rule only if unavoidable." Mommsen further adapted this formula to the decolonization period (after World War II), when the international system ceased to tolerate military interventions by imperial powers: "informal control whenever possible, while formal control no longer applies."[59]

Imperial structures suppressed religious, interethnic, and tribal conflicts, which then exploded after independence was granted or with the creation of new nation-states (India and Pakistan; Israel and the Arabs; African tribal conflicts). One can easily apply this model to the interethnic strife in the former Soviet republics and within Russia, long suppressed under the thumb of the imperial system. These conflicts began to explode as soon as the system started unraveling.

Mommsen focuses on the legacy of dislocation of economic development which creates a forced linkage between the economies of the peripheries and that of the metropole. This can take the form of forced growth of agricultural monoculture (cotton in Egypt and Uzbekistan) or overdevelopment of certain types of extracting or heavy industries, often of a character conflicting with the overall direction of development of the periphery.[60] The concept of "establishment of economic bridgeheads" by the metropolis in the periphery can be applied to the Soviet case. Industrial plants and combines were run extraterritorially in the republics by the union ministries, not only bonding the republics to Russia, but also employing a "colonist" workforce that established a permanent colonizing presence in the republics, such as heavy and chemical industry in the Baltics and extracting industries in Central Asia.

Another contribution of the pericentric approach to the study of empires is the concept of the "turbulent frontier" developed by John S. Galbraith. He argues that local conflicts with indigenous populations on the periphery constantly give rise to an extension of territorial control on the grounds of restoring law and order. The borders of colonial territories are generally not clearly defined, and chronic instability thus leads to the further extension of imperial rule. The home governments often view these developments with great anxiety or even extreme displeasure, but they are generally unable to curb the subimperialism on the periphery and in the end nearly always have to sanction the results.[61] The recent examples of Trans-Dniester, Tajikistan, Chechnya, and a turbulent frontier developing in the Crimea, eastern Ukraine and northern Kazakhstan indicate the importance of these phenomena for the postimperial period.

Empire and Emancipation

In an attempt to combine the analyses of the metropolitan dispositions and the processes in the peripheries (such as twentieth-century decolonization), the Dutch scholar Jan P. Nederveen Pieterse offers an incisive dialectic analysis of these phenomena while rejecting orthodox Marxism.

Marxists put the blame for imperialist wars on the vicissitudes of monopoly capitalism and threats to bourgeois hegemony, while, according to Nederveen Pieterse, it was the crisis of *aristocracy*, of aristocratic order, that set the stage for World War I. The European nobility was deeply involved in obtaining infusions of new wealth, career opportunities, and military glory from the empire. In contrast to the Marxists, Pieterse claims that

War and "the bloodstained fetish of Empire" are not simply expressions of economic dynamics, they are primarily political phenomena, a manifestation of political will. Economic theories of imperialism, while elucidating many pertinent dynamics, at the same time conceal the political logic in the course of affairs. By focusing on economic interests they fail to examine political interests. Thus they fail to address the question of power, which lies with the "will to power," especially with the will to power of strata who feel insecure in their status. By failing to see power clearly in the past, this perspective clouds the future.[62]

Marxist views on ethnicity and race share the same weakness as Marxist views on nationalism: Essentially, they are class reductionism, what Tom Nairn called "Marxism's great historical failure."[63] Without adequate theories of nationalism and race there is no hope for an adequate explanation of empire and emancipation. Yet an empire can be defined as an *ethnic status hierarchy* and analyzed in terms of the politics of race.[64]

Nederveen Pieterse sympathetically views the work of W.F. Wertheim.[65] In an empire dominated by the metropolitan, ruling set of values, "beneath the dominant theme there always exist different sets of values, which are, to a certain degree, adhered to among certain social groups and which function as a kind of counterpoint to the leading melody."[66] Social evolution is a two-way process, propelled and nourished not only from above, but also from below. The emancipation theory—in contrast to "dialectic materialism"—attaches great importance to ideas in history.

Wertheim is a "probabilist" who rejects the concept of history "programmed" by class struggle to inevitable outcomes. One easily perceives how these concepts are applicable to an analysis of the emancipation processes in the Soviet Union and Eastern Europe, where a two-way affair of reforms from the top and the push of popular initiatives (emancipation) from below resulted in the disintegration of the biggest contiguous empire of our time.

Nederveen Pieterse dedicates a great deal of attention to two patterns of imperial behavior: "divide and conquer" and "divide and rule." He documents how the British deployed oppressed nationalities (for example, Irish in India, Gurkhas in New Zealand) to capture new realms, similar to the ethnic Russian officer corps posted from Poland to Kirghizstan.

Sometimes colonial generals boost their careers in the capital: from the Roman empire, where power fell into the hands of the provincial military commanders, to Francisco Franco, who brought his Moroccan troops to Madrid in the Spanish civil war.[67] Similarly, General Boris Gromov, who commanded the troops dealing with the preservation of the Soviet empire abroad (in Afghanistan), was put in charge of the Interior Ministry troops that attempted to deal with the preservation of the Soviet empire at home. The hard-line General Albert Makashov was an Afghan war veteran who commanded the Volga military district during the August 1991 coup. He might have been far more dangerous if he had been near Moscow. In 1993, Makashov was Alexander Rutskoi's "defense minister." Another Afghan war hero, Alexander Lebed, was put in charge of pacifying Azerbaijan, Georgia and the Trans-Dniester region. Lebed became a presidential candidate in 1996.

"Social imperialism" is defined as an attempt to delay emancipation at home by means of expansion abroad. Slogans such as *La Grande Nation* in France and *Machtpolitik, Weltpolitik,* and *Lebensraum* in Germany exemplify demographic and political considerations leading to imperialist expansion. One might add to this group of powers Russia and the Soviet Union, whose leadership, from Count Witte to Stalin and Brezhnev, pursued expansion as a result of a combination of foreign policy, economic, and political (antidemocratic) considerations. The ideology of national grandeur permeates the minds of the decision makers and dissipates from the top down to the consciousness of the lowest classes.[68]

Why, then, do empires, so successful and intimidating, collapse after all? Imperial supremacy is temporary, because—among other things—the technology, economic organization, and politico-military structures upon which they are founded do not belong exclusively to them forever. They are only the managers and transmitters of these modes of collective competence, despite the fact that they claim their domination is ordained by nature, God, race, and destiny.

Oppression, as power, represents a level of collective competence, and forces of liberation have to match it to win.

Systems of domination survive by adjusting to the demands of emancipation movements: by mimicking emancipation, systems of domination attempt to forestall more fundamental change. Emancipation movements emulate the oppressor in order to subvert oppression. Together domination and emancipation, empire and liberation constitute a force field in which they increasingly interpenetrate one another, and in the course of backstage negotiation the actual process of humanization of social relations takes shape. Thus time and again we see today's emperor wearing the clothes of yesterday's emancipation. Naked, except for the clothes of yesterday's emancipation.[69]

One can see selective applications of this theory to the Russian and Soviet cases. The Bolsheviks, posing as a liberation movement, installed one of the most oppressive societies known in the twentieth century. As the Soviet empire unraveled, mass movements working for its destruction did indeed surpass mass mobilization of the Communist party and its morale. But at no point did they match it organizationally or militarily. The anti-imperial faction in Russia simply pulled over parts of the state machine to its side and neutralized the rest.

Historically, after some time, divide-and-rule and collaboration, which represent the logic of empire, start to unravel. "Mutinies and rebellions mark the moment where the logic of empire begins to yield to the logic of resistance. To understand this moment is as important as understanding the logic of the empire itself."[70] The USSR had its own imperialist system, Eastern Europe. And while Eastern Europe was the external and to a degree informal empire, the non-Russian territories of the union were the *internal* and *formal* empire. Emancipation culminated in Berlin, Prague, and Budapest in 1989, and in Moscow in August 1991. These were the watersheds that indicated the end of the Soviet empire.

SYSTEMIC THEORIES

Systemic Approach: Imperialism as a Power Game

Another attempt to create a theory of empires was undertaken by B.J. Cohen in the early 1970s. His approach to the study of empires goes back to the works of Baumgart and Ranke.[71] According to Cohen, "Imperialism refers to those particular relationships between inherently unequal nations which involve effective subjugation of some nations by others." Cohen stresses the operational character of the concept, in which inequality is the necessary condition, and active affirmation of superiority and inferiority is the logical condition of sufficiency. Other scholars wrote about the "relationship of domination and subjection" or the "image of dominance, of power asserted."[72]

There are two characteristics one has to be aware of in dealing with imperial relationships: One is the *form* of dominance and the other is the *forces* from which a particular relationship stems, and which maintain it. Cohen broadly considers imperialism to be *any relationship of effective domination or control, political or economic, direct or indirect, of one nation over another*. This definition is extremely broad. Therefore, one should examine the relationships of forms and forces. A goal in analysis should be to determine which forms are the most prevalent, which forces are the most potent, and what the connections really are.[73]

The paradigm explaining imperialism, according to Cohen, is "the good old game of power politics." Thus, international inequality has been actively affirmed by *stronger nations*, not by the economic needs of private business, as would be argued by Marxists. Many writers have pointed in this direction, with varying degrees of analysis, including W.H.B. Court, Hans Morgenthau, David Landes, and Raymond Aron.

The aspect of interruption of vital relations of a given state with other nations by an imperial power is considered by Cohen to be crucial to measuring the degree of dependence, economic as well as political, of the weaker nation. The more interruption one nation can impose upon another without significant retaliation, the stronger is its power position. Conversely, the more exposed a state is to the interruption of its vital relations, the more dependent it is upon others.[74] The Soviet sanctions against Lithuania in 1990 and 1991, which involved halting the supply of oil and electricity, are a vivid illustration of this point.

To follow this logic, a state should attempt to decrease its own dependence upon others and to increase others' dependence upon itself, which means to increase its dominance over others. In Cohen's words, *imperialistic behavior is a perfectly rational strategy of foreign policy*. It is a wholly legitimate and rational response to the uncertainty surrounding the survival of the nation. However, this behavior is contingent upon the availability of resources at the disposal of the nation's decision makers, as well as the resources at the disposal of competing powers. Thus power and influence become a result of a *relative* disequilibrium of resources.

Additionally, calculations of the costs and benefits of imperialism define the bottom line of imperialist behavior (or lack thereof). Therefore, world domination rarely figured as an operational goal of imperial powers, as the costs of such a policy would be exceedingly high. But where the costs are not too high, superiority over dependent nations will be actively affirmed.[75]

To sum up the position of the "power school," including, in addition to the above mentioned theorists, Robert Tucker, Lionel Robbins, and J. Viner, imperial domination has as its root *the anarchic organization of the international system of states*.[76]

Systemic Approach: the Four-Dimensional Model

One of the more successful attempts made to create a coherent theory of empires was undertaken by Michael W. Doyle. He stressed, inter alia, the similarity of domestic and international political elements in the complexity of empire. Imperial societies are similar to domestic ones because they have one sovereign—the imperial government. Parts of an empire resemble international order in their imperfect integration of social interaction and culture; in other words, in their lack of community. Empires are different from federations and confederations because of prevailing political inequality: one nation's government decides who commands another nation's political life.

Imperial control involves both political processes and political outcomes. To quote Machiavelli, "there are three ways of holding [conquered states]. The first is to despoil them, the second is to go live there in person [direct rule], the third is to allow them to live under their own laws, taking tribute of them, and creating within the country a government composed of a few who will keep it friendly to you [indirect rule]."[77]

As far as decision-making processes go, Doyle notes that "the formal control of the effective sovereignty of a subordinate society involves controlling its political decision-making, a complex process with many points of influence. The social, economic, and cultural environments of the metropole penetrate those of the periphery through metropolitan forces and actors—missionaries, merchants, soldiers, and bureaucrats."[78] Some decisions are made in the colonies, others in the metropole. After a decision has been taken, the colonial bureaucrats rally support for that decision and its implementation.[79]

Doyle suggests the application of "Patrick Henry's rule" and "Jefferson's rule" to characterize an empire. Patrick Henry's rule holds essentially that imperial tyranny often results in widespread political resistance; and that a successful response to peripheral resistance is a sign of effective imperialism.

To illustrate this point, it is enough to remember the Soviet suppression of the independence of Ukraine in 1918–1919, of the Transcaucasian republics in 1920, and of the Basmachi movement during the 1920s; the annexation and harsh handling of the Baltic republics before and after World War II; the suppression of the Hungarian revolution of 1956; the "Prague Spring" of 1968; and the Soviet support of repressive action against Solidarity in Poland in 1981. The weakness of response to peripheral challenge in the late 1980s indicated imperial decay and the approaching collapse of empire.

Jefferson's rule states that empire can be identified by a "long train of abuses" which testify to a design to render or keep one country subject to another. The goal of such a design is political, even if the means of such domination can be military, economic, or cultural.[80] Many Soviet republics at any time probably would have preferred the rule of the most offensive governor sent by the Court of St. James rather than the local NKVD commissar sent from Moscow.

A useful distinction made by Doyle is between imperialism and hegemony. Control of both foreign and domestic policies means effective imperialism, whereas control over foreign policy alone amounts to hegemony. The first to draw the distinction was Thucydides, noting that Sparta's allies exercised a significant amount of domestic autonomy—unlike the "imperialized allies" of Athens which were dictated to regarding both their foreign and domestic policies.[81]

The tools of implementing imperial control draw on both domestic and international power domains and range from persuasion, through bribes and coercion, to gunboat diplomacy and the direct application of force.

Combining all available resources of the metropole and peripheries, and using less than absolute force, the imperial power becomes more cost-effective than the power of a smaller nation-state.

In distinguishing between imperial control and dependency, Doyle points out the possibility of a mixed dependency/control situation, wherein economic domination is so strong, and attempts to withdraw would cause such severe economic dislocation, that they force a breakaway periphery to rejoin the imperial fold. One who read Gorbachev's diatribes against breakaway republics and followed the economic sanctions against Lithuania should wonder if this is the scenario the Soviet leaders had in mind. Furthermore, by witnessing the current economic hardships in the Caucasus and Ukraine one can easily see the economic factors working for reintegration of these areas into a future postSoviet Russian empire.

Empire, therefore, is "a relationship, formal or informal, in which one state controls the effective political sovereignty of another political society. It can be achieved by force, by political collaboration, by economic, social or cultural dependence. Imperialism is simply the process or policy of establishing or maintaining the empire."[82]

Systemic Approach: The Rise and Fall of Empires

Another quintessential systemic approach to the question of the rise and fall of empires was applied by Paul Kennedy in his popular *The Rise and Fall of the Great Powers*. Kennedy concerns himself with the interaction of economics and strategy, assuming that the major players in the international system are seeking to maximize and perpetuate their strength, security, and wealth. Kennedy argues that historically the ascendancy of one power and the collapse of another was usually the consequence of a prolonged military conflict. The rise of a great power was also a result of the more or less efficient utilization of a state's economic resources and industrial capacity prior to and during wartime. The long-term economic performance of states aspiring to dominant status therefore becomes extremely important.

> The relative strengths of the leading nations in world affairs never remain constant, principally because of the uneven rate of growth among different societies and of the technological and organizational breakthroughs which bring a greater advantage to one society than to another. The history of the rise and later fall of the leading countries in the Great Power system shows a very significant correlation *over the longer term* between productive and revenue-raising capacities on one hand and military strength on the other.[83]

It is the *relative* strength between the major players that is of paramount importance. Holland overtaken by England in the seventeenth and eighteenth centuries, France surpassed by Germany in the nineteenth, and England left behind by the USSR and the United States in the twentieth century are all good illustrations of this point. The relative wealth of the USSR in the late 1970s and early 1980s deteriorated compared with Japan, Western Europe, the United States, and even China.

When great powers perceive themselves to be in relative decline due to economic pressure, they tend to spend more on security, thus exacerbating the economic situation; and they are also inclined to cut investment, so that their long-term dilemma becomes more intractable.

There is evidence that relative economic strength and military power do not rise and fall in parallel, and that a lag exists between the state's economic power and its military and territorial position. An economic rising star—Britain in the 1860s, the United States in the 1890s, and Germany and Japan in the 1980s—might prefer to be rich rather than heavily armed. Several decades down the road, foreign economic commitments (the need to protect sources of raw materials and maintain markets, alliances, bases, and colonies) bring with them more military spending. Both the United States and the USSR, according to Kennedy, appeared to run up high national security tabs in the second half of the twentieth century.[84] What Kennedy seems to have missed was the much higher rate of Soviet GDP allocation for its military compared with the United States. Even Soviet and Russian statisticians do not know the real figures, but estimates range from 16 to 40 percent of the GDP. The U.S. indicators were approximately 5 percent.

Whereas economic determinants are paramount in the rise and fall of great powers, other factors can also become key: geography, military organization, national morale, and the individual characteristics of political and military leaders. Economics become most important *during* a long coalition war, in which victory goes to those great powers that have the deeper pockets, such as in the case of Habsburg Spain.[85]

The lag between economic decline and deterioration of the strategic-military posture in the case of the USSR was quite short, and the resultant collapse of the empire in Eastern Europe and in the Third World, along with the concurrent turmoil in the republics fit into the systemic model of relations between the metropole, the individual peripheries, the international system, and transnational factors.[86]

THEORIES OF EMPIRE—CONCLUSIONS

There is clearly a continuity in the study and theories of empires over the last hundred years, stemming primarily from the work of Hobson, Lenin, and Schumpeter. A fundamentally new approach to the question was pioneered by the British historical school studying the peripheries.

According to Doyle, neither the metrocentric analysts (Hobson, Lenin, and Schumpeter), the pericentric school (Gallagher et al.), nor the adherents of international system theories (B.J. Cohen and Paul Kennedy) provide a complete answer to the question of why empires rise and fall, and they do not examine *all four* components involved in political interaction: the metropole, the peripheries, the transnational system, and the international context.[87] Therefore, to provide an adequate analysis of an empire, one needs to examine the nature, forms, and channels of power relations between the system of an imperial center and one or more its peripheries in the four dimensions suggested by Doyle. This is a legitimate model that deserves attention when applied to the case of the USSR.

Mommsen points out that the theory of forced capital export, first advanced by Hobson and then adopted by Lenin, as well as arguments on the link between financial and industrial capital have been convincingly refuted. Similarly, Schumpeter's argument of free trade capitalism being inimical to imperialism does not stand up to close scrutiny.

Mommsen admits that "the interplay of interests which contributed to imperialist policy was highly complex and could at no time be clearly associated with particular social groups, either at the metropolitan countries or in colonies or semi-colonies."[88] He calls for the development of a new theory of imperialism that would take into account the interaction of endogenous and peripheral factors, as well as manifold varieties of formal and informal imperialist domination, colonial or otherwise.[89]

If we accept the notion that there can be no monocausal explanation of such a complex historical and political phenomenon as an empire, it clearly follows that any attempt to find a single cause for the collapse of an empire (or, as Alexander Yanov argued, the end of a civilization) would miss other, no less important, facets of this epochal event. To analyze the development and the endgame of the Soviet Union exclusively in terms of ideology, the competition of interest groups, the spread of technology, or even such undeniably important parameters as economic performance or nationalism, is to follow the example of the eight blind men of Indian lore, each of whom tried to describe an elephant from the experience he had with the one body part he managed to examine by hand—a trunk, an ear, a leg, or a tail. Therefore, in an attempt to provide a comprehensive explanation of the Soviet imperial collapse, all relevant theories mentioned in this section will find application in Chapters Four and Five.

NOTES

1. Robert Wesson, *The Imperial Order* (Los Angeles: University of California Press, 1964), p. 500.

2. John Starchey, *The End of Empire* (London: Victor Gollanz, 1959), p. 319.

3. Michael W. Doyle, *Empires* (Ithaca, N.Y.: Cornell University Press, 1986), p. 19.

4. Maxime Rodinson, quoted in Jan P. Nederveen Pieterse, *Empire and Emancipation* (New York: Praeger, 1989), p. 245.

5. Benjamin J. Cohen, *The Question of Imperialism* (New York: Basic Books, 1973), p. 10.

6. At the turn of the century, some Americans referred to their country as the "Empire of Liberty," while the literature of "captive nations" treated the USSR as an oppressive empire.

7. Cohen, *The Question of Imperialism*, p. 10.

8. Doyle, *Empires*, p. 20.

9. Doyle, ibid.

10. V. I. Lenin, *Imperialism: The Highest Stage of Capitalism* (Moscow: International Publishers, 1988), pp. 10–11.

11. Ibid., pp. 118–19.

12. J. Schumpeter, "The Sociology of Imperialism," in *Imperialism and Social Classes*, quoted in Doyle, *Empires*, p. 24.

13. E.M. Winslow, *The Pattern of Imperialism: A Study in the Theories of Power* (New York: Octagon Books, 1972), p. 232.

14. A.P. Thornton, *Imperialism in the Twentieth Century* (Minneapolis: University of Minnesota Press, 1977), pp. 4–5.

15. Ibid., pp. 30–31, 68.

16. Ibid., p. 132.

17. D.C.M. Pratt, quoted in Thornton, *Imperialism in the Twentieth Century*, p. 81.

18. W.W. Rostow, *The Stages of Economic Growth* (London: Cambridge University Press, 1971), p. 156.

19. George Lichtheim, *Imperialism* (New York: Praeger, 1971), pp. 88–89.

20. Ibid., pp. 90–91.

21. Wolfgang J. Mommsen, *Theories of Imperialism* (New York: Random House, 1980), pp. 71–72.

22. David K. Fieldhouse, *The Colonial Empires* (New York: Macmillan, 1982), p. 102.

23. Wesson, *The Imperial Order*, p. 22. Russia's insistence on intra-CIS peacekeeping and control of the borders is consistent with this paradigm.

24. Ibid., p. 7.

25. Vladimir Zhirinovsky, who is calling for Russian expansion south as well as restoration of the USSR, is a classic empire builder.

26. Wesson, *The Imperial Order*, pp. 7–10, 20.

27. Ibid., p. 11.

28. Ibid., pp. 20–21. Zhirinovsky's treatise, *The Last Thrust South*, promulgates precisely this approach.

29. Ibid., pp. 46–47.

30. Ibid., pp. 47–50.

31. Ibid., pp. 27, 35.

32. Personal interviews conducted with Soviet political scientists Andrey Bystritzky, columnist for *Literaturnaya gazeta* and advisor to the RSFSR Parliament, and Leonid Sedov, Senior Fellow, Institute of Sociological Research (ISI), Moscow, in Autumn 1990.

33. Wesson, *The Imperial Order*, pp. 123–24.

34. Personal interviews conducted at the Institute for International Economics and International Relations (IMEMO), the USA-Canada Institute, and with representatives of the Russian media, Moscow, 1992–1993.

35. Wesson, *The Imperial Order*, pp. 126–27.

36. Ibid., p. 139.

37. For more on Soviet front activities, see Leonard Schapiro, *International Front Organizations and Peace Campaign*, unpublished, and Ariel Cohen, "Front Organizations as a Tool of Soviet Power Projection in the Third World," Master's thesis, Fletcher School of Law and Diplomacy, Tufts University, 1989.

38. Wesson, *The Imperial Order*, p. 153.

39. Ibid., p. 155. Wesson notes that letters between today's Peru and Ecuador were delivered faster in the Inca times than in the twentieth century.

40. In 1990–1991, fax machines, even when available, lacked phone lines.

41. Wesson, *The Imperial Order*, p. 197.

42. An anti-communist activist, Novodvorskaya was prosecuted for criticizing Gorbachev. The chief editor of *Argumenty i fakti* was removed for publishing a poll showing that Gorbachev was unpopular. However, in both cases, the prosecution failed.

43. Wesson, *The Imperial Order*, p. 227.

44. Ibid., p. 234.

45. Quoted in ibid., p. 258.

46. Ibid., p. 260.

47. Ibid., p. 293.

48. Ibid., p. 320.

49. Ecumene, from the Greek *oikumena*, is a term indicating the known inhabited universe—that to the domination of which a "dominant state" or "universal empire" is striving. If ecumene is global, the bid for domination would be global.

50. Geoffrey Parker, *The Geopolitics of Domination* (London: Routlege, 1988), p. 64.

51. Ibid., pp. 68–69.

52. Ibid., pp. 70–75.

53. Y.M. Goblet, *Political Geography and the World Map* (London: George Philip, 1956), p. 201, quoted in Parker, *The Geopolitics of Domination*, pp. 147–52.

54. J.A. Gallagher and R.E. Robinson, "The Imperialism of Free Trade," *Economic History Review*, 2d Series VI, I (1953), pp. 1–15.

55. Anil Seal, preface to John A. Gallagher, *The Decline, Revival and Fall of the British Empire* (London: Cambridge University Press, 1973), p. viii.

56. Seal, ibid., page viii.

57. Seal, ibid., p. x.

58. Seal, ibid., p. xi.

59. Wolfgang J. Mommsen, "The End of Empire and the Continuity of Imperialism," in W.J. Mommsen and Jürgen Osterhammel, eds., *Imperialism and After* (Boston: Allen and Unwin, 1986), p. 344.

60. Ibid., pp. 345–46.

61. John S. Galbraith, "The 'Turbulent Frontier' as a Factor in British Expansion," *Comparative Studies in Society History*, vol. 2, no. 2, January 1960, pp. 150–68.

62. Nederveen Pieterse, *Empire and Emancipation*, p. 216.

63. Ibid., p. 226. Beyond conceptual inadequacy, what can one possibly make of such remarks by Marx and Engels about nations such as the Spaniards ("indeed degenerate"), the Scandinavians ("the brutal, sordid, piratic old Norse national traits"), the Chinese ("History had first to make this whole people drunk before it could raise them out of hereditary stupidity"), the Mexicans ("All vices of the Spaniards are found in the Mexicans raised to the third power"), and the Bedouins ("a nation of robbers"), as well as such individuals as Lassal ("a Jewish Nigger")—quoted in Nederveen Pieterse, ibid., p. 253.

64. Ibid., p. 245.

65. W.F. Wertheim, *Evolution and Revolution: The Rising Waves of Emancipation* (Harmondsworth: Penguin, 1974); *Emancipation in Asia: Positive and Negative Lessons from China* (Rotterdam: Comparative Asian Studies Program, 1983), quoted in Nederveen Pieterse, *Empire and Emancipation*, p. 83.

66. Wertheim, *Evolution and Revolution*, quoted in Nederveen Pieterse, *Empire and Emancipation*, p. 86.

67. Nederveen Pieterse, *Empire and Emancipation*, pp. 119, 188.

68. Ibid., p. 205.

69. Ibid., pp. 366–67, 380.

70. Ibid., pp. 121, 355.

71. Winfried Baumgart, *Der Imperialismus, Idee und Wirklichkeit der englischen und französischen Kolonialexpansion 1880–1914* (Wiesbaden: 1975), quoted in Mommsen and Osterhammel, *Imperialism and After*, p. 156.

72. Cohen, *The Question of Imperialism*, p. 15; other quotes are by George Lichtheim and A.P. Thornton, ibid.

73. Ibid., pp. 15–16.

74. Ibid., pp. 242–43.

75. Ibid.

76. Quoted in Cohen, ibid., p. 245.

77. Niccolò Machiavelli, *The Prince*, quoted in Doyle, *Empires*, pp. 36–37.

78. This is Doyle's modification of a governmental process presented in G. Almond and G. Powell, *Comparative Politics: A Developmental Approach* (Boston: Little, Brown, 1966).

79. Ibid.

80. Doyle, *Empires*, pp. 39–40.

81. Ibid.

82. Ibid., pp. 44–45.

83. Paul Kennedy, *The Rise and Fall of the Great Powers* (New York: Vintage Books, 1989), pp. xv–xvi.

84. Ibid., p. xxiii.

85. Ibid., p. 55.

86. Transnational factors include the level of technology and business practices, social norms, values, beliefs and ideas, political and human rights, and cultural issues that are shared in the global environment and are instrumental in determining the overall level of development of a state.

87. Kennedy, *The Rise and Fall of the Great Powers*, p. 46.

88. Mommsen, *Theories of Imperialism*, pp. 144–45.

89. Ibid.

2

Historical Development of the Russian Empire

THE METROPOLE OF THE MONGOL EMPIRE AND THE DEVELOPMENT OF RUSSIAN POLITICAL CULTURE

An investigation into the roots of Russian imperialism reveals the fascinating story of a fragmented imperial periphery learning the lesson of its imperial masters. In very few other cases has the elite of a subjugated people assimilated the ways of its ruler as thoroughly as the Russians learned from the greatest conquerors of all times—the Mongols.

Russia belonged to the political universe of Medieval Europe prior to the Mongol invasion through the Byzantine and Norman connections. Europe was only one of the centers of civilization at the time, and not the most developed one at that. The Arabic Middle East, India, and China were more populous, organized, and advanced. Moreover, Kyivan Rus',[1] Russia's predecessor, was the least developed periphery of Europe. Its Slavic tribes, embattled by nomadic invaders from the south and east, were ruled by invited Norman chieftains. Its culture, religion and alphabet were influenced by the Byzantine Greeks. The Mongol invasion occurred in 1237 against a backdrop of internecine feuding among the Eastern Slavic princes.

At the end of almost 250 years of domination (1237–1480), Russian political culture was radically transformed. Initially a classical European feudal system of principalities, it evolved under Mongolian tutelage into a centralized and expansionist state. Wesson's observation regarding Chinese imperial administration having been copied by the Mongols, Ottomans, and Russians is correct, and in the Russian case is supported by numerous examples.

The Russians also emerged as the heirs to both the Byzantine and Mongol metropoles. After 400 years of expansion both eastward and westward, the Russian empire covered roughly the same areas of Northern Eurasia as the Ulus of Juchi, part of the western Genghizid empire. It was also known as the Kipchak Khanate, which included the steppes of Central Asia and the conquered khanate of Khorezm (Khiva).[2] This vast realm was ruled in the thirteenth century by Batu, Genghis's grandson, in the empire of Genghis Khan.

Between 1237 and 1480, the territory of today's Russian core was under Mongolian control. These were formative years for the Moscow principality. No similar influence was exerted by the Mongols upon other regions of Europe. Few historical events elsewhere created a national trauma—as well as transformation—comparable with that of the "Mongol yoke" of the Russians.

The Russian political elite (the princes) were involved in bloody conflicts even prior to the Mongol intervention. These rivalries were exacerbated by the conquerors, who tried to exploit the feuds for their own purposes. Thus, at the early stages of Russian statehood, Gallagher and Robinson's model of imperial forces exploiting divisions in the local elites and Kennedy's argument that weak peripheries come under the influence of more technologically and culturally advanced metropoles seem highly relevant.

When in 1257 the new Great Khan Kubilay, Batu's brother, decided to expand military operations into Persia, Mesopotamia, and Southern China, it was demanded that the Rus's vassals provide troops. There was resistance to this in Novgorod. Prince Alexander Nevsky enforced the recruitment with the help of Russian (peripheral) and Mongol (imperial) troops. Thus, Russian infantry participated in the Chinese campaign of Kubilay. This is a function typical of imperial peripheries—India, for example, was a long-term manpower reservoir for the British Raj.

With the Tatar conquest, the Orthodox Church replaced the Byzantine emperor in its liturgy with the name of the Kipchak Khan.[3] The Mongol policy toward the church was lenient. The church was formally granted judicial powers. Sacrilege was punishable by death. Recognized as legal servants of the khan, convents became the largest and richest landowners under the Tatars.

When the Moscow princes took over as the sovereigns of Russia after the Mongols, they continued the same protective policy toward the church. The Metropolitans of Moscow were almost always the faithful allies of the grand princes.[4] Thus, both the Mongols and their Russian heirs successfully enlisted a transnational factor (religion) in the service of their imperial interests—the Mongols in the multidenominational context of a multinational empire, and the Russians in the context of ideologized Christian Orthodox expansion.

As happened before with other nomadic empires, the Golden Horde showed signs of early decay. Berke Khan, the first Moslem khan of the Mongols, died in 1266, and the Kipchak Khanate de facto split in two. In this historic period, *the Russian princes were local collaborators of the imperial rulers, quite often sacrificing the security and well-being of their people, and the interests of other princes, to promote their own power and position.* This has often been the case among local chieftains collaborating with imperial powers in a colonial context, from Latin America, to the Middle East and India.

The Mongolian metropole provided the Russian peripheral elite with possibilities to improve its relative position in the society and advance its own interests in exchange for the enforced malleability of the population, yearly monetary contributions (*yasak*), and the occasional supply of manpower for

Mongolian military ventures. Vernadsky points out that the Russian princes showed "much unbending persistence and abundant energy together with total unscrupulousness in the means of fighting" for metropolitan recognition.[5]

The Muscovite Danilovichi dynasty, the most pro-Mongol faction in the Russian elite, finally won domination of the periphery under the auspices of the Tatar metropole.

Prince Ivan Kalita based his regime on the support of Mongol troops to implement an ambitious program of strengthening the Moscow principality. This activity included land and town acquisitions, the eradication of crime, an improvement of the position of the Russian treasury, and last, but not least, the transfer of the Russian Orthodox center from Vladimir to Moscow, which granted Moscow both political and spiritual dominance over other Russian cities.[6]

The decline of the Golden Horde began in 1357, when Janibek Khan was killed by his son Berdibek. A wave of murders followed, resulting in the first round of disintegration of the khanate. Nevertheless, with imperial inertia holding the provinces in its grip, the contending Russian princes proceeded to compete for "licenses" to rule from whomever was formally in charge in Saray.

The khans held future grand princes (heirs to the Moscow throne) as bonds. In captivity, they learned the language and political culture of their captors. According to Ostrovsky, "when grand princes faced the need to administer the regions for which they were responsible, they would naturally adopt and modify institutions that they had seen work so well at Saray."[7] The Russian administrative structure of the fourteenth century is an outstanding example of borrowed political culture and institutions. Little similarity can be traced to either the Kyivan Rus' or Byzantine political structures.[8]

Not only the structure, but also the relationships and functions of Muscovy were very close to the Mongol original. The Russian princes accepted the language, culture, administrative system, and military innovations of the Mongols. The diplomatic ceremony of the grand princes reflected Mongolian practices until the sixteenth century, such as the famous *chelom bit'ye* (headbeating), a linguistic calque and administrative borrowing of the Turkic *bas ur,* which in turn was a borrowing of the Chinese *kow tow*[9]—"technology transfer," in which administrative innovation tends to spread as fast as military inventions.

The wide use of the institution of collective responsibility (*poruka*), in which extended families were held responsible for the behavior of an individual member, became prevalent under the Mongol influence. This hydralike institution was an unmistakably Oriental form of political control. Similarly, in the Soviet period, Stalin's use of the "family members of counter-revolutionaries" as hostages in Article 58 ("Treason") of the USSR Penal Code, as well as the punishment of whole peoples, are examples of *poruka*'s influence on Russian political life.

In the military sphere, Russian tactics, strategy, formations, weapons, and materiel were all imitations of those of the Mongol imperial masters. The Russian system of privileges being attached to service of the prince predated the communist system of state and party *nomenklatura* privileges, which expired as soon as the apparatchik left his post—as opposed to the Western idea of private property.[10]

In the mid-fourteenth century, the international equation in Eastern Europe was changing. In approximately 1350, the Lithuanians, under the command of Grand Duke Olgerd, began expanding toward the east and southeast, clashing with the Golden Horde and the great principality of Muscovy.

Lithuania consisted of principalities populated by Letts as well as by Eastern Slavs. Olgerd installed his son Vladimir in Kyiv and defeated the Mongols on the lower Dnieper; the Lithuanians reached the Black Sea. The weakened Horde, meantime, sought an alliance with the Lithuanian principality against the unreliable Russians. Some Tatar princes with their troops defected to the service of the Lithuanian grand duke. They received lands in the steppes near the northern Black Sea coast.

This was the beginning of the imperial disintegration of the Horde, with Lithuania and Muscovy competing for the role of the emerging metropole.

As a result of Lithuanian expansion, the consolidation of the international regional system, including Poland-Lithuania, on one hand, and the grand principality of Moscow and the Horde, on the other, began. Thus, the relationship of a province with its imperial metropole has to be addressed from this time in the context of the international environment, per the Doyle and Kennedy hypotheses.

Increasingly, in the last quarter of the fourteenth century and the first quarter of the fifteenth century, the Moscow principality became involved in a diplomatic quartet with united Poland and Lithuania, on one side, and Russia and the weakening Golden Horde, on the other. The former unconditional domination of the Horde was over. Applying Paul Kennedy's model, one can see that the decline was relative. It was the growth of Russian and Lithuanian strength, not only the decline of the Horde's power, that defined the conditions of the emerging regional system.

Lithuania's Grand Prince Vitovt died in 1430 without an heir, and with his death the might of Lithuania collapsed. The Catholic kingdom of Poland, with its links to the European political system and Rome, was to take its place as the dominant force in the western part of Eastern Europe. Poland lacked Lithuania's ability and historical connections (such as a vast Eastern Orthodox population) to expand eastward and challenge Russia.

The objectives of Muscovy's Prince Dmitrii at the time of the emergence of this international subsystem were to ensure his position as the grand prince, as well as to secure his domain from both excessive Tatar control and Lithuanian expansion.

By the 1430s, the Horde was collapsing rapidly. The new prince, Vasiliy Vasilyevich, who was in the habit of living in Saray for lengthy periods of time, assimilated the Tatar culture and spoke the language. He was trusted by the Tatars and received the title of grand prince. After assuming office, Vasiliy began hiring his former friends from the Horde—the Tatar khans with their military detachments—as servicemen of Muscovy. Early in the development of the Russian state machine, the rulers of Moscow began to build the autonomous state apparatus vital to future imperial development.

As Michael Doyle points out, separation of the interests of the imperial servants and the ruler from those of the society is a prerequisite for successful empire building. The alien ethnic origin of the prince's Tatars helped to keep the nascent military-bureaucratic structure isolated from the rest of the population. The Tatars did not have any allegiances in Russia, and they treated the population as an occupying force in the service of the Russian prince. A similar ethnic separation between the bureaucracy and the rest of the population would occur later under the Romanovs when the Russian imperial bureaucracy became inundated by Germans. Such a dichotomy resulted in a pattern very typical of Russia: The bureaucracy treats the population as would an occupying force.

The Tatars even got a small principality southeast of Moscow, in a border area with the Kazan' khanate, with the purpose of encircling and fighting it.

The roles had reversed. Now Russia was using one Tatar prince against another, Russia was granting licenses to the Tatar princes to rule, and Russian princes were using other people's soldiers to serve their political ends.

While some historians note the corrupting influence of the Mongol yoke, it appears that the process was that of the fusion of two political cultures rather than the corruption of one by the other.[11]

As Vasiliy was consolidating his power, the pope and the emperor of the Eastern Roman Empire (Byzantium) negotiated a union between the Roman and the Orthodox churches with the Orthodox Patriarch of Constantinople (Florence, 1439). The objective was to unite the Christians in a struggle against the ascending Ottoman empire. The reaction of the Russians shows that they were well outside the European political system. For generations indoctrinated by the Greek Orthodox to hate Rome, and on friendly terms with the (Moslem) Horde, isolationist Muscovy refused to join the all-Christian cause, thereby indirectly precipitating the fall of Constantinople in 1453. The Russian political elite displayed unmistakable hostility to the Christian political universe of the West and its goals.[12]

The rulers of Moscow were most persistent enemies of Russian medieval democracy (the *veche* city self-rule typical of Novgorod and Pskov preserved by the Lithuanian princes). They rejected any attempts toward an alliance with Western powers, which at the time granted their nobility, burghers, and peasants far more rights and privileges than either the Tatars or their pupils, the Russians.

Prolonged contact with the Mongols created a dislocation in Russia's politico-administrative development precisely in the formative years of statehood and has influenced its behavior ever since. Above all, the Russian rulers inherited the insatiable hunger for territorial acquisition that would motivate them and their heirs to create one of the largest contemporary land empires.

THE TSARDOM OF RUSSIA—THE MOSCOW PERIOD: THE EMERGENCE OF A NEW METROPOLE (FIFTEENTH–SEVENTEENTH CENTURIES)

As heir to the Ulus of Juchi, the emerging Russian state under its first ruler, Ivan III Vasilyevich, was politically oriented to the East. According to Vernadsky, the broad Eastern policy conducted by this grand prince was influenced by close contact with the Tatar khans in the service of Moscow. Ivan III increasingly immersed Russia in the international system of the time, with Russian ambassadors appearing as far away as Persia.

The wars of conquest against the Tatar khanates of the Golden Horde and Kazan indicate that the Russian rulers *from the beginning of statehood* were concerned not so much with nation building as with territorial acquisition. A purely Slavic "patriotic" policy would have dictated a totally different course—that of assembling the former Kyivan lands.

Moscow-led Russia could not proceed to become a dominant power until other Russian principalities were brought under its sway. After the Kazan khanate was pacified in 1469 and a proRussian khan installed,[13] Ivan III turned against his ethnic brothers and coreligionists in Novgorod.

Novgorod was the stronghold of a historical Russian form of government—the *veche* city democracy, not dissimilar to that of the Hanseatic free cities. The pro-Lithuanian sympathies of Novgorod's boyars (especially when they signed an alliance treaty with Lithuania in 1471) were feared in Moscow. Eastern Orthodox Moscow interpreted the signing of this pact as "not only political, but also religious and national treason" and a defection to Catholicism.[14] Ivan III's mobilization against Novgorod continued until 1478, when he besieged the city again, demanding the termination of democratic rule and dismantling of the *veche*. By 1489, Moscovite troops had gained control over the vast Novgorod lands, conquering the resisting town of Vyatka (a Novgorod offshoot). The means of establishing metropolitan domination were particularly harsh, demonstrating the tactics of occupation learned by the Russians from the Tatars.

A year after the conquest, Ivan exiled Novgorod's archbishop. Many boyars were also exiled to Muscovite territories and their lands given out to Moscow military and servicemen. The peasants were organized into tax-paying communities in the manner customary in Muscovy. The trade Novgorod had pursued with the West vanished; German merchants were exiled following the Moslem tradition of isolation from the West. The population of the city shrank from 200,000 to 20,000.

Novgorod's inhabitants, who traded with Europe and were democratically governed, were formerly known for their politeness and fairness. When the Muscovites moved in, manners in the city drastically deteriorated. A similar phenomenon occurred with the occupation of Pskov by the Muscovites in the sixteenth century.[15] "Thus ended Novgorod's nobility, and with it the memory of Novgorod's freedom," says Platonov.[16]

The exile of political opponents accompanied Russian territorial expansion.

This pattern continued with the banishment of political and other undesirables to Siberia under the tsars, and the practice would become one of Stalin's most favored "political instruments" against the kulaks, Crimean Tatars, Greeks, Volga Germans, and other "enemies."

After Novgorod, the consolidation of Russian lands continued unhindered, with most formerly independent princes petitioning (*bili chelom*) to be accepted as serving nobles (*boyare*) of the Moscow ruler.

Thus Moscow, after securing its independence from the Tatars, concluded the unification of the northeastern Russian lands, becoming the metropolitan center of an expanding, Russo-Turkic and Finno-Ugric multinational empire.

From being a conglomerate of feuding principalities, northeastern Russia became a vast state looking for its place in the international system. As elsewhere in the Middle Ages, "matrimonial diplomacy" was to play a role in this process. In 1472 Ivan III married Zoe-Sofia Paleolog, niece of the last emperor of Byzantium. This resulted in an increase of the Greek influence, as well as more imperial behavior and protocol at the Moscow court. The Byzantine two-headed eagle appeared on the Moscow shield of arms. In addition, connections between the Russian principality and the West were increased, as a large number of Western merchants, diplomats, and craftsmen appeared in Moscow. For the first time, Russia had dealings with Denmark, Hungary, and the Venetian Republic.[17]

To use Michael Doyle's model, a fusing of the transnational cultural factors and changes in the international system provided the basis for Moscow's imperial growth in the late fifteenth century. The ascendancy and consolidation of Moscovy resulted in her becoming a neighbor of several major European players. Byzantine and to some extent Western, rather than Tatar, culture was established as a dominant influence in the capital for the first time. Muscovy became increasingly recognized in the international arena.

1480 was a key year in the history of Muscovy as it is considered the official year of the termination of Mongol domination. A polycentric system had been created in Eastern Europe, with Russia allied with the Crimean Khan Mengli-Girey (at that time already a vassal of the Ottoman Turks), while the Golden Horde, extremely weakened by internecine struggle, aligned itself with the unstable Duchy of Lithuania. Ivan III also maintained diplomatic relations with the Persians and the Nogay Horde, located between the Volga and the Aral Sea. Effectively, the Golden Horde was isolated by Russia. Vernadsky stresses Ivan III's reliance on the expertise of his Tatar vassals in forging a coalition of all neighbors of the Horde against it.

Ivan III continued the war with Lithuania, which pitted a strong Russian-Crimean coalition against a Lithuania supported by the German knights of the Livonian Order (which ruled what is today Latvia and Estonia). During the reign of Ivan III, Russia commenced its offensive toward the West. With the exception of the setbacks of the early seventeenth century (the Time of Troubles) and the postrevolutionary period (1920–1939), this offensive, which began circa the 1500s, was carried on for almost five centuries and later became one of the most stable and unchanging characteristics of Russian/Soviet imperial political strategy.

Ivan bequeathed the rule of the state to his older son, Vasiliy III, who continued his father's policies of centralized state building. He terminated self-rule in always loyal Pskov and exiled 300 prominent families, replacing them with 300 Muscovite clans. In this manner, any effectively independent nobility was subjugated throughout Russia.[18]

Under Ivan III and Vasiliy III, Russia effectively crossed what Doyle calls the Augustan threshold of empire, as the interests of the ruler and the empire became the only ones exercised in Russian foreign and domestic policy. Still, suspicion of the nobility on the part of the monarch remained, as would be demonstrated by Vasiliy's son Ivan IV the Terrible.

Under both Vasiliy and Ivan IV, the role of the *dyaki*—low-born but literate bureaucrats, sons of priests and peasants—increased, and so did the role of government "ministries" (*prikazi*). Thus, the role of the bureaucracy in Russia was important from the sixteenth century on. The rights of all other strata of the society were increasingly curbed, with burghers, craftsmen, peasants, and merchants being subject to the whim of the crown and heavy taxation. This was in contrast to the strengthening of the aristocracy and the Magdeburg rights for the cities in neighboring Poland and Lithuania. Russian empire building was in the works.

The members of the *duma* were uneducated by Western standards, and the boyars were illiterate.[19] The secretaries of state for foreign affairs and defense were *dyaki* and not boyars. The role of the *dyaki* as policymakers was important, and they were nominated directly by the tsar. The *duma* was the supreme legislative, executive, and judiciary organ of the realm, and it also listened to private appeals.

The number of *duma* council members was not fixed by law.[20] The delineation of authority between the council of state and the more than forty "ministries" was not clear-cut. Similarly, the provincial (*oblast*) governors did not have a clearly delineated authority, and their decisions were subject to appeal to Moscow—to *prikazi* and *duma*, as well as direct appeal to the tsar. The city of Moscow was run directly by the *duma* (similarly to the Politburo nominating the Moscow party committee chief in the Soviet period).

As in other empires in all times, law and justice were not separate from the executive. "Courts, as well as other branches of government, were seen as a way to 'feed' the nominee (*kormleniye*), i.e. as a source of income," says Kluchevsky.[21] In other words, a noble would buy a judiciary position and would "feed" himself off bribes and court taxes.

In the seventeenth century, *kormleniye* was replaced by the nomination of government appointees, but those continued to see public service as a way to quick enrichment. Nevertheless, the institution of tsar-appointed governors and *voyevody* (military rulers), who were not supposed to have personal pecuniary interest in the job, was another step in the creation of a government bureaucracy with only imperial interests in mind.

This view of government service as a way to personal enrichment struck deep roots in the Russian/Soviet empire. Buying and selling party, government, economic, judicial, and academic positions took place throughout the USSR's history until its dissolution.[22]

Court seats were not public service positions, but private domain; they were separated (murderers would be judged in one court and thieves in another) and sold out as concessions, similar to tax farming. Judges sold sentences to the highest bidder. There was no crime that could not escape punishment with the help of money. This was the case not only in the lower-level courts—large-scale corruption was rampant at the tsar's court.[23]

As in the Soviet Union, a crime against a servant of the state was treated as a crime against *the state*. The level of cruelty in law enforcement and in the justice system was shocking even to medieval European visitors. The degree of physical punishment and use of torture was staggering.

With the ascendancy of Ivan IV (*Grozny*—the Terrible), Muscovy started to expand simultaneously east, south, and north, and only in the west was colonization checked by Poland and Lithuania for awhile. With his council of boyars, Ivan embarked on an expansionary course against the heirs of the Golden Horde. In 1552 Kazan was stormed and captured, and in 1556 Astrakhan, the key to eastern trade and expansion, followed suit.

This thrust eastward brought under Moscow's control, in addition to the Tatars, a number of Turkic and Finno-Ugric peoples, some of them pagan and some Moslem, who inhabited the Kazan khanate. These included Mordva, Chuvash, Cheremis, Bashkir, Mari, and others.

Russia was further evolving into a multiethnic state. Empire building, rather than Russian nation-state building, became the goal of the tsar and the political elite. Russian expansion, as adequately described by Parker, continued into the middle and lower Volga, and on to the Don, Kuban, and Terek areas, as well as the Urals.

Siberia was conquered by a private expedition of the Volga Cossacks hired by the mercantile Stroganov family in the style of the British East Indies Company. Eight hundred forty Cossack mercenaries, armed with firearms, defeated (conquistador style) tens of thousands of Siberian Tatars.[24]

Invading bands of Tartars and other nomadic tribes constantly jeopardized the security of the settlers in many of the frontier areas. The Russian state hence needed to reorganize the defense of its southeastern borderlands. In forty years, Russian defense lines moved quickly from the north to the southeast, complete with forts, observation posts, and ramparts. In the mid-sixteenth century, the entire southeast of Russia became one large military camp.[25]

Ivan the Terrible also turned against the west. In early 1558, Muscovite troops invaded the lands of another weakening periphery—the Livonian Order. These troops were headed by the Kasimov "tsar" Sheikh-Ali and two Tatar princes, Abdallah and Tokhtamysh. The use of the Tatars as proxies of the Russian tsar is similar to the British use of Indian troops elsewhere in the empire.[26] The Tatars crushed the resistance of the Baltic Germans in two years, but a political complication turned a victorious war into a major strategic fiasco.

The Livonian Order disintegrated; its parts were transferred to Russia's neighbors. Kurland became a vassal of Poland. Livonia (Lifland) arranged for a union with Lithuania. Part of Estonia (Estland) turned to Sweden, while still another part became a protectorate of Denmark. Lithuania and Sweden demanded that the Russians vacate Livonia, and Russia refused.

In 1559 the tsar started military operations against Lithuania and in 1562 invaded Byelorussia. The Lithuanian nobility, terrified of Ivan the Terrible's reputation for executing noblemen, sought union with Poland.

As the Russian threat became imminent in the Baltic region for the first time, Poland and Lithuania merged in the Congress of Lublin (1569). Russia, because of its aggressive policies toward its neighbors, had succeeded in turning the international system against itself.

In 1576 a capable Polish general, Stephan Batoriy, was elected king of Poland. In 1578 he defeated the Russians in Lifland. Batoriy recaptured Polotsk and Velikiye Luki and cut off Moscow from Pskov. The war moved into the Russian homeland. In 1581 Batoriy besieged Pskov but could not capture it.[27] At the same time, the Swedes invaded Karelia and Estonia, took Keksholm on Lake Ladoga, and captured all of the Russian towns previously established in the area by Ivan III.

Ivan appealed to the pope to mediate for peace, and the papal legate Possevinus succeeded in arranging a truce. Under the peace of 1582, Russia lost Polotsk and all earlier conquests and failed to reach the Baltic.[28] Grozny's aggressive war turned out to be a strategic catastrophe.

Even more disastrous were the results of Ivan's domestic policies. Russia could not continue the war despite the fact that, since the early 1560s, Ivan IV had turned the land into one giant military camp. Grozny exiled hereditary nobility en masse from their estates and settled them in border areas, fragmenting their large land holdings and giving them out to his servants. Although Ivan III and Vasiliy had used this technique against internal "enemies," such as Novgorod, mass transfers of the old nobility had never before been applied against loyal Russian princes.

Ivan the Terrible, like Stalin, used to say that he was sifting through people as sand between his fingers, raising some, dropping some.[29] Grozny physically eliminated the boyars "as a class". Thus, absolute power, decried by Wesson in *The Imperial Order*, was unleashed by one of the bloodiest tyrants of Russia, with disastrous consequences both at home and abroad.

Under Grozny's rule, the status of Russian Orthodoxy improved, having been mobilized to provide an ideological basis for the Russian empire. The political philosophy of the church was establishment of the Russian Orthodox kingdom, with the Russians being the new chosen people, *novyii Izrail* (New Israel). The importance of the Russian people was taking on universal, messianic significance.[30]

Grozny crowned himself tsar (caesar/emperor) in accordance with the Byzantine rite followed by the Russian Orthodox Church. Thus he formalized the empire launched by his grandfather, Ivan III. There was a need to nominate a patriarch (head of the church) to emphasize the importance of the new tsardom. The policy of turning Russia into the center of Eastern Orthodoxy continued under Grozny's son, Feodor Ioannovich, and his regent and successor, Boris Godunov. For this purpose, the concept of Moscow as the Third Rome was formulated: the Two Romes—the second being Constantinople—had fallen, the Third is standing (Moscow) and the Fourth will not be.[31]

In 1589, after intensive political bargaining, the Moscow patriarchate was established. The purpose of this dual arrangement (patriarchate-monarchy) was to expand state and cultural domination throughout the known political universe (the *ecumena*). Muscovy thus positioned herself, as other states bidding for universal imperial domination before her, as not only a military, but also a cultural force with a universal mission.

In 1564-1565, Grozny disappeared from Moscow, surfacing in a monastery, from which he declared that he was abdicating because of a "treasonous conspiracy" of the boyars. Muscovites sent a delegation begging him to continue to rule. He agreed to stay on condition of receiving extraordinary powers, which he immediately used to launch a reign of terror. He established *oprichina*, an apparatus of repression he personally directed. Operating as a state within a state, it included its own villages, somewhat similar to the later NKVD/MGB structures under Stalin. The *oprichina* waged a campaign of extermination against numerous "enemies of the crown," employing torture, assassination, and exile, foreshadowing Stalin's later exploits. Thus, the institution of the purge *(chistka)* was introduced as part of Russian imperial governance. As in other empires during periods of mass mobilization, immense economic decline accompanied the repressions. Grozny's colonization policy depopulated traditional Russian centers of economic activity. In unprecedented recruitment drives, Tatars, Cossacks, priests' sons and peasants were accepted into military service, elevated to serving nobility status, and granted estates. Huge tracts of land in the central regions of Russia lay fallow and could not support their owners as there was no one there to cultivate them.

Grozny introduced *prikrepleniye* (attachment to the land), first instituted to facilitate the tsar's tax collection, and later to enforce the personal dependence of the serfs upon their landlords.[32] This was the precursor of Stalin's *propiska* (police residence permit). The peasants began to desert Russia as a result. There ensued a swelling of the Cossack ranks, the appearance of large masses of lumpen and a rise in crime. These strata of the society would later play an active role in the civil strife of the Time of Troubles.

From Grozny to Peter the Great to the Bolsheviks, considerations of economic development were subjugated to politico-military goals, often resulting in economic deprivation and destruction of the productive base of the country.

While the rulers of Russia managed to promulgate a coherent (though not necessarily successful) foreign and military policy, they failed abysmally to provide a workable economic or trade framework, and to correlate the two so that military requirements would not decimate the national economy.

By decimating the country's ruling class and exhausting its resources, Ivan the Terrible contributed to the first systemic collapse in the history of the Russian state, the Time of Troubles. The destruction of the elite had brought debilitating results upon the state (as was the case with the Roman empire). A similar slaughter of the elite occurred in Russia after the revolution of 1917, when the "old" upper classes were annihilated or exiled, and more so in the 1930s, when the new postrevolutionary elite was exterminated in Stalin's purges. The princely aristocracy had been destroyed by Grozny, and power shifted to the nonprincely boyars (the Zakharyin/Romanov family and the Godunovs).

There was political continuity between Grozny's rule and Godunov's. Boris Godunov, Grozny's prime minister, was a descendant of a Tatar noble (Murza-chet). Like Ivan IV, he continued to harass the top boyars and princes, while lower ranking personnel were promoted.[33] The imperial government, therefore, systematically pursued the destruction of alternative power centers in the state, strengthening the tsar's autocracy and the imperial bureaucracy.

Godunov succeeded in regaining the towns on the Baltic coast which Grozny had ceded to Sweden. He was forced to make peace with Russia's neighbors after decades of devastating war. Peace talks with Poland were under way. The southern borders and Volga territories were settled. Voronezh was founded in 1586, Samara in 1586, and Saratov in 1590. The town of Ufa was started in 1586 to establish a Russian presence in Bashkiriya. The empire began to expand into faraway Siberia.[34]

However, all of this expansion took place amidst great internal turmoil. Godunov's election to the throne by the Congress of Lands (*Zemskoy Sobor*) had been far from unanimous. The princely clan of the Shuiskys openly opposed him. Intrigues against the tsar soon began, and the Shuiskys eventually grabbed power.

Then came the famine of 1601, which produced unprecedented chaos.[35] The Time of Troubles had begun. Russia was invaded by Polish mercenaries and by the Swedes, hired by competing contenders for the throne as well as by King Sigizmund of Poland. The middle classes appealed to Sigizmund to allow his son, Crown Prince Vladislav, to become tsar of Russia. The Polish defeat of the Russian forces led by Dmitrii Shuisky turned the people against the tsar, Vasiliy Shuisky. He was dethroned and forcibly sent to a monastery.

For a limited period of time, the Polish king became the most powerful political force in Russia, with parts of the society ready to swear allegiance to him.[36] As was the case before 1480, in a period of weakness of the state, the Russian elites were ready to seek the protection of an external power to ensure their privileged position.

The Russian state fell into disarray. In the hinterland, those Russian cities not under foreign occupation maintained constant contact with each other regarding the future. Thus, the revival of Russian political will and the reestablishment of the state toward the end of the Time of Troubles was a bottom-up process in which the Russian urban polity, anxious to stop the turmoil, was much involved.

This widespread political participation and mass involvement is characteristic of Russian imperial crises—from the time of the struggle against the Poles in 1611, to the 1917 revolutions, to the recent breakdown of the communist regime. It is also typical that, when the systemic crisis is over, the power that assumes control fails to renew its popular mandate and legitimacy, instead erecting a wall between the rulers and the people.

The Time of Troubles was indeed a crisis of overextension. As the subsequent installation of the popular Mikhail Feodorovich Romanov (1613) by the Congress of Lands as the first monarch of that dynasty demonstrates, Russia behaved like other empires which needed to reinstate a new regime after years of disarray.

In 1617 Russia signed a peace with Sweden in which the Swedes gave up all ambition to the Russian throne, but collected a contribution and kept the Russian cities that Ivan III had established. The battle for access to the Baltic Sea would be won under Peter the Great a century later.

In the summer of 1617, despite a terrible economic situation at home, the Russians attacked the Poles, but the war was indecisive. A truce was signed in 1618. Thus, Poland and Sweden, due to their own lack of resources, did not take advantage of Russia's prolonged weakness nor impose domination as did the Western great powers in the cases of India and China.

Muscovy, by the seventeenth century, had become the largest European state. In the mid-fifteenth century its area was approximately 15,000 square miles; however by the early 1600s its territory was approximately 155,000 square miles.[37]

Hundreds of thousands of people were relocated by the government to colonize new areas. A great economic burden was imposed on the crown, as colonization of the north and Siberia was primarily government initiated, and not based on the economic interests of the population. The rise of the two major ports, Archangel and Astrakhan, contributed to increased trade with the West and expansion into the Caucasus and Central Asia.

The new colonial power was "very satisfied with the famine and disease that exterminated up to one hundred thousand men [Nogays], and helped them [the Russians] to displace the nomads from the steppes."[38] Avril also points to another "benefit of civilization"—the widespread drinking introduced by the Russians.[39]

Universal empires destroy the economic well-being of the population by ever-increasing taxation. Under the rule of Mikhail Feodorovich (Romanov), as a result of the wars with Poland, a new high tax, one-fifth on all property, was introduced. It remained in place during the rule of Alexei Mikhailovich. Among the more important sources of income for the crown—as was true for the Soviet state—were alcohol taxes and the revenues from innumerable public houses it owned.[40]

By the sixteenth century, Russia had started to fall behind Western Europe technologically. Major Russian exports were raw materials such as beeswax, flax, salt, hides, salmon and cod, seal and whale fat, lard, walrus tusks, iron, hemp and hemp rope, and furs; all manufactured goods and luxury items were imported. The price of many Western manufactures in Muscovy was 300 percent higher than in their countries of origin.[41]

The traditional structure of Russian exports, with its heavy emphasis on commodities combined with reliance on the West for consumer goods, contributed to Russia's long-term dependence upon Western industrial innovation. Due to the political and geographical barriers to entry (many Western merchants were barred from trading with Russia), supply imbalances were created, causing great price fluctuations and resulting in both superprofits and considerable losses. Another source of pricesetting distortion lay in the predominance of barter trade, so popular with nonmarket economies to this day. These patterns, which first started to form in Russia in the sixteenth century, continued to complicate trade with the former Soviet Union.[42]

While the Moscow tsars had pretensions, in Kluchevsky's words, to "get included among Augustus's descendants" and "join the family of Christian European states," Western visitors were met with Asiatic suspicion and contempt.[43]

METROPOLITAN AND PERIPHERAL ELITE INTERACTION IN THE SEVENTEENTH CENTURY: THE CASE OF UKRAINE

In the seventeenth century, the concentration of landholding by the nobility and the spread of serfdom were under way in Muscovy and Ukraine. Over the centuries, the old Russian Orthodox nobility there had undergone a conversion to Catholicism and was culturally Polish.[44]

The military hierarchy of the Cossacks was Orthodox and of peasant origin. In 1648 the Cossacks rebelled against Poland under the leadership of Hetman (supreme military commander) Bohdan Khmelnitzky. An independent state was proclaimed, and in 1654 the pro-Russian Khmelnitzky arranged for union with Russia. The *Peryaslav Rada* (congress) approved the union by swearing allegiance to Tsar Alexei Mikhailovich.

In June 1656 the regional international system started to unravel when King Charles X of Sweden invaded Poland, allied with Friedrich Wilhelm, elector of Brandenburg, Prince Georg II Racoszy of Transilvania, and Bohdan Khmelnitzky.

Russia, already suffering from a Swedish blockade in the Baltics that barred much needed maritime trade with Western Europe, concluded an armistice with Poland in April 1656. War was declared on Sweden one month later; war with the Poles was also eventually resumed.

In 1660 dissatisfaction with Moscow's rule caused a faction of the Cossacks, led by Hetman Petro Doroshenko, to establish an Ottoman protectorate over Ukraine. The Crimean Tatars (vassals of the sultan) and Doroshenko's Cossacks attacked the Polish garrisons and plundered cities on both banks of the Dnieper.

Entrance by the Ottoman empire, a great power at the time, into Ukrainian politics threatened both Poland and Muscovy. The ensuing peace negotiations resulted in the Andrusovo Treaty, signed on January 13, 1667. Moscow retained Smolensk but ceded Byelorussia to Poland. The right bank of Ukraine, except for Kyiv, was also ceded to Poland. The Cossack state of Zaporozhye was put under joint Russian-Polish authority. This treaty was of lasting importance. The boundaries between Poland and Russia agreed upon at Andrusovo were confirmed by the "eternal peace" of 1686 and lasted for almost a century until the partition of Poland.

In 1672 Turkish and Crimean troops, invited by Hetman Doroshenko, ravaged right-bank Ukraine. Under the treaty of Buchach, Poland ceded Podolia to the sultan and had to pay yearly tribute to the Porte.

In the same year (1672), a pro-Russian Cossack, Samoilovich, was elected hetman of both banks. Russia was planning a major war against Turkey with the aim of conquering the Crimea, or at least bringing in Bakhchisaray as a Russian vassal.[45]

Plans were laid out by Samoilovich and Grigoriy Romodanovsky for an army of 90,000 troops, including Cossacks, *streltsy* (infantry), Bashkirs, and Kalmyks to attack the Crimea. In 1676 Tsar Alexei died. As a prelude to the war, Romodanovsky and Samoilovich defeated Hetman Doroshenko's troops and captured him. In the meantime, Turkey and Poland signed another peace treaty (Zuravno, 1676), under which right-bank Ukraine was partitioned between them.

The thirty years of civil strife in Ukraine resulted in innumerable casualties and massive suffering. Hundreds of thousands were killed, captured, or sold into slavery. The lack of drive for independence, the absence of a national renaissance leader, and attempts to enlist help from the adjacent empires illustrate how Gallagher and Robinson's peripheral model of empire is applicable to the Ukrainian case. Members of the Ukrainian elite (the *starshina*), which was always split against itself, were willing to cooperate with whoever promised to maximize their power, and actively promoted the imperial influence of their masters.

Russian politics, such as the need to deny escaping serfs a safe haven in the Cossack country, played an important role in Moscow's attempt to take over Ukraine. Ukraine became a prize for which the Ottoman empire, Russia, and Poland competed. While Russian policy toward Ukraine was influenced by the ideology of the Third Rome and attempts to incorporate "Little" and "White" Russia under the scepter of the Orthodox tsar, decisions of war and peace were taken based on realities of the battlefield, considerations of regional power competition, and geopolitical issues.

Before Alexei Michailovich, Russia was seeking a balanced position between the Moslem East and the Catholic West. However, from the second half of the seventeenth century on it joined a "Latin-Uniate coalition" with the aim of fighting the Ottoman empire, thus ending the idea of Moscow as the Third Rome.[46] The results of this policy were unimpressive at first. Prince Golitsyn's campaigns against the Crimea in 1687 and 1689 ended in defeat. Nevertheless, in the long term, the anti-Turkish orientation contributed to Russian acceptance into the European concert of nations and resulted in vast territorial gains and influence.

RUSSIA'S EASTWARD EXPANSION IN THE SEVENTEENTH CENTURY

The principal states of Central Asia in the seventeenth century were Bukhara and Khiva, populated by Turkic-speaking Uzbeks and Persian-speaking Sarts and Tajiks. Both were in decline throughout the seventeenth century. These khanates, whose golden age had occurred prior to the Mongol invasions of the thirteenth century, were by then typical Asian feudal aristocracies—corrupt, culturally stagnating, and militarily inefficient.[47]

In Central Asia, Muscovy conducted "diplomatic reconnaissance" by sending political missions and merchant caravans. The Central Asians sent twelve missions from Bukhara and fourteen from Khiva in the first part of the seventeenth century. Trade flourished, with an annual turnover of about 50,000 rubles, and included Oriental luxury items and slaves.

Russian-Chinese and Russian-Manchu relations in the Far East developed from the second half of the seventeenth century on. Expeditions were sent to explore Dauria in the upper Amur region (Khabarov, 1649–1653) and contact was established with the Manchu, who at the time had completed their conquest of China. Russian expansion in eastern Siberia and the Far East was based primarily on economic considerations. In the second half of the seventeenth century the fur supplies of western Siberia were in decline. The treasury, dependent on the fur trade for at least one third of its income, desperately needed to open new taiga areas for more hunting and trapping.[48]

Eastward expansion brought the Russians into contact with eastern Mongols, the Kalmyks, and Kazakhs. The Kazakhs, whose chieftains traced their ancestry to Genghis Khan, were a Turkic nomadic, pastoral people. They were divided into three hordes (*orda* in Russian), each led by a khan. The khans were involved in constant quarrels and power competition with each other.[49] Using these internal rivalries, the Russian state would eventually establish its authority in the Kazakh steppes.

Relations between the Kalmyks and Moscow were initially chilly due to Moscow's fears of Kalmyk raids against Kabarda and the Don Cossack areas, and because of the possibility of an alliance between the Crimean Tatars, the Ottomans, and the Kalmyks. The turning point came in 1654 as a result of the war with Poland, when the tsar had to mobilize available resources from all quarters, including the nomad tribes. Overall, Moscow's policy toward the Kalmyks was a success, preventing their alliance with either Persia or the Ottomans and enlisting their considerable military force against the Crimean khan and his allies, the Poles.[50]

Pressure against the Crimea and the Ottomans eventually resulted in the storming of Azov by Peter's troops in 1698 and the occupation of the Crimea by Catherine II in the 1780s.

As in the case of Ukraine, Russian expansion in the east was characterized by interaction with tribes or stateless peoples, nomad states, and decaying kingdoms or empires, such as Persia and China.

In Asia, as in the case of Poland, Russia came into contact with deteriorating state systems, which hardly could control their peripheries. It was only natural for Moscow to take advantage of the opportunities.

RUSSIAN EXPANSION IN THE EIGHTEENTH CENTURY

Peter the Great: Revolution From Above

Some foreign influence was felt in Russia even before the reign of Peter the Great (1689–1725), but the young tsar's desire to expand the empire was crucial to bringing it into the European constellation of great powers. For the second time in its history, Russia embarked on extensive borrowing in the military, technological, administrative and cultural spheres to upgrade its capabilities as a military power.

The pre-Petrine decades were characterized by a gradual introduction of Western ideas and technology from the top down. This was an osmotic assimilation of Western thought and concepts by part of the elite, which came in contact with Western books and people. The clergy, the boyars, and the merchants were extremely suspicious of the new influences.

It was clear that, if Russia were to engage one of her three potential Western rivals (the Porte, Poland, or Sweden), she could end up fighting two others. Despite Peter's failure to capture the Ottoman fortress of Azov in 1695, which prevented Russia from gaining access to the Black Sea, his army recovered. He ordered a fleet of ships built that would isolate Azov from the Turkish resupply sea line. The first Russian navy was constructed on the Voronezh River in 1695–1696. The second siege of Azov succeeded. Europe was duly impressed, and so was Russia.[51]

The victorious Peter could now move with ease against his retrograde opponents, as the boyars and the clergy were in the process of disintegration.

On his unprecedented tour abroad, which lasted more than a year, Peter studied various applied disciplines to be used later in the creation of the new Russian military machine. He gave impetus to the development of modern science in Russia, importing experts and technology.

The redesigned Russian army and navy became the instruments of imperial expansion that propelled Russia to the rank of first a European, and then a global great power. Reliance on military might, preoccupation with Turkey, the Balkans, and the Mediterranean, as well as an active role in European affairs, continued throughout the twentieth century.

During his European tour, Peter attempted to build a new coalition against the Ottomans, but France, an ally of Turkey and Austria, would not agree to his plans. Instead, Peter embarked upon a path toward war with Sweden, together with Augustus, the king of Poland.

Nevertheless, Peter remained convinced that Russia was to face the Ottomans and a campaign, though unsuccessful, followed in 1711. The Europeans, especially the French, were treating the Ottomans as a status quo power and distrusted Peter's designs, which included the liberation of the southern Slavs. Thus, in the midst of Peter's reign, the concept of pan-Slavism was formulated not so much as an ideology, but as a politico-military doctrine that would be adhered to by the expansionist segment of the Russian ruling class for the next two and a half centuries. Victorious Russian military operations against the Turks came later, in the eighteenth and nineteenth centuries.

In Peter's absence, a palace coup was plotted by conservative elements in Moscow, but this attempt was mercilessly crushed on his return. The purpose of the reforms was not explained to the masses of Russia. The introduction of European dress and culture created a schism between the ruling class and the people (*narod*). Peter was often rough and impatient. The famous incident of the tsar's seizing a scissors and cutting off the beards and caftan sleeves of the boyars was revolting to the clergy, the boyars, and the tradition-oriented strata of the society.

Thus, Peter's reforms put Russia on the path of Westernization from above, isolating the ruling class from the rest of the population. Russia has had to pay the price to this day. The schism between the ruling class and the masses, as well as the incompleteness of Westernization, remain impediments to successful Russian integration into the world community.

After Russia negotiated peace with the Porte, Peter attacked the Swedish fortress of Narva, only to see his 40,000-man army defeated by some 8,000 Swedes under young King Charles XII. After this defeat, Peter succeeded in capturing some of the Livonian littoral and parts of the Gulf of Finland. St. Petersburg, established in 1703, became the new Russian capital in 1713. The city became a sentinel of the newly conquered territories, "the window to Europe," and a symbol of a new Russian historical phase, that of Westernization and European political orientation.

King Charles pursued Peter, who lured him into the Eastern European hinterland. The Swedish forces were finally defeated by the Russians at Poltava between June 27 and July 8, 1709. Charles fled to Turkey, leaving behind 2,000 troops and his general staff as Russian prisoners of war.[52]

In addition to the army, Peter reformed the institutions of the empire. The objective was to facilitate military and financial administration by creating territorial "governments"—and concentrating power in the hands of the generals. All cities and towns over one hundred *versts* away from Moscow were assigned by region to Kyiv, Smolensk, Kazan, and Archangel. Peter borrowed the idea of local governments and their responsibility to maintain the regiments assigned to them from Sweden, as he did other aspects of military administration, but the Russian implementation often fell far behind the Swedish example.

One of the innovations introduced by the first Petrine reform was the priority of central government revenues (necessary for waging war), over the income of the local governments that conducted the collection. This measure put the local governments at a permanent disadvantage vis-à-vis the capital, a feature that was very much part of the scene in the Soviet period.

As Peter was often away from the capital conducting war with Charles, the empire was ruled by the council of boyars, which later evolved into the Russian Senate.[53]

As the financial crunch was growing, the Senate established an institution of *oberfiscal*—a network of agents to conduct surveillance of the citizens, initially on tax matters. A centralized apparatus of informants, so typical in absolute empires, became a permanent fixture in Russian, and later in Soviet, political life.

Despite the reform efforts, the new government system was extremely confused. Accounting was rudimentary, while lines of reporting and responsibility were obfuscated. As in the current Russian Westernization attempts, the transition from the old ways to the new ones created a chaos that took several years to sort out.[54] Unfortunately, the Swedish system of government was ill-suited to Russia's needs.

The last round of Peter's reforms was based on a sound foundation of practices already being applied in the West. These included commercial and industrial policy, the establishment of a chamber of industry, appointing commercial consuls in major European cities, establishing free domestic trade, and terminating state monopolies. But it was also under Peter that the internal passport system was introduced, primarily to account for all the tax-paying peasants and to facilitate collection. This system hampers the mobility of the Russian workforce to this day.

Still, Peter's reforms contributed to a remaking of the Russian ruling elite and the society. He fused the upper classes, demanded service to the state first and foremost, humiliated the old noble families, and promoted many commoners to high ranks.

Peace with Sweden was not concluded until 1721, after three seasons of Russian "punishment expeditions" against the Swedish core. Sweden ceded Livonia, Estonia, and a part of Karelia to Russia. The peace was hailed by Peter as a major accomplishment of his reign. The Senate granted him the title of "Father of his country, Emperor and the Great."

Even before the war with Sweden ended, Peter had launched reconnaissance missions into the Caucasus and the Caspian Sea. His dream was to find a land route to India.[55] The emperor designed plans to establish protectorates over the Christian Georgians and Armenians and to prevent the Porte from moving into the Caucasus and the Caspian. In 1722 Peter, with a 125,000-member army, advanced against Persia on the Caspian coast, past Baku, and up to the fortress of Derbent, which surrendered without a fight. Russian acquisition of the Caspian coast was recognized by the Porte in the treaty of June 1724. Russian attempts to penetrate Transcaspia and Central Asia at this point failed due to an extremely difficult climate and the resistance of local tribes. A small Russian expeditionary force was defeated, and its commander was beheaded in Khiva.

As was true of many other of his policies, the Central Asian project was ahead of Peter's time. He was an empire builder par excellance.[56] In the sixteenth and seventeenth centuries Russia set off on the painful road toward absorbing the transnational factors of culture and technology that would give her the competitive edge needed in order to become a great power. Peter's was an outstanding contribution along this route.

As a result of Peter's reforms and due to his ruthless energy, Russia emerged as a major continental power to be feared and respected for the next three centuries. For the first time, the larger international system, which included the great powers of the time—England, France, the Porte, and the Netherlands—had to be faced by the Russian political elite. The process of Westernization started by Peter was destined to transform Russia into the global power that she remained into the 1980s.

Peter's Heirs and Catherine II

After Peter's death, Russian expansion slowed for several decades. There were succession crises. The state was overstretched, the treasury exhausted, and the administration in shambles. As in other historical periods, expansion and war contributed to an economic turndown.

Despite her troubles, Russia stayed the course of imperial aggrandizement. For example, Russia was involved in intrigues around the Polish succession, and achieved the dethronement of the proFrench Stanislaw Leszczynski (1733) by military force. The proRussian King Augustus III was crowned.

The war with Turkey (1735–1739) cost Russia 100,000 lives and resulted in little territorial or political progress. The Turks were to destroy and evacuate Azov.

The war with Sweden, unprovoked and unwanted in Russia, was considered a diplomatic failure. More successful was Russia's performance in the Seven Year War, when she cooperated with Austria and France against Prussia. After this, Russia returned to the "big league" of European powers.

It took the appearance of another ambitious monarch, Catherine II, to reform the Russian system of administration and resume territorial expansion. Catherine, born Sophia Augusta Frederica Anhalt-Zerbst, was a Prussian princess who married a German-born grandson of Peter the Great, the duke of Schlezwig-Holstein, Carl-Peter-Ulrich, known as Peter III, a mentally and physically weak man.

Soon after the arrival of Peter III and his future wife to Russia, the personal qualities of the two became obvious to the court. Catherine became the center of a strong political faction. Her coup, in which Peter III was killed, was viewed favorably by the Russian nobles and the military.

The first years of Catherine's rule were spent conducting comprehensive administrative and legislative reforms. For nearly 100 years, the Code of Alexei Michailovich had remained untouched, and it was in dire need of change.

The empress reformed the Senate into a more efficient branch of the executive government. She repaid state debts, restored credit, and ended up with a budgetary surplus. An in-depth reform was undertaken in the provinces (*gubernii*), with separation of administrative, judicial, and tax/fiscal functions.[57] Merchantilist policies were replaced under Catherine by a more laissez-faire approach.

The empress pursued a policy of Russification and centralization in the frontier areas. In 1764 she expressed the opinion that, while Ukrainian and Baltic autonomous rights could not be abolished immediately, "to call these regions foreign and to treat them as such would be more than a mistake; it would be indeed plain stupidity."[58]

Under Catherine, the Zaporozhye, Volga, Don, and Urals Cossacks lost their freedoms. Their regiments were absorbed into the Russian army. The Ukrainian Cossacks were settled on the Kuban River. In 1781 left-bank Ukraine lost the remnants of its independence, becoming a governor-generalship of three provinces under the control of Great Russian officials. The Baltic provinces were denied autonomy in 1783.[59] The process of imperial consolidation was proceeding at full speed.

Russia had grand designs upon the Orthodox lands of Byelorussia and Ukraine, ruled by Poland. Playing the European balance of power game in a masterly fashion, Catherine's foreign minister Count Panin implemented his "Northern system," which guaranteed Russo-Prussian domination in northeastern Europe and ensured the weakness of Poland and Sweden.

In order to forestall Russia's annexation of Poland, Austria and France provoked an Ottoman declaration of war on Russia. This war ended in land and naval victories for Russia, as well as in territorial gains.

Catherine pursued the so-called Greek Project, under which the Ottoman Porte would be driven out of Europe and dismembered, and in its stead a Greek empire, ruled by Catherine's grandson, appropriately named Constantine, would be restored, and with it the glory of ancient Byzantium. For this purpose, she sought the support of Emperor Joseph II of Austria. In 1795, according to a secret Austro-Russian agreement, the Porte was to be dismembered and Constantinople seized by Russian troops. Only Catherine's death prevented this from actually being attempted.

The Crimean khanate, last survivor of the Ulus of Juchi, was neutralized and declared independent from the Porte, only to be occupied and annexed by the Russians in 1783. With the occupation of the Crimea, the Russian navy was strengthened and construction of its Sevastopol naval base began, watched anxiously from Constantinople.

The Ottomans attacked southern Russia in 1787, demanding the return of the Crimea. France, supporting the Sublime Porte, provoked Sweden to open a second front. But Russian military power in the last quarter of the eighteenth century was unrivaled. In the Jassy peace treaty (1792), the sultan renounced all his territorial claims to the Crimea and Georgia. Vast territories in the northern Caucasus were annexed to Russia and immediately opened for colonization.

As war with the Ottoman empire was winding down, a 100,000-strong Russian army invaded Poland to oppose the May Constitutional Reform that Catherine had branded "revolutionary." Russian troops, led by Alexander Suvorov, brutally suppressed a popular revolt led by Kosciuzko in 1794. The stage was set for the final partition of Poland (1795). Russia negotiated the agreement with Austria and dictated the terms to Prussia. Catherine acquired Lithuania, Kurland, and parts of Podolia and Volynia, so that all eastern Slav lands with the exception of Galicia were now under the Russian scepter.[60] Within 100 years, the Westernization of Russia had paid tremendous dividends. The absorption of Western technology and military skills turned her into a major European power. It also prepared Russia for the confrontation with Napoleonic France and participation in the European concert of powers (1815–1914).

Many Russian and Soviet historians hail Catherine's expansion as the "achievement of natural borders of the empire" and a "successful solution of Russian foreign policy questions": the Polish and the Turkish ones.[61] Nevertheless, this brutal policy of territory grabbing was a harbinger of Russian pan-Slavism in the Balkans and of the harsh treatment of (Slavic) Poland in the nineteenth and the twentieth centuries. Catherine's Great Russian "patriotism" certainly did not make her the favorite empress of Ukrainians, Poles, Crimean Tatars, and Lithuanians.

Eighteenth-Century Expansion in Siberia and Kazakhstan

While the major thrust of eighteenth-century expansion was in the west and in the south, the Russian "turbulent frontier" also moved south and east in Siberia. There was a creeping transformation of the agricultural borderland into a fortified defense line. By the eighteenth century, what had begun as several forts on the Irtysh had turned into a long chain, extending more than 4,000 kilometers from the Caspian all the way to the Altay Mountains. From the 1720s through the 1740s, major mining towns and forts went up in the Kazakh steppe and the Altay to support the northern war effort.

Russian expansion into the grasslands of Kazakhstan was initially invited by the Kazakhs (Kirghizs), who wanted assistance against the invading Dzhungars, who in turn were pursued by the Chinese (1726–1729). A weak peripheral elite was seeking protection from an expanding Russian metropolis.

As the Russian troops and forts moved in, fortified lines that separated the Bashkirs, Kalmyks, and Kazakhs were built. The Kazakh nomadic movement to protected pastures was blocked, and they were forced to assume a sedentary lifestyle, with dire consequences, as they began dying out. Still, Russian forts provided markets for their livestock surplus and animal husbandry products. What began as a Russian-Kazakh cooperation ended in catastrophe for the nomadic peoples of the steppe. The total subjugation of the Kazakhs occurred in the nineteenth century.

RUSSIAN EXPANSION IN THE LATE EIGHTEENTH–NINETEENTH CENTURIES, THE WAR WITH FRANCE, AND THE HOLY ALLIANCE

The French revolution of 1789 was a central event that continued to influence European politics for at least half a century. In 1798 Russia under Catherine's son, Paul I, joined a coalition of Great Britain, Austria, and the Ottoman Porte against France, which threatened the status quo countries and the international balance-of-power system. Its general, Napoléon Bonaparte, had invaded Egypt on his way to India.

As part of the anti-French effort, Admiral Ushakov's squadron was allowed by the Ottomans into the Ionic and the Adriatic seas in 1799. The Ionic Islands were turned into a Russian-protected republic. Russia acquired a naval base in the Mediterranean for the first time. Montenegro asked to be accepted into the Russian empire. Paul also took the Maltese Order under his auspices. Russian strength in the Balkans and the eastern Mediterranean suddenly reached unprecedented proportions. The Greek Project was closer to its implementation than ever. However, Emperor Paul was assassinated by guard officers loyal to his son, Alexander, in 1801. In 1805 Russia reentered the coalition war against Napoleonic France. In 1806 the Porte, which was allied with France, declared war on Russia, only to lose Bessarabia to Alexander. Another French ally, Sweden, declared war on Russia only to forfeit Finland. Despite these peripheral victories, the main Russian armies were defeated in Central Europe by Napoléon.

After the peace of Tilzit (1807) divided Europe into two spheres of influence, Russian and French, Alexander became Napoléon's ally in the so-called continental system that isolated England from European trade. This alliance was not popular in Russia, as preparations for war with Napoléon were under way. There are certain parallels between the situation in Europe in 1812 and 1941. In both cases, Russia seemingly acquiesced to the ruler of Europe, but was aware of the possibility of invasion. In both cases, England was isolated and waiting for the fatal mistake of the hostile conqueror. Russia's retreat into the hinterland, the size of the country, and the severity of its winter were similarly devastating for the invading army.

After Napoléon's invasion of Russia (1812) and the spectacular victory of the coalition arms over the French, Russian troops for the first time reached Paris. While the victors were dividing the spoils of war in the Congress of Vienna (1815), Napoléon attempted to restore his rule but was defeated at Waterloo. Russian troops were reintroduced into France to maintain order. Russia thus ensured its status as a major European power, and Alexander was compensated with the Duchy of Warsaw, which was renamed the Tsardom of Poland. Poznan was ceded to Prussia and Galicia to Austria.

The status of Russia was further strengthened by the principal of intervention agreed upon by the members of the Holy Alliance to intercede in each other's internal affairs in order to maintain the political status quo. The revolutions of 1830 in Belgium and France led to an uprising in Poland, but the armies of Russia and Prussia crushed the insurgents. In a deliberate affront, Tsar Nicholas I (who succeeded his brother Alexander I in 1825), awarded the Russian General Paskevich, who had conquered Warsaw, the title of Prince of Warsaw and Viceroy of Poland.[62] Mass exiles of Poles to Siberia followed.

Russia's reputation as the "gendarme of Europe" was strengthened in 1849, when Nicholas I sent his troops to suppress a revolution against the Habsburgs that broke out in Hungary. For the next several decades, Russia was intensely disliked by revolutionary and liberal circles throughout Europe.[63]

The defeat in the Crimean War (1855) ended Russia's status as the predominant European power, especially in Balkan and Ottoman affairs, which she had enjoyed from the time of Catherine II. The Russian imperial protectorate over the Danubian provinces and Balkan Orthodox Christians was ended. Austro-Hungarian influence in these areas was on the rise. Russia lost her access to the Danube delta and the Black Sea. The Aaland Islands were demilitarized, and Kars was surrendered to the Ottoman empire.[64]

There are parallels between the repercussions of the Soviet defeat in Afghanistan and the aftermath of the Crimean War. As in the case of Gorbachev, the new ruler, Alexander II—very much a product of the previous era—stunned his contemporaries with his demands for a "frank presentation of all defects," the abrogation of "petty limitations on the press," and his stated desire for "openness, enlightenment, truthfulness and free voice."[65] However, there was more to the reforms of 1861 than mere progressive disposition. "Reform had been embarked upon to help reverse the decline in international standing Russia had suffered in the Crimean War, to prevent the Russian Empire from going the way of the Ottoman Empire, and to make Russia in actual fact into the great power she claimed to be."[66]

There was an understanding that serfdom had brought the state to a dead end. If economic and administrative development were to be achieved, reforms could not be avoided. A need for "realism" in international relations—several years of peace to undertake a major housecleaning—was recognized. In addition, modernization of the armed forces and railway building were vital to maintain Russia's status as a great power.

Thus, the reforms were primarily an attempt to *maintain imperial power* through government-initiated measures aimed at extricating the country from a systemic crisis.[67] They were influenced by the requirements of legitimacy the Russian society was quick to present to the government once the rigid controls of the Nikolayevan epoch were relaxed.

Similar to postcommunist Russia, the mid-nineteenth-century great power shift from an aristocracy to an emerging bourgeoisie and middle class was accompanied by a redistribution of wealth. Today, emergence of the postcommunist elite is accompanied by a redefinition of property relations and the redistribution of productive assets. In both cases, poor military and foreign policy performance led to major reform efforts.

RUSSIAN NATIONALISM AND PAN-SLAVISM

The Polish War of 1863 and Its Repercussions

One of the central slogans of Alexander II's reforms was *glasnost*. It created, similarly to the Soviet case, informed public opinion and a flurry of newspapers critical of the government. The public soon was split among liberal, conservative, Slavophile, and radical-democratic camps. Most of these groups were in opposition to the bureaucracy. Despite this, very few people were ready to give up autocracy and move toward a Western-style representative democracy.[68] Nationalism could provide an alternative to autocracy as a unifying force for the Russian people. It was co-opted (in the second half of Alexander II's rule, but especially under his son, Alexander III, and his grandson, Nicholas II) to represent a coalescing factor known as the "populism" (*narodnost*). The slogan Orthodoxy, Autocracy, Populism (*Pravoslaviye, Samoderzhaviye, Narodnost'*) came to reflect the Russian national ideology.

A deep contradiction developed between the regime and the diverse nationalities constituting its multinational empire. While Alexander II was aware of this, his heirs were not. The militant Russian nationalism of the governing elite brought with it the seeds of the empire's destruction half a century later. As was suggested by Gallagher in *The Decline, Revival and Fall of the British Empire*, the dependent elites learned their own nationalism from the metropolitan nation (the Russians) and opted first for autonomy and then (after the Bolshevik revolution) for independence. Although in the second part of the nineteenth and for most of the twentieth century attempts to secure national self-determination were thwarted, events in Gorbachev's USSR proved the validity of Nederveen Pieterse's hypotheses in *Empire and Emancipation* regarding the long-term influence of liberation ideas.

When a challenge from Poland arose in the early 1860s, it created a unifying effect on polarized Russian public opinion, which turned dead against the Polish aspirations. The Poles had suffered persecution for twenty-five years. The "thaw" under Alexander II renewed their hopes for independence. European and Siberian exiles were allowed to return home. The "tsar-liberator" was willing to grant the Poles home rule.

As in the past, supporters of moderate reforms in the Polish society were quickly outnumbered. By December 1862–January 1863, there were demands for the reestablishment of the independent Polish crown and historical borders reaching to the Zapadnaya Dvina and the Dnieper. An assassination attempt was made against the grand duke. A clandestine "national government" was in charge of the rebellion.

Soon, shopkeepers in Finland and the Baltic lands began to display portraits of Garibaldi. The Russian government decided that a tough line against the Poles would unify the otherwise fragmented Russian society. Foreign denunciations of the Russian treatment of the Poles only contributed to the rising xenophobia, as the specter of yet another war with the European powers seemed a realistic possibility.

The popular anti-Polish and anti-European feelings were captured by Slavophile writers, such as Katkov, to create Russian national solidarity. A hysterical campaign against Polish arsonists, spies, and well-poisoners was a harbinger of both the "Black Hundreds" of the 1900s and the Zhdanovite persecution of the "cosmopolitan" Jews in the 1940s and 1950s.

The Polish insurrection was severely suppressed by Russian troops. Thousands of Poles were hanged. The kingdom itself was abolished and instead a "Vistula Region" was created.

The Russification of Poland and Lithuania was pursued intensively. Russian agricultural settlers were brought in. The Polish language was banned from schools.[69] In 1864 administration of the kingdom was revised. Ten provinces and eighty-four Russian-style counties (*uezdy*) were created. All properties of the Catholic Church in Poland were confiscated and the monasteries were closed.

A campaign of suppression aimed at the nascent Ukrainian nationalist movement was also launched. In 1875 an official commission recommended a series of anti-Ukrainian measures. All publications and concerts in the Ukrainian language were banned.

Following the Polish war, the forces of Russian nationalism began to attack previously loyal, though culturally separate, ethnic groups: Baltic Germans, Finns, Armenians, and others. The traditional privileges of the Baltic Germans—loyal servants of the crown under Nicholas I and Alexander II—were assailed. Russian was introduced as the official language of the administration.

The opposition of the Baltic peoples to their former German masters and Russian overlords in national language newspapers and literature began to shape the consciousness of the Estonians and Latvians.

The Balkan Wars, Growth of National Awareness and the Seeds of Destruction

Once the Polish "threat" was over, the Slavophiles formulated another set of goals. Without renouncing the 300-hundred-year-long objective of seizing Constantinople and the Straits, they argued that the coming clash would be between the Slavs and the Teutons (the Germans). This ideology had important ramifications. Internally, there was considerable Baltic German influence at the court, in the bureaucracy, and especially in the foreign service. Externally, Vienna was in the way of the liberation of the Slavic brethren yearning for unification with the Russian elder brother under the scepter of the tsar.

Economically, Russian goods could not compete with those turned out by the industrial powerhouses of the Ruhr, Silezia, and Bohemia, and cries abounded for stricter protectionist policies so that Mother Russia would not deteriorate into an agricultural appendix of the Reich. After the Prusso-Austrian war of 1866 and the Franco-Prussian war of 1870 it was clear that the Russian army could not match Bismarck's military machine. Thus, Slavophilia transformed itself into Germanophobia.[70] Simultaneously, Russian relations with Britain and France had been strained since the debacle of the Crimean War. It is little wonder that Russian nationalism began assuming defensive and desperate overtones.

Similarly to the ravings of Vladimir Zhirinovsky today, the declarations of the pan-Slavist leaders were often embarrassing to the bureaucracy and the crown. They not only attacked the government in the name of the nation, but also continually questioned the very existence of the Russian diplomatic interlocutors—the Ottoman Porte and the Austro-Hungarian empire, thus putting Russia in an awkward position in the *Dreikaiserbund* (the Union of the Three Kings) reconstituted by Bismarck.

Russia's leadership was aware of the restraining factors afflicting its foreign policy, such as economic weakness, a debt ridden budget, and an underequipped and poorly trained military. At the same time, it was under pressure to act as a great power and appeal to the traditional elite's quest for imperial grandeur with its career-enhancing opportunities.

Once Serbia and Montenegro started military operations against the Ottomans (1877), with the Serbian army commanded by a retired Russian general, there was an outburst of popular support for the Slavic cause. The tsar, after deliberations, called the Russians to fight for "Russia's holy mission."

For the first time since the Polish rebellion, Russian public opinion rallied behind the emperor, who proceeded to march to war and win a military victory at Plevna and a short-lived diplomatic triumph at the peace conference of San Stephano.

The future was imbued with uncertainty, as Russia resisted a clear demarcation of spheres of influence in the Balkans. While sober politicians in St. Petersburg recognized that securing the eastern Balkans from economic penetration by the German speaking nations would satisfy Russian interests, an "activist" school won the day. It argued against limitations being placed on Russia's ability to come to rescue of the Balkan peoples.[71] History proved this decision to be disastrous, as the Russian commitment to Balkan expansion and domination of the Straits eventually contributed to the calamity of World War I.

The process of Russification and greater central control of the provinces intensified after the assassination of Alexander II in March 1881. Official policy now proclaimed that the Russian people, the Russian language and the Orthodox religion must enjoy predominance in the empire. The underlying rationale was to create a new basis of legitimacy for the regime in the name of the Russian nation.

Vladimir Solovyev summarized the development of Russian nationalism in 1889:

> (It was) adoration of one's people with a direct negation of the very idea of universal truth—these are the three gradual stages of our nationalism, represented in succession by the Slavophiles, by Katkov and by the latest obscurantists. The first of these taught pure fantasies; the second was a realist with imagination; the last are realists without any imagination but also without any shame.[72]

The Russian chauvinist reaction continued unhindered until the revolution of 1905, at which point a certain liberalization took place. But already by 1907, with the appointment of Stolypin to the post of prime minister, nationalism had returned to rule. Stolypin considered that the minorities of the empire should be Russian patriots in a modern Russian nation-state. He tolerated the virulent anti-Semitism of the extreme right, was preparing to do away with the Finnish autonomy, and was planning to deal decisive blows to the Polish and Ukrainian nationalist movements—all in the name of combating socialism.

The Russian ruling elite, as arrogant as it was isolated from the bulk of the society and the people, did not excel in developing either the American "melting pot" or the Austro-Hungarian culturally autonomous coexistence.

While several nations—the Poles, the Jews, the Ukrainians and the Tatars—were treated harshly even before the emergence of nationalism, from the 1880s even the loyal Armenians, Baltic Germans, and Finns were alienated and suffered from Russification. As a result, the intelligentsia of these nations became determined to bring the masses of peasantry into nationalist struggles.

Russia was entering the twentieth-century world of mass politics with all the attributes of, in August Bebel's words, "the socialism of imbeciles." Anti-Semitic, demagogic, nationalist socialist movements were rampant. The curse of Great Russian chauvinism, which threw masses of *inorodtsy* (non-Russians) into the thick of the revolutionary struggle, as well as the appalling lack of attention to and sensitivity for the national and cultural needs of the minorities, was digging the empire's grave.

EXPANSION IN THE CAUCASUS, CENTRAL ASIA, AND THE FAR EAST

Expansion in the Caucasus

Christian Georgia appealed to Russia for help against the dual expansionist threat of the Moslem Ottoman Porte and Persia. In 1804 a Persian-Russian war started which, due to the Russian involvement in the Napoleonic wars, continued until 1813. Under the Gulistan peace treaty of that year, Georgia, Guria, Imeretia, Mingrelia, and Abkhazia, as well as Dagestan and Azerbaijan, were ceded to Russia.

In 1826, under Nicholas I, the war with Persia began again. Under the Turkmanchai peace treaty of 1828, the Erivan' and Nachichevan khanates were ceded to Russia and a contribution was to be paid by Teheran.

The Moslem mountaineers of the north Caucasus, including the Chechens, declared a holy war (*gazavat/jihad*) against the Russian infidels, under the able leadership of Imam Shamil. Only during the rule of Alexander II was the rebellion put down.[73] However, the rebellious spirit never died in the mountains of the Caucasus.

Expansion in Kazakhstan

Throughout the eighteenth century, the Russians maintained pressure on the Kazakh steppe. By the nineteenth century, the khans of the Younger and the Middle Hordes were being appointed by the Russian tsar.

In 1822 the territory of the Middle Horde was annexed to the Omsk *oblast*. The Kazakh khan was replaced by a council of sultans responsible to the commander of the Russian Siberian Army Line in Omsk.[74]

Eventually, the Kazakh clans were restricted in their freedom of movement, and each was assigned to a permanent *okrug* administered by a Russian garrison. The *okrug* offices were manned by Siberian Cossacks, who were effectively turned into the imperial policing force. The Cossacks also were granted (Kazakh) land for their livelihood. A Kazakh rebellion followed in 1838.

In 1846 the Elder Horde, which suffered military pressure from the Kokand khanate, allied itself with Russia. Russian control over Kazakhstan was finalized after 1860 in the border demarcation treaty with China and after the building of a fortress line against the Turkestan khanates (1864–1865).

After military control was secured, the floodgates of Slav peasant colonization opened. The new code of 1868 allowed for the expropriation of Kazakh lands. While Russian settlers were granted free land and timber for house building, only those Kazakhs who would accept Christian Orthodoxy and join agricultural communities were granted similar privileges.[75]

Between 1906 and 1915 more than one million peasants from Russia and Ukraine migrated to Kazakhstan, when the new Trans-Siberian railroad made the steppe more accessible. The building of the Turkestan railroad encouraged even deeper penetration by Russian colonists into the steppe.

Expansion in Central Asia

Russian intellectuals and Orientalists in the second half of the nineteenth century produced a wealth of writings justifying Russia's "historical mission" in Asia. M. Pogodin, in the wake of the Russian defeat in the Crimean War, called for a redirection of the expansionist drive to the east, "so that Japeth may rise above his brothers." Solovyev and Kluchevsky saw Russian expansion as a salient feature of Russian historical destiny. Miliukov considered colonization a process that would lead to the creation of a Great Russian nation.

The Slavophiles saw the Russian destiny in Asia in the apocalyptic context of struggle with both the West and the Islamic East. By the 1880s, Russian aspirations in East Asia had become a focus of discussion.

The question of assimilation of the Turkic peoples into the Slavic ethnic universe was a touchy one. It was viewed positively by the more liberal intelligentsia as long as the Russian birthrate was very high, around the turn of the century, but was often frowned upon later.

The relationship of Russia with Asia and its unique role in the world formed the centerpiece of the Eurasianist movement that flourished in the Russian emigré community in the 1920s and 1930s. The Eurasianists advocated a fusion of Russia's Greco-Byzantine and Mongol-Turkic heritages.

Eurasianist concepts influenced the Soviet ideologists of the Khrushchev era, with their advocacy of *sliyaniye* (merger) and *peremeshivaniye* (mixing) of ethnic groups, culminating in the creation of "Great Russian culture."

Russian expansion in Central Asia started long before the pronouncements of the Slavophile ideologues. The preoccupation of eighteenth-century Russian rulers primarily with Europe made the Russian advance into Central Asia possible only by the mid-nineteenth century. After General Perovsky's unsuccessful campaign in 1839, a policy of encirclement and steady advancement was undertaken. A new geographic unit was created, named Turkestan, under a capable military ruler, Governor General von Kaufman. In 1867 he was granted the authority to conduct foreign affairs with and wage wars upon the neighboring Central Asian kingdoms.

The Russian conquest of Central Asia proceeded in steps, from 1866 to 1895. The khanates were taken one by one. An encirclement then followed, cutting the khanates off from the Persian and Afghan borders. This Russian move, threatening the western foreposts of the British Raj in India, almost caused a war between the Russia and the British empire. An agreement establishing the border of the Russian empire was signed between the two powers in 1895.[76]

Russia achieved control of Turkestan with relatively small forces. After the military operations were over, a 50,000-man military contingent sufficed to control 8 million natives. Slavic agricultural colonization followed in the footsteps of the soldiers. One requirement for successful subjugation of the steppe, as in other cases of expanding empires, was a local peripheral elite which served as a conduit of Russian influence.

A Case of Imperial Overextension: Russian Policies in the Far East

In the Far East, Russia took advantage of the weakening of the Chinese empire due to its defeat in the Opium Wars (1839–1842).

While the foreign ministry was anxious not to antagonize the European powers and the Chinese, Captain Nevelskoy, disregarding his orders, established Nikolayevskii Post in the mouth of Amur (1850). He was threatened with demotion to a sailor, but Nicholas I pardoned him with a famous quote, "Where the Russian flag has flown, it must not be lowered again."[77]

In April 1853, the Russian-American Company was instructed to take over the administration of Sakhalin. Under the Shimoda treaty (1855), the Kurile Islands were divided between Russia and Japan. Sakhalin was declared a common possession; the ports of Shimoda, Hakodate, and Nagasaki were opened for Russian navigation. Two more treaties were signed in 1857 and 1858.

Now it was time to convince the Chinese to recognize the Russian acquisition of the Amur delta. Through skillful negotiations, the Chinese were persuaded to cede Russia territory between the Ussuri River and the Pacific, thus allowing the construction of the warm water port of Vladivostok (Master of the East in Russian).

The only territory abandoned by Russia in the Far East was Alaska. The sea-otter population had been depleted due to unmerciful exploitation by hunters and the territory was not producing any revenue. The Russian government spent large sums to lobby the American congress and media to support the purchase of Alaska for $7 million. The treaty finalizing the transaction was signed on March 30, 1867, and the United States assumed sovereignty on October 18.

Russia undertook a new stage in its Far Eastern advance with the announcement of the construction of the Trans-Siberian Railway on March 17, 1891. The railway, to be the longest in the world, was justified in terms of Siberian economic development and as a channel for grain distribution, especially after the great famine of 1891.

Despite the stated economic goals, this was an expansionist program, promulgated by Finance Minister Sergei Witte. He believed that Russia would be able to penetrate the Chinese market and preempt the British, who were rumored to be preparing to build a south-north railway into Manchuria.

Witte chose to compete with Britain in the Far East, an area where British communications were the most stretched and the British positions the weakest, while Russia's geographical proximity and the intended railway should have produced the best results. However, despite his plans, Russia was to suffer a resounding defeat in the region.

When China and Japan clashed over Korea in 1894, both countries sent in their troops. After the Chinese were routed, Japan demanded the Liaotung Peninsula including Port Arthur, which was already a Russian concession. Witte maintained that the establishment of a Japanese stronghold on the mainland would increase her power, and demanded that Russia play for time until the Trans-Siberian Railway was completed. Until then, Russia had to prevent the annexation of Chinese territory by Japan and bring the pressures of Berlin and Paris on Tokyo. The Japanese government finally yielded and abandoned the Liaotung Peninsula.

Russia advanced into Manchuria, but also tried to keep its positions in Korea. When a new bout of territory grabbing by the great powers in China began in 1898, Russia secured for itself Liaotung Peninsula and Port Arthur for twenty-five years, and received a concession for the South Manchurian Railway from Kharbin to Port Arthur, thus securing a land link to the port and expanding its sphere of influence into northern China.

Confrontation between St. Petersburg and Tokyo was again avoided by an agreement in 1898, in which Russia and Japan recognized Korean independence, while Russia acknowledged Japanese economic interests in Korea. However, this only papered over Japan's alarm concerning the Russian expansionist course in the Far East, which was understandable in light of Russian claims for "sphere d'action exclusive" not only in Chinese Turkestan and Manchuria, but also in all of northern China, including the capital, Beijing.

When the anti-Western Boxer rebellion erupted, Japan came out in defense of China, and the Russians backed off, signing a treaty with China (April 2, 1902) under which the Russian troops were to be withdrawn by October 1903.

The Japanese, sensing Russian intransigence over Manchuria, concluded an alliance with Britain on January 30, 1902, that recognized Japanese interests in Korea and provided for a military alliance.

A disastrous influence on Tsar Nicholas II, Alexander's successor, in the Pacific policy was exercised by Captain A.M. Bezobrazov, who got Nicholas involved as shareholder in timber concessions on the Yalu River through the East Asiatic Development Company and the Russian Timber Company of the Far East. While Bezobrazov lost his sway with the tsar in July 1903, he contributed to the dismissal of Witte in August and to the collapse of Witte's Far Eastern policy.

The Russians did not withdraw from Manchuria on the planned date of February 1903. The Chinese recruited American and Japanese assistance, and the Manchurian question became the focus of the Russo-Japanese confrontation. On October 8, 1903, diplomatic exchanges dead-ended, with China signing treaties with Japan and the United States. The planned Russian evacuation from Manchuria never happened.

Russia was not ready to recognize Japanese hegemony in Korea, while Japan had never accepted the Russian occupation of the Liaotung Peninsula.

Russia's policy of peaceful penetration was a debacle. Initiated by Witte, its aim was to open economically underdeveloped areas with a vacuum of political authority. Witte treated economic development as a category of power, and he pursued it by securing foreign loans and providing expertise for railway construction. Russia attempted to create its own zone of economic domination, but it failed.

Witte's policy also could be analyzed from the perspective of the Russo-British competition over the Eurasian landmass, in which Russia, seen geopolitically as heir to the Genghizian land empire, controlled the "heartland" while maritime Britain and Japan controlled the "rimland." Russia's limitations were multifaceted. Her economic base was founded on an impoverished agricultural sector. Her industrialization was based on capital imports and could not support a forward imperialist policy. Her autocracy did not develop policy-making institutions adequate to the process of imperial policy formulation and implementation. In short, Russia's systemic weakness led to a systemic crisis which proved fatal for the empire.

Hostilities in the Far East were initiated by Japan, beginning in early February 1904. Russia had vastly overestimated her ability to project power over such a great distance. Her navy suffered a series of humiliating defeats, including a rout in the Tsushima battle. The Japanese army landed in Korea and breached the Yalu River. The Russian army, under General Kuropatkin, was defeated at Liaolian and the Shakha River.

On December 19, 1904, Port Arthur surrendered to the Japanese. The Japanese army then moved to the Manchurian front, where it soundly defeated the Russians at Mukden.

Russian policy in the Far East lay in shambles. Japanese hegemony in Korea was recognized, while Russia abandoned Manchuria and gave up Port Arthur and the South Manchurian Railway. Japan also received "eternal and full ownership" of the southern half of the Sakhalin Islands (up to the 50th parallel).

Even more important, the war exposed the feebleness of Nicholas II's regime. After the Russo-Japanese war, the revolutionary and nationalist movements in Russia severely shook the foundations of the autocracy, and it is only due to the reforms forced on the establishment, and later the consolidation and further economic reforms of the Stolypin era, that the end of the empire was postponed for a decade.

CONCLUSIONS

The Russian empire was different from its Spanish, British, and French counterparts in that it expanded over land, not overseas—and with outstanding results. In 300 years (1600–1900) Russia grew by 17 million square kilometers. It resembled the great empires of the past: China, Rome, and the Ottoman empire. In its nature it was a universal empire, a contained geographical and historical unit that measured its political values and successes in relation to itself, not in comparison with other countries.[78]

Unlike the Western European colonial empires, profits, markets, and sources of raw materials were not the central motives for expansion. On the other hand, not all the aggrandizement was based on military conquest either. Most of Russia's thrust along the east-west axis was undertaken against the hunters and gatherers of the Urals and Siberia and the nomads of the Asian steppes, who lacked state organization. These tribes, like the ones in the Americas, could be easily exterminated or subjugated.

Expansion along the north-south axis was characterized by the steadfast movement of fortified lines south and southeast.

Russia began her expansion earlier than the northern European powers—approximately in the same time as the Spanish *reconquista*. Initially this aggrandizement followed four riverheads that led the Russian settlers, troops—and borders—toward the four seas: the Black, the Caspian, the White, and the Baltic.[79] Russian imperial growth ended about the same time as that of the other European powers. At that point, she had reached her natural geographic limitations and had experienced overextension in the Far East. Russia failed to develop Western-style capital-driven imperialism. Nor is there any historical precedent to indicate that this would have saved her empire, as the experiences of Britain and France demonstrate.

Similarly to her Ottoman and Habsburg contemporaries, Russia, while succeeding in conquest, failed at the assimilation of the major nationalities of the realm. Moreover, the Great Russian chauvinist policies antagonized the majority of the *inorodtsy* (non-Russians), who opted out of the imperial arrangement.

Without the Bolshevik coup and the subsequent ruthless military activities of the Red Army, the empire might not have been reconstituted in the form it existed between 1921 and 1991. The processes of Russification continued in the contiguous Russian/Soviet empire longer than similar cultural and linguistic influences in the European dominions overseas primarily due to the "reassembly" of the empire by the Soviet regime. It seems reasonable to conjecture that these processes would not have taken place with the same intensity if a federal or confederate, rather than a centralized structure, had been created in the wake of World War I.

The failures in the foreign policy area, from overextension in the Far East to preoccupation with the Straits, the Middle East, and India, and the "adventurist" Balkan policies, brought upon the Russian empire the debacle of World War I. Due to its internal feebleness, the state could not sustain such a disaster. By 1917 Russian nationalism had exhausted its resources, and the national minorities were not interested in dying for an inept autocrat. The empire that the tsars had built disintegrated, only to be reassembled with renewed ferocity under a seemingly antithetic regime.

The next chapter will examine how the Russian empire was reconstituted under the rule of Lenin's and Stalin's Communist party and received yet another lease on life.

NOTES

1. The modern Ukrainian spelling of Kyiv is used throughout this book.

2. Daniel Ostrovsky, "The Mongol Origin of Muscovite Political Institutions," *Slavic Review*, vol. 49, no. 4, Winter 1990, p. 525. Throughout his article, Ostrovsky uses the term Kipchak Khanate instead of the Golden Horde, which he calls a sixteenth-century Muscovite propagandistic term. Ostrovsky is correct; however, since the term Golden Horde appears in the majority of the sources used for this book, the terms the Golden Horde, Ulus of Juchi, and Kipchak Khanate are used interchangeably.

3. Ibid., p. 529.

4. Ibid., p. 529.

5. G. V. Vernadsky, *Nachertaniye Russkoy Istorii*, (Prague: Yevraziyskoye Knigoizdatel'stvo, 1927), p. 87.

6. Ibid., p. 88.

7. Ostovsky, "The Mongol Origin," p. 528.

8. Ibid., p. 529.

9. Interview with Dr. Harold Rhode, Office of the Secretary of Defense, Pentagon, September 1990.

10. Ostrovsky, "The Mongol Origin," pp. 535–36.

11. Russian imperial historians, as well as their Soviet counterparts, differ with this assessment. Nevertheless, Rambaud recognized that "the first tsars of Muscovy were the political descendants not of the Russian princes [of Kyivan Rus'] but of the Tartar khans." (Ibid., p. 172).

12. S.O. Platonov, *Lektsii po Russkoy istorii*, 9th ed. (Petrograd, Iv. Blinov, 1915), p. 153.

13. One hundred years later, Kazan would be stormed by the Russian troops of Ivan IV (Grozny), never again to recover the status of an independent Tatar capital.

14. Vernadsky, *Nachertaniye Russkoy istorii*, p. 118.

15. V.O. Kluchevsky, *Skazaniya inostrantzev o Moskovskom gosudarstve* (Petrogram, Literaturno-Izdatel'skii Otdel Kommissariata Narodnogo Prosveshcheniya, 1918) pp. 241, 243.

16. Platonov, *Lektsii po Russkoy istorii*, p. 159.

17. Ibid., pp. 163, 165.

18. Ibid., p. 166.

19. Anthonius Possevinus, quoted in Kluchevsky, *Skazaniya*, p. 128.

20. A. Olearius, *Relation du Voyage d'Adam Olearius en Moscovie, Tartarie et Perse*, pp. 181, 221; Augustin, Baron de Mayerberg, *Relation d'un Voyage en Moscovie*, II, p. 107; Grigoiy Kotoshikhin, *O Rossii v Tzarstvovanie Alexeya Mikhaylovicha*—all quoted in Kluchevsky, *Skazaniya*, p. 130.

21. Ibid., pp. 131–35.

22. Kluchevsky mentions that in the seventeenth century, the *Razryadniy Prikaz* (ministry of defense) was in the business of selling governorships (*voyevodstva*). After spending extremely high sums to attain their jobs, the governors would in turn take bribes on a grand scale, knowing that the head of the *prikaz* would not investigate complaints about their misconduct as he benefited from the arrangement. Those who did not take themselves allowed their wives and relatives to serve as conduits for bribes (pp. 155–57).

For information on how similar arrangements were in practice quite recently, see, for example, *Radio Liberty Soviet Area Audience and Opinion Research (SAAOR) Reports*, 1984–1990.

23. Kluchevsky, *Skazaniya*, p. 157.

24. Vernadsky, *Nachertaniye Russkoy istorii*, p. 148.

25. Platonov, *Lektsii po Russkoy istorii*, p. 185.

26. Compare this usage of troops with the use of the Cubans by the Soviets in Africa in the 1970s and 1980s.

27. Vernadsky, *Nachertaniye Russkoy istorii*, pp. 143–44.

28. Raymond Beazley, Nevill Forbes, and G. A. Birkett, *Russia* (Oxford: Oxford University Press, 1918), pp. 128–29.

29. Platonov, *Lektsii po Russkoy istorii*, p. 211.

30. Vernadsky, *Nachertaniye Russkoy istorii*, p. 149, and Platonov, *Lektsii po Russkoy istorii*, p. 190.

31. Platonov quoting *Poslaniye startza Filopheya k dyaku Munekhinu* in *Lektsii po Russkoy istorii*, p. 245.

32. Ibid., pp. 213–15.

33. For a detailed discourse on the relationship between the boyars and the monarchy, see Platonov, *Lektsii po Russkoy istorii*, pp. 190 ff.

34. Vernadsky, *Nachertaniye Russkoy istorii*, pp. 147–48.

35. For a detailed description of the Time of Troubles, see Platonov, *Lektsii po Russkoy istorii*, pp. 250–80.

36. Ibid., pp. 281–83.

37. Kluchevsky, *Skazaniya*, p. 41.

38. Ibid., pp. 208–9.

39. Ph. Avril (S.J.), *Voyage en divers etats d'Europe et d'Asie enterpris pour decouvrir un nouveau chemin à la Chine* (Paris, 1691), quoted in Kluchevsky, *Skazaniya*, p. 212.

40. Ibid., p. 166.

41. Ibid., pp. 280–91.

42. S. Herberstein, *Rerum Moscoviticarum auctores varii*, quoted in Kluchevsky, *Skazaniya*, pp. 300–301. Herberstein complained about the Moscovites, who habitually indulged in questionable business practices, such as price gouging, misrepresentation, mediating in business transactions with obvious conflict of interest on the part of the middleman, and so on.

43. Ibid., p. 174.

44. Vernadsky, *Nachertaniye Russkoy istorii*, pp. 166–67.

45. For a detailed description of Ukrainian infighting and the intrigues in Moscow, see Vernadsky, *The Tsardom of Moscow, 1547-1682* (New Haven: Yale University Press, 1969), pp. 636–38.

46. Ibid., p. 181.

47. Ibid., pp. 649–50. The standing armies were small and consisted of guards and infantry. Although the emir of Bukhara, in case of an emergency could mobilize as many as 150,000 people, most of them did not have firearms.

48. Ibid., pp. 547–48.

49. Ibid., p. 646.

50. Ibid., pp. 549–54.

51. Paul Miliukov, Charles Seignobos, and L. Eisenmann, *Empire of Peter the Great*, vol. 1 (New York: Funk and Wagnall, 1968), pp. 221–22.

52. Ibid., 240–41.

53. Ibid., p. 256.

54. Ibid., pp. 262–64.

55. Peter was seeking ways to invade India and China and even shipped the Vilster expedition to capture Madagascar and to establish a naval route to "Bengalia."

56. Vernadsky, *Tsardom*, pp. 191–94. Vernadsky notes that Peter's military reform, with its emphasis on the use of masses of troops and concentration of artillery, was rooted in the Genghizian tradition on which the Moscovite military machine was initially based.

57. Florinsky, *Russia* (New York, 1953), vol. 1, p. 555, as quoted in David MacKenzie and Michael W. Curran, *A History of Russia and the Soviet Union* (Homewood, Illinois: The Dorsey Press, 1977), p. 234.

58. Ibid., p. 234.

59. The peace of Kuchuk-Kainarji, in 1774, was the first to mark Ottoman decline and give Russia vast territorial gains. In this treaty, the sultan recognized the Russian right to intervene to protect the Balkan Christians, thus opening an avenue for subsequent Russian interventions in the Balkans.

60. MacKenzie and Curran, *A History of Russia*, p. 240.

61. Platonov, *Lektsii po Russkoy istorii*, pp. 639–43.

62. Hugh Setton-Watson, *The Russian Empire 1801–1917* (Oxford: Clarendon Press, 1967), pp. 281–88.

63. S. G. Pushkarev, *Rossiya v XIX veke* (New York: Izdatel'stvo imeni Chekhova, 1956), p. 193.

64. Dietrich Geyer, *Russian Imperialism: The Interaction of Domestic and Foreign Policy 1860–1914* (New York: Berg, 1987), p. 19.

65. Platonov, *Lektsii po Russkoy istorii*, p. 701.

66. Geyer, *Russian Imperialism*, p. 32.

67. Ibid., pp. 19–20.

68. Ibid., p. 28.

69. Platonov, *Lektsii po Russkoy istorii*, pp. 719–21.

70. Geyer, *Russian Imperialism*, p. 57.

71. Geyer, *Russian Imperialism*, p. 106.

72. V.S. Solovyev, *Sobraniye Sochinenii*, vol. V, p. 228, quoted in Setton-Watson, *The Russian Empire*, p. 486.

73. Pushkarev, *Rossiya v XIX veke*, p. 177.

74. For such as crimes against the state, robbery, and murder. See I. Stebelsky, "The Frontier in Central Asia", in James H. Baker and R.A. French, eds., *Studies in Russian Historical Geography* (London: Academic Press, 1983), p. 154.

75. Ibid., p. 157.

76. Ibid., pp. 163–64.

77. Setton-Watson, *The Russian Empire*, p. 297.

78. Personal interview with Andrei Bystritzky, advisor to the Supreme Soviet of the Russian Federation, Moscow, October 1990.

79. Milan Hauner, *What is Asia to Us? Russia's Asian Heartland Yesterday and Today* (Boston: Unwin Hyman, 1990), p. 70.

3

The Soviet Empire: 1917–1985

COLLAPSE OF THE ROMANOV EMPIRE

By 1916, with the Romanov empire weakened as a result of World War I, the nationalities problem, together with the questions of peace and land, had emerged as a central issue on the political agenda. The Russians, the dominant nation of the empire, constituted 43 percent of the total population. The Russian political class was unwilling to fathom autonomy, let alone independence, for their non-Russian fellow citizens. Nevertheless, many of the non-Russians had embarked upon the path of national self-realization, seeking political representation and building national institutions.

The 1917 struggle for power in St. Petersburg between the Bolsheviks and the provisional government prompted many of the non-Russians to seek solutions to their political aspirations through the creation of separate nation-states. A wave of secessions occurred. The Romanov empire, known as a "prison of peoples," collapsed less than two years before Austria-Hungary and the Ottoman Porte. While Russia ostensibly was part of the winning Entente, it in fact lost the Great War together with Turkey and Austria.

LENIN, STALIN, AND THE END OF THE TSARIST EMPIRE

From the beginning of his political career, Lenin fought for a monolithic party to control a centralized state. Expounding upon "the national question," he pointed out that "our unreserved recognition of the struggle for freedom of self-determination does not in any way commit us to supporting every demand for national self-determination. The Social-Democratic Party considers it to be its positive and principal task to further the self-determination of the proletariat in each nationality rather than that of peoples and nations."[1]

After the Bolsheviks split the Social Democratic party and united under Lenin's leadership, they would go on openly to demand the subordination of democratic principles to the needs of the revolution.

Thus, as early as the 1900s, Leninism denied national liberation to peoples of the tsarist empire in order to provide them with "social liberation." This contradiction would take almost a century to sort itself out—in favor of national liberation. It seems that Lenin grossly misread the relative weight of the national problem, treating it with a mixture of naiveté and ruthlessness. But he adroitly exploited the issue in 1917, and used it to grab power.

In August 1912 (at the Vienna Conference under the chairmanship of Leon Trotsky), Stalin's professed solution to the nationality problem was the much-touted "right of nations to self-determination." In the pre-revolutionary Caucasus this was a winning position.

Stalin stressed that, although a nation had the right to autonomy, this would not always be beneficial to its majority, "i.e., the toiling strata." He was particularly opposed to the self-determination of the Azeris and to the secession of Poland.[2] Thus, while the formula of national self-determination proclaimed by the Bolsheviks declared the right of separation in theory, Stalin made sure that all steps were taken to prevent it from taking effect in practice.

In "The Right of Nations to Self-Determination,"[3] Lenin assumes that if nationalities are granted the right to self-determination they will not exercise it, as it is in their interests to remain (voluntarily) in large economic and state units.

With the start of World War I, Lenin advocated turning the "imperialist war" into a "civil" one. In order to do this, he stepped up his calls for self-determination of the non-Russians to rally support for his program. He resolutely denounced Russian attempts to "throttle Ukraine and Poland," but in the same breath stated that "we are decidedly for centralization."[4] He further clarified his position in "The Socialist Revolution and the Right of Nations to Self-Determination" (March 1916), stating that the moment the bourgeois-democratic revolution was complete and the socialist revolution was on the march, the interests of the workers of the oppressor and oppressed nations would coincide, *and the demand for secession from that point on would be reactionary.*[5]

Lenin's stance prior to the February Revolution was fairly consistent. While using "the right of nations to self-determination" as a slogan to weaken the tsarist regime, he clearly advocated a centralized state, without committing the Bolsheviks to recognizing the secession of any particular nation. This position would perpetuate the Russian empire in a new social guise: that of the "workers' state" ruled by the Communist party elite. Several factors would serve to ensure the subjugation of the national interests of the non-Russians to the Russian-led Bolshevik revolution and its "vanguard." These were the antidemocratic and centralist bent of the Bolshevik model; the messianic ideology of social liberation, which would justify intervention abroad; the geostrategic advantage of the Russian imperial expanse with its pan-hemispheric reach; the commitment to state ownership of the means of production; and finally, the predominantly Russian composition of the Communist party.

Thus, amidst the death throes of the Romanov empire, a new group emerged with a substitute paradigm for metropolitan imperialist ideology. This group, victorious in the October 1917 coup, would accomplish the reassembly of the imperialist Romanov empire in less than ten years.

BETWEEN THE TWO REVOLUTIONS

For the provisional government which assumed control in March 1917, the war against the Central Powers remained a high priority. The Great Russian imperialists, such as Foreign Minister Paul Miliukov, failed to attract the nationalities of the empire to the side of the Provisional Government, which proved to be a fatal mistake.

Parties enjoying the widest popular support—the Socialist Revolutionaries (SRs) and the Mensheviks—were in favor of "territorial-national autonomy" and were against the right of nations to self-determination and secession.[6]

Ukraine took prompt steps to assert its position. In March 1917, a Central Rada (council) was founded in Kyiv, backed by the Ukrainian National Congress, which expressed its willingness to negotiate a confederation, or even a federation, with Russia. However, the provisional government dragged its feet, postponing decisions "until after the Constituent Assembly."[7]

Byelorussian organizations set up a National Committee at Minsk, which in July of 1917 took the name of the Central Rada of Byelorussian Organizations. In October 1917, this body was transformed into the Great Byelorussian Rada and declared itself the representative of the Byelorussian people. The independent Byelorussian republic was proclaimed only after the Bolshevik coup in Petrograd.[8]

The Russian imperial administration of Transcaucasia all but disintegrated after the February Revolution. Georgian, Armenian, and Azerbaijani local revolutionary committees, mostly affiliated with the Mensheviks, took over. The provisional government established a Special Committee for Transcaucasia headquartered in Tiflis (Tbilisi).

The provisional government also restored Finland's abrogated political rights, but negotiations had not been concluded before the Bolshevik takeover.[9]

The "bourgeois-democratic" national intelligentsia led the national councils in Tataria. A military committee *(Harbi Shura)* was formed in Kazan in May 1917. In August the All-Russian Moslem Military Congress voted to replace the old Russian army with a popular militia. The Bashkirs followed suit, and established an All-Bashkir Congress in Orenburg in July.[10]

Bessarabia, the Crimea, Kirghizstan, and Turkestan underwent similar developments.

The political vacuum that existed in Russia of 1917 allowed individual parties to formulate nationality policies of their own. Thus, on May 29 (June 13) 1917, a soviet of the national socialist parties of the Ukrainian, Byelorussian, Baltic, and Caucasian peoples, the Jews, and the Moslems was constituted in Petrograd. The Russians were represented by the SRs. The program of this council envisaged national autonomy on the territorial or individual level.

A Congress of the Peoples of Russia was to be convened by the Ukrainian

Rada in September.[11] It met on September 6–15 (September 19–28) in Kyiv. The congress decided by unanimous vote to transform Russia into a democratic federal republic, and the provisional government was asked to issue a proclamation to this effect. However, on September 14(27), Kerensky proclaimed Russia a republic, leaving the question of whether the republic was to be unitary or federative until after the convention of the Constituent Assembly.[12]

The Kyiv congress declared that it was the nationalities, not national territories, that were supposed to become subjects of the federation, adopting the Austrian-style national-personal autonomy model.

In April 1917 Lenin, sensing the weakness of the provisional government, set the course toward a "proletarian" (socialist) revolution by way of military insurrection. Bolshevik national policies therefore were to be subordinated to the supreme task of seizing power. While the provisional government was incoherent, the Bolsheviks advocated "proclamation and immediate realization of complete freedom of secession from Russia for all the nations and peoples who were oppressed by tsarism, or who were forcibly joined to, or forcibly retained within, the boundaries of state, i.e. annexed."[13] In 1917 Lenin had no reservations about promising the right of secession to any particular nationality.

At the April 1917 party conference, Stalin presented a resolution on the nationality question. Drafted by Lenin, it ensured that the suppression of "bourgeois nationalism" would become possible in due course.[14]

The question of the right of nations freely to secede must not be confused with the question of whether it would be expedient for any given nation to secede at any given moment. This latter question must be settled by *the Party of the proletariat* in each particular case independently, from the point of view of the interests of the social development as a whole and the class struggle of the proletariat for socialism...[15]

The resolution effectively put forth the *Russian* Bolshevik party as the only arbiter of the expediency of secession of any particular nationality. In addition, it made no mention of the right to self-determination publicly upheld earlier. National cultures were denounced as "bourgeois nationalist."

Despite this stance, in hopes of securing the future development of their nationalities under Russian socialist tutelage, many non-Russian socialists participated in the civil war on the side of the Bolsheviks.

IN THE AFTERMATH OF OCTOBER: THE RECONQUISTA

After the October coup in Petrograd, the Bolsheviks attempted to win the sympathies of the non-Russians by issuing the Declaration of Rights of Peoples of Russia on November 2, 1917. Lenin and Stalin, the People's Commissar of Nationalities (*Narkomnats*), signed the declaration, which called for

open and truthful policy, leading to the complete mutual trust of the peoples of Russia.

Only as the result of such trust can an honest and strong union of the peoples of Russia be created. The Council of People's Commissars decided to put at the basis of its activities on the nationalities question the following principles:

1. Equality and sovereignty of the peoples of Russia.

2. Right of the peoples of Russia for free self-determination, including secession and creation of independent states.

3. Cancellation of every and all national and national-religious privileges and limitations.

4. Free development of national minorities and ethnic groups populating the territory of Russia.[16]

This declaration was a propaganda sham. The only policy carried out in the non-Russian territories was subversion followed by military conquest by the Red Army.

Stalin ordered the creation of Polish, Finnish, and Baltic sections in the Commissariat for Nationalities, disregarding all the proclamations about the recognition of the right to secede. Even a Czechoslovak section was organized. These sections soon generated Bolshevik "governments" that were sent to the respective provinces along with the advancing troops of the Red Army.[17]

The anti-Bolshevik majority of the non-Russian borderlands initially rejected the Bolshevik propaganda. The Ukrainian Rada refused to grant Lenin's government any kind of recognition and on November 6(19) proclaimed the establishment of the Ukrainian People's Republic, which was to be part of an envisaged pan-Russian federation.[18] But the Soviet government was not about to accept the establishment of an independent Ukrainian state. The Bolsheviks of Kyiv attempted an insurrection on October 30 (November 12) 1917, but were repelled.

On November 22 (December 5) 1917, Lenin, addressing the First All-Russia Congress of the Navy, explained the Bolshevik *realpolitik* vis-à-vis Ukrainian self-determination: "We are going to tell the Ukrainians that as Ukrainians they can go ahead and arrange their life as they see fit. But we are going to stretch out a fraternal hand to the Ukrainian workers and tell them that together with them we are going to fight against their bourgeoisie and ours."[19]

How was the "fraternal hand" going to help? The First All-Ukrainian Congress of Soviets adopted a resolution on December 12, 1917, calling for nonrecognition of the Central Rada and proclaiming Ukraine a republic of soldiers', workers', and peasants' soviets.[20]

On December 17, 1917, the Rada was presented with an ultimatum by the Soviet government, and it was threatened with the use of force if the conditions were not accepted. The Soviets demanded Ukrainian assistance in the Bolshevik military action against the Whites in the Don region. These demands were rejected not only by the Rada, but even by the All-Ukraine Congress of Workers' and Peasants' Deputies, originally convened by the Bolsheviks.

The Soviet-inspired Ukrainian communists set up a rival government in Kharkiv and commenced military action against the Rada. On December 25, 1917, Soviet troops invaded Ukraine. The Rada first negotiated with the Entente, but in the end had to sign a peace treaty with the Central Powers on February 9, 1918. This agreement was recognized by the Soviet Republic in Article 6 of the Treaty of Brest-Litovsk. At the end of April 1918, the government of the Rada was replaced by the pro-German regime of Hetman Skoropadsky. In the aftermath of the German defeat, an independent government, the so-called Ukrainian Directory, led by Volodimir Vinnichenko and Simon Petlura, was established in Kyiv. The directory enjoyed considerable popular support, but was militarily weak.

Despite a Soviet-Ukrainian armistice signed in Kyiv on June 12, 1918, the Soviet government created a Provisional Workers' and Peasants' Government of Ukraine in the Russian city of Kursk, headed by the Russian Bolshevik Grigorii Pyatakov. Stalin got himself appointed to the Central Committee of the Ukrainian Communist party. Despite People's Commissar for Foreign Affairs (*Narkomindel*) Chicherin's assurances to the Directory of Russia's respect for Ukrainian independence, a Soviet invasion resulted in the fall of Kyiv on February 4, 1919. A bitter struggle for Ukraine ensued. Ultimately, the directory was forced into exile, and the Soviet Ukrainian republic was forced to join the USSR in 1922.[21]

In other non-Russian territories, all expressions of national self-determination were severely suppressed by the Bolsheviks.

Poland, together with Finland, was supposed to be a showcase of the Bolshevik interpretation of the right to self-determination. Nevertheless, the primary reason for Lenin's "liberal" posture was the German occupation of Poland. By a decree of the Council of Peoples' Commissars of August 29, 1918, the Russian republic abrogated all treaties and arrangements made by the former tsarist government regarding the partition of Poland. But it took the bloody war of 1920, in which Poland miraculously defeated the invading Red Army troops, to temporarily settle the feud between communist Russia and the Poles. In the fatal events of August-September 1939, Poland was partitioned again, this time by Stalin and Hitler.

The plight of the Moslems was particularly bitter. In the Crimea, the Moslem Executive Committee established a National Tatar Directory in November 1917. This embryonic government was dominated by the moderate socialist *Milli Firka* (National Party). In Kazakhstan, independence was pursued by a socialist national party *Alash Orda* (Horde of Alash, the legendary founder of the Kazakh tribes). In Central Asia a People's Council (*Khalq Shurasy*) was convened in Kokand. The Volga Tatars had several committees in Petrograd, Kazan, and Ufa who represented their interests.[22]

The Bolshevik attack against the Moslems started in the Crimea in January 1918, when the Tatar Executive Committee was disbanded and the Tatar leader assassinated. In Kazakhstan, *Alash Orda* leaders were dispersed by Russian Red Army units in January 1918. In February the Orenburg Bolsheviks arrested the Bashkir leader, Zeki Validov. In the same month, the Russian soviet of Tashkent initiated action against the Moslem government in Kokand.

On February 6, 1918, Soviet troops stormed Kokand. Tens of thousands of people were slaughtered. The escaping Moslem leaders started the Basmachi guerilla movement which continued until the early 1930s.

The Tatar National Front was so demoralized by Bolshevik propaganda that on February 27, 1918, the Kazan soviet could arrest the majority of the *Harbi Shura* leaders. Those who escaped were crushed by 300 Kronshtadt sailors sent in by the Bolshevik government. Within two months all branches of the Tatar nationalist organizations in Kazan and Petrograd were shut down. This was the first time that *Narkomnats* Stalin showed how ruthlessly he could *purge*. In March 1918, the Bolsheviks, Armenian Dashnaks, and pro-Bolshevik Moslems from the Hummet party attacked the Azeri quarters in Baku. Three thousand Azeris were killed, after which the Commune of Baku was established.[23]

Nevertheless, when the civil war started, most of the Moslems allied themselves with the Bolsheviks, as the other side seemed even less attractive. The majority of anti-Bolshevik Russians marched under the banner of *Rossiya yedinaya i nedelimaya* (Russia One and Indivisible). The religious conservatives, the Naqshbandis in the North Caucasus and the Basmachi in Turkestan, fought against all infidels, red or white, and for Islamic independence.

After the Bolshevik victory in 1920, a second round of Russian-Moslem strife began, in which conservative Islamic society and clergy came under severe pressure in the northern Caucasus and Central Asia.[24]

When the Red Eleventh Army occupied the lowlands of Dagestan in 1920 and committed innumerable atrocities, including the destruction of mosques and rape of women, Dagestan and Chechnia went up in arms. The Naqshbandi sheikhs, together with former Dagestani officers of the tsarist army, led the rebellion.[25]

Two Bolshevik field armies, as many as 40,000 troops, were deployed against the poorly equipped locals. The few Chechen leaders who remained alive escaped to the mountains, where they continued resistance until 1925, when they were finally captured and executed.[26]

The old Roman imperial principle of divide and rule was applied to the Moslems of the northern Caucasus. Administrative mergers were conducted among linguistically dissimilar peoples. Only in 1936 did the republican and provincial capitals become the seats of local administration.[27]

In the Transcaucasus, the local revolutionary committees refused to recognize the legitimacy of the Bolshevik government in St. Petersburg, and the national committees of Georgia, Armenia, and Azerbaijan created a Federation of Transcaucasia.

Russia recognized Georgian independence under the Supplementary Treaty to the Treaty of Brest-Litovsk (Article 3). Article I of the Russo-Georgian Peace Treaty, signed in Moscow on May 7, 1920, proclaimed: "Russia recognizes without reservation the independence and the sovereignty of the Georgian State and voluntarily renounces all sovereign rights which belonged to Russia with respect to the Georgian people and territory."[28] However, after the collapse of the

Central Powers, the Soviet government made three attempts to invade Georgia. In the spring of 1920, communist coups were engineered in Baku and Tiflis. By that time, Georgia had already been recognized by the Allied Supreme Council (January 27, 1921). Finally, on February 11, 1921, a massive invasion of the Red Army from five directions took place.

Despite Lenin's numerous promises to recognize Armenian independence[29] when the Armenian National Council proclaimed the country's sovereignty, there was no response from Moscow. Moreover, Lenin dropped his initial promises to demand reparations from Turkey and the return of Armenian refugees to eastern Anatolia. The Kemalist revolution seemed a saving grace for the Bolsheviks, as it tied the forces and attention of the Allies and turned them away from Russia. Stalin, an open opponent of independence for Transcaucasia, created an Armenian section in the Commissariat for Nationalities.

In May 1920, communists organized unsuccessful riots in several Armenian towns, and the Red Army invaded amidst peace negotiations. In a Soviet effort to placate Kemalist Turkey, Armenia lost the regions of Karabakh, Nakhichevan, and Zangesur to communist Azerbaijan (August 10, 1920). On November 18, 1920, Armenia signed an armistice with Turkey. Ten days later, the Soviets invaded again. A Bolshevik Military Revolutionary Committee was proclaimed after the overthrow of the legal government. At the same time, the Turks resumed military operations. The Armenians were thus coerced into signing the treaty of Erevan on December 2, 1920, which "guaranteed" Armenian territory and sovereignty as an independent Soviet socialist republic.[30]

Azerbaijan proclaimed independence on May 29, 1918. On December 7, 1918, the Azeri parliament was elected. There was an attempt to install a Soviet regime, but it failed due to lack of support on the part of the workers. On April 27, 1920, the Red Army invaded, and promptly proclaimed an Azerbaijani Soviet independent republic.[31]

With the defeat of Admiral Kolchak's Siberian army, the Soviet republic recognized an independent Far Eastern republic (DVR). Another independent zone was established with Japanese support on Russia's Pacific coast. The administration of the zone, which was inclined to join the DVR, was overthrown by a right-wing group in April 1921. In the same month, the DVR adopted a democratic constitution, but came under increasing pressure from the Soviet government to dissolve itself and incorporate into the Russian federation,[32] which it finally did on November 10, 1922.[33]

A complex situation developed in the Baltic territories under German occupation. When Estonia, Latvia, and Lithuania declared their independence, Soviet troops attempted to install communist regimes through a terror campaign directed by Lenin. After a defeat, Lenin described the Peace of Dorpat (with Estonia) as a "remarkable victory over international imperialism, a window on Western Europe for the Russian worker."[34]

Finland was the most adamant among all the former Russian provinces in its decision to secede from the former imperial master. As early as December

18 (31) 1917, the Soviet government promulgated a decree granting Finnish independence. Lenin and other Bolshevik leaders hoped that the Finns would stage a proletarian revolution and join the Russians in a socialist republic. However, by the end of November 1917, a right-wing government, led by Per Svinhufvud, had been formed. On December 6 (19) 1917, Finland proclaimed independence. Lenin's recognition was outward only. He intended to set up a Bolshevik government by employing pro-Bolshevik troops stationed in Finland. In the end of January 1918, these troops occupied large parts of southern Finland and set up a Finnish Soviet government. Civil war broke out.

After General Mannerheim's victorious Finnish troops entered Helsinki in May 1918, the Peace Treaty of Tartu was signed on October 14, 1920. The Russian troops left until the Soviets invaded Finland in 1939.[35]

On the other end of the empire, in Central Asia, the Bolsheviks fought to retain Turkestan. The confrontation was between ethnic Russian workers, who supported the Bolsheviks (and their links to Russia), and the local Moslems, who fought for independence. Some Moslems desired a traditional Islamic state, while others opted for a national republic in the spirit of the educated national intelligentsia (the Jadids).

The Basmachi movement never could unite under one leader, not even as widely hailed a military commander as Enver Pasha of the Ottoman empire. The movement was plagued by interethnic friction among the Uzbeks, Tajiks, Turkmen, and Karakalpaks.

The Red Army reconquered Turkestan after defeating Kolchak in 1919. The communists applied a sophisticated policy of divide and rule, opening wide the doors of the local party cells to native revolutionaries and reformers. The local elite was split and used by the imperialist power in order to install its control, on one hand, while the metropolitan state was used by parts of the local elite to promote their reformist policy, as Gallagher and Robinson suggest in "The Imperialism of Free Trade."

Throughout the civil war, Lenin's position remained, at least in theory, quite consistent. For propaganda purposes, he advocated "the right of nations to self-determination" and urged care in treating with the small nations. With that, Lenin did not lose sight of the dual goals of the global revolution and strengthening the Bolshevik grip over the former Romanov empire. Still, Lenin's position was more complex (and devoid of Great Russian chauvinism) than that of Stalin, Dzerzhinsky, or Bukharin. Polemicizing against key members of his own party, Lenin said,

To reject the self-determination of nations and insert the self-determination of the working people would be absolutely wrong, because this manner of settling the question does not reckon with the difficulties, with the zigzag course taken by differentiation within nations. If we were to declare that we do not recognize any Finnish nation, but only the working people, that would be sheer nonsense. We cannot refuse to recognize what actually exists.[36]

Half a year later, with the situation on the fronts of the civil war seeming rosier, and the Denikin threat from the south collapsing, Lenin began shifting his position. In an appeal to the communists of Turkestan (who, in the absolute majority, were ethnic Russians and other nonindigenous peoples), the chairman of the Soviet of People's Commissars (*Sovnarkom*) urged:

It is no exaggeration to say that the establishment of proper relations with the peoples of Turkestan is now of immense, epochal importance for the Russian Socialist Federative Soviet Republic.

I earnestly urge you to exert every effort to set an effective example of comradely relations with the peoples of Turkestan, to demonstrate to them by your actions that we are sincere in our desire to wipe out all traces of Great Russian imperialism and wage an implacable struggle against world imperialism, headed by the British. You should show the greatest confidence in our Turkestan Commission and adhere strictly to its directives, which have been framed precisely in this spirit by the All-Russia Central Executive Committee.[37]

This is vintage Lenin: on one hand, calling for cautious treatment of the locals and, on the other, setting his sights on using Soviet Central Asia as a showcase to attract the developing nations and strategically threaten Western (and especially British) imperialism in India and China.

To sum up, almost immediately following the October Revolution, Russia under the Bolsheviks shrank to the borders of the Grand Duchy of Muscovy under Ivan the Terrible. The first Russian empire, that of the tsars, effectively disintegrated after the Bolshevik coup of 1917.

It took Lenin's single-mindedness and Trotsky's military mastery to reconquer the empire and in fact to prolong the existence of the "prison of nations" for another three generations. In doing so, the Bolsheviks co-opted the representatives of the local elites, who were seeking positions of power for themselves. They did so with varying degrees of success, depending upon the existence of indigenous Bolshevik and socialist organizations. Overall, with the exception of the Baltic states, Finland, and Poland, the local elites were not particularly effective in opposing the new imperial masters.

EMPIRE REBORN: THE CREATION OF THE SOVIET UNION

Initially the Bolsheviks, including Lenin and Stalin, advocated a centralist (unitary) state and opposed the idea of a federation. However, concrete political reality in the wake of the October coup, demanded that a federative state at least be declared. An outline for the first Soviet constitution, which allowed for a federation, was submitted to the Third Congress of Soviets in January 1918.

The civil war resulted in the reoccupation of Ukraine, Byelorussia, the Caucasus, Turkestan, and the Far East. All provinces formed centralized Soviet republics that were closely connected with the core of the Soviet state.[38] The extreme hardship of the civil war, combined with economic chaos, put the country in 1920–1921 on the brink of widespread popular rebellion against the Bolshevik regime. The Tambov region peasant uprising and the Kronshtadt sailor revolt were brutally crushed by immense military force.

Lenin undertook a volte-face, bringing the country to the "safe landing" of the New Economic Policy (NEP). The attitude toward the national republics changed accordingly. They were to be exploited to improve the economic situation in Russia. In a letter to the Caucasus communists, Lenin stressed the differences in the position of the Russian Soviet Federal Socialist Republic (RSFSR) and that of the Caucasus republics and warned against copying the Russian tactics. He openly called for the initiation of trade and "cohabitation" with the capitalist West "sooner and with greater ease."

The anxiety of the Moscow communists with regard to the situation in the Caucasus is understandable. For several years after the communist takeover, the Mensheviks remained a dominant political party in Georgia. In August 1924, an uprising broke out in which 3,000 Georgians perished. Western Georgia and the Chiaturi Manganese Works were the center of the anticommunist resistance, which was crushed by the Red Army within several days.[39]

The Bolshevik government understood that the prerevolutionary economic ties with the borderlands had to be preserved and restored. Russia needed Central Asian cotton, Azerbaijani oil, Georgian ores and fruit, and Ukrainian coal and wheat. To achieve Soviet foreign policy goals, the strategic position of the Caucasus, Central Asia, and Ukraine were also vitally important.[40]

In the process of "integration" with Russia, the republics were ordered to delegate to the RSFSR "on the basis of unbreakable brotherly ties, etc.," diplomatic representation in the Genoa Conference (1922).[41] Thus, while the affairs of state were conducted de facto as if it were a unitary state, no union existed de jure, and one had to be created.

In the summer of 1922, Stalin secretly formulated a plan to merge the "independent" republics of Ukraine, Byelorussia, Georgia, Azerbaijan, and Armenia with the Russian federation. The process became known as "autonomization" *(avtonomizatzia)*. The republics were supposed to transfer to the RSFSR exclusive control over foreign affairs, foreign trade, military questions, the railways, finance, and postal and telegraph services. Food, labor, and economic functions were also to be submitted to the RSFSR jurisdiction. Local matters, such as internal affairs, justice, education, agriculture, workers' and peasants' inspection, health, and social welfare were to remain under the authority of the "autonomies."[42]

In August 1922, Stalin advocated control of the republics through the unitary party and "arranging" for the local Congresses of Soviets or TsIKs (Central Executive Committees) to adopt his resolution "as the will of these republics." Stalin's conception of the union was based on deception from the very beginning.

On September 22, 1922, Stalin wrote a letter to Lenin advocating autonomization. He explained that there were only two options: either the republics would have full and real independence—which was totally unacceptable to the communist leadership—or they would have fictitious independence, which was the essence of his autonomization plan.[43]

Stalin's letter stresses the "formal" character of the independence. While the formal structure and semantic meaning of the words dealing with independence were to be preserved, the real content and substance would be removed.[44]

Stalin discussed his proposal with Lenin on September 26, 1922. Lenin completely endorsed his idea of subordinatng all of the key functions of the republics to Moscow. However, he persuaded the *Narkomnats* to adopt the concept of union, in other words, "a federation of republics with equal rights," wording that was supposed to be more palatable to the republics.

The agreement of the USSR's founding fathers was signed on September 26, 1922, by Stalin, Ordzhonikidze, Miasnikov (Miasnikian), and Molotov. Each republic retained the (formal) right to secede from the Union.[45] A day after the agreement was signed, Kamenev, in a memo to Lenin, referred to the formal character of the right to secession:

In my opinion, either we should not address the question of "independence" at all (which, clearly, is already impossible), or we should construct the Union in such a way as to maximally retain *formal independence*, that is, more or less according to the proposed scheme [Stalin's autonomization plan]. The Union Treaty should definitely contain: a) a provision on the right to unilaterally secede from the Union, and b) a clear delineation of the sphere of administration [*oblasti vedeniya*].[46]

While none of the Bolshevik leadership in Moscow took the right of secession seriously, rifts developed between Lenin, who supported the formal (as opposed to real) right to secession, and "centralists" Stalin, Dzerzhinsky, and Ordzhonikidze, who opposed this right. Stalin accused Lenin of promoting "national liberalism"—a serious charge in the language of the time.[47] Lenin castigated his opponents as "dominant nation [Great Russian] chauvinists." The struggle between the dying master and his apprentice continued until Lenin's death.

As a preliminary step, the Transcaucasus Soviet republics (Armenia, Georgia, and Azerbaijan) created a union among themselves that was supposed to deal with military affairs, finances, foreign policy, transportation, and fighting counterrevolution (March 1922). All the national People's Commissariats (*narkomaty*) of the Transcaucasus republics were united, with the exception of the republican Chekas (secret police).[48] Congresses of Soviets in Ukraine and Byelorussia adopted a series of resolutions calling for the creation of the union. This union, the declarations maintained, would be the first step toward creating a World Soviet Republic of Labor.[49]

The final steps in the creation of the Soviet Union took place during the Tenth All-Russian Congress of Soviets. The congress declared in paragraph 2 of the resolution on the formation of the USSR that "in the basis of the unification lie the principles of voluntary association and equality, with preservation in each case of the right of free secession from the union."[50]

The Tenth Russian Congress proceeded to reconstitute itself as the First

All-Union Congress of Deputies, and on December 30, 1922, adopted the Treaty on the Creation of the Union of Soviet Socialist Republics. The ailing Lenin was elected honorary chairman of the congress. Theoretically, this was supposed to be one of the pinnacles of his career, a happy day in his life. In reality, Lenin dictated on that day, and the day after, one of his grimmest works: "The Question of Nationalities or 'Autonomization'."[51]

Lenin expressed his "greatest apprehension" about the Georgian mission of Dzerzhinsky, Stalin, and Ordzhonikidze. The Moscow squad had used physical violence and insults against the Georgian communist leaders, to Lenin's great dismay. His work is worth quoting at length, as it illustrates the difference between the nation-building (Leninist) policies implemented until the early 1930s, and the Stalinist Great Russian chauvinism unleashed thereafter:

If matters had come to such a pass that Ordzhonikidze could go to the extreme of applying physical violence, we can imagine what a mess we got ourselves into. Obviously, the whole business of "autonomization" [proposed by Stalin] was radically wrong and badly timed.

It is quite natural that in such circumstances the "freedom to secede from the union" by which we justify ourselves will be a mere scrap of paper, unable to defend the non-Russians from the onslaught of that really Russian man, the Great Russian chauvinist, in substance a rascal and a tyrant, such as the typical Russian bureaucrat is. The Soviet and sovietized workers will drown in the tide of chauvinistic Great-Russian riffraff as a fly in milk.

A distinction must necessarily be made between the nationalism of an oppressor nation and that of an oppressed nation, the nationalism of a big nation and that of a small nation.

In respect of the second kind of nationalism we, nationals of a big nation, have nearly always been guilty, in historic practice, of an infinite number of cases of violence; furthermore, we commit violence and insult an infinite number of times without noticing it.

A detailed code [for struggle against Great Russian abuses] will be required, and only the nationals living in the republics in question can draw it up at all successfully. And then we cannot be sure in advance that as a result of this work we shall not take a step backward at our next Congress of Soviets, i.e., retain the union of Soviet socialist republics only for military and diplomatic affairs, and in all other respects restore full independence to the individual People's Commissariats.

It must be borne in mind that the decentralization of the People's Commissariats and the lack of co-ordination in their work as far as Moscow and other centers are concerned can be compensated sufficiently by Party authority, if it is exercised with sufficient prudence and impartiality; the harm that can result to our state from a lack of unification between the national apparatuses and the Russian apparatus is indefinitely less than that which will be done not only to us, but to the whole International, and to the hundreds of millions of the peoples of Asia, which is destined to follow us on the stage of history in the near future. It would be unpardonable opportunism if, on the eve of the debut of the East, just as it is awakening, we undermined our prestige with its peoples, even if only by the slightest crudity or injustice towards our own non-Russian nationalities.[52]

Lenin on his deathbed managed to be quite sophisticated in relation to the nationality problem. First, he attempted to balance the autonomy of the socialist republics with the centralizing role of the party. Second, he put Soviet federalism into an international context (of revolution in the East). This would become increasingly unacceptable to Stalin, who after 1923 became the champion of "socialism in one country." Lenin's choice of Trotsky to present the Georgian problem at the party congress (i.e., an alliance against Stalin of the two most senior figures in the party) indicates that Lenin had embarked upon Stalin's political elimination. Lenin's illness and death not only saved Stalin, but also precluded any retreat on the unification of the USSR.

NATIONAL DEVELOPMENT OF THE NON-RUSSIANS, 1920s THROUGH THE EARLY 1930s

After the victory in the civil war, numerous concessions had to be made to establish the Soviet regime in the borderlands. Stalin's formulas on the predominance of non-Russians in the ethnic provincial party and in the administrative and economic organs, stipulated under Lenin's supervision, were accepted as the prevalent party doctrine.[53]

The Twelfth Party Congress (1923) reaffirmed Stalin's position against that of the Georgian and Ukrainian communists (supported by Lenin). Stalin understood the Russian chauvinist sentiment in the party better than his opponents, and he had fewer scruples against using these sentiments in his power struggle against them.

Nevertheless, in the 1920s, Stalin and other leaders of the party advocated policies of nation building (*natsional'noye stroitel'stvo*) and "nativization" or nationalization (*korenizatsiya*), which put non-Russians in privileged positions in their titular union republics and autonomous republics of the RSFSR.

Efforts to recruit ethnic cadres were successful until 1932, when their percentage reached 53.8 percent of the "non-Russian" territorial party organizations. At that point, the attempted political empowerment was reversed, and by 1937 the percentage had dropped to the pre-1927 level of 45 percent.[54] The policy of nationalization was abandoned prior to achieving its goals. Stalin was remaking the party. The 1933–1934 purge resulted in its "re-Russification."

New recruitment of party membership from 1937 on, and especially during World War II, favored Great Russians, and to a certain degree Armenians and Georgians. The percentage of Ukrainians, Byelorussians, and Central Asians (with the exception of Kazakhs) continued to decrease. In Central Asia, only about 10 percent of the Uzbek and Tajik republican party apparatuses consisted of titular nationalities.[55]

There was a clear correlation between the length of time a particular nationality was under Russian imperial control and its success in taking over the administrative functions of the Soviet institutions. There also was a correlation between Russification of the nationality in question, and the success of administrative nativization.

In most national territories nativization succeeded only at the lowest level, that of the village soviet. The higher the administrative level of the territorial unit, the lower the percentage of nationals allowed in the government agency. While the most prominent functionaries often belonged to the titular nationality, the apparatus would be predominantly Russian.[56]

Even in those republics where a non-Russian proletariat existed prior to the Bolshevik takeover, it often supported Menshevik organizations (Dashnaks in Armenia, the Bund among the Jews, Social-Democrats in Georgia, and so on). In Ukraine nation building was given especially high priority. Nevertheless, G. Simon shows that in Ukraine *korenizatsiya* had stopped by the late 1930s.[57]

One part of the nation building policies pursued by the Bolsheviks was language development of the non-Russian nationalities. The creation of forty-eight written languages, which allowed printing literature in these languages for the first time in history, was an impressive achievement by any standard.

Policy considerations, both foreign and domestic, came into play in language policy decision making: The Ukrainian and Byelorussian languages were supposed to maintain unity of the respective nations across the Soviet-Polish border.

In the Moslem lands, especially in Tatarstan, Bashkiria, and Central Asia, the language policy served to prevent the creation of a Turkic-Islamic nation, and to undo whatever Moslem or pan-Turkist solidarity had already been achieved. The Bashkir intelligentsia was heavily under Tatar cultural influence, and Tatar was used as the written language. In the 1920s, the Bashkir dialect farthest from Tatar was adopted as the standard Bashkir written language, and declared, together with Russian, as the "state language."[58]

The introduction of Latin script, instead of Arabic, in the 1920s and 1930s caused an upheaval in the linguistics of the Soviet Moslems. The Latin alphabet was declared "revolutionary" and "the alphabet of the communist world society." The reform affected the sixteen Islamic peoples of the former Russian empire: the Azeris, Tatars, Uzbeks, Tajiks, Kazakhs, Chechens, Ingush, and other peoples of the northern Caucasus. With about 90 percent of these peoples illiterate, and extensive secular literature in Arabic script existing only in Azeri, Tatar, and Uzbek, the transition to the Latin script, following the example of Turkey, might have had its logic.

The Tatar and Azeri intelligentsia and the clergy, as well as national communists, fought for the preservation of the Arabic alphabet tooth and nail.[59] In the 1990s, the Central Asian republics and Azerbaijan, shifting their cultural orientation from Russia to Turkey, have once again changed their alphabets—from Cyrillic to Latin. This time it was done not in the name of international revolution, but Turkic solidarity.

Then, in 1937, the Latinization of scripts was abruptly stopped. Latinized alphabets were forcibly changed back to Cyrillic, and the process was completed by 1939. In the mid-1930s, the shift in language policy indicated a broader change towards zenophobic totalitarianism.

The progress of non-Russian postelementary and college education was modest. The enrollment of national minorities into institutions of higher learning was achieved through quotas and lower entrance examination scores.

The quota system was suddenly abandoned in 1934, which signaled a policy shift in favor of the Russians. The percentage of non-Russian students, which had peaked by 1933–1934, had dropped by 1939.

Peoples without their territorial units and peoples residing outside their national republics and Autonomous Soviet Socialist Republics (ASSRs) achieved considerable social and cultural advancement in the 1920s and the first half of the 1930s. But the year 1937 signaled, as in many other areas, a drastic policy shift.

To conclude, the 1920s and the first half of the 1930s witnessed the national development of non-Russians as part of the creation of a Soviet federation. These policy guidelines were initiated by Lenin and other union and republican leaders and implemented prior to the ascendancy of Stalinism. In promulgating these policies, the USSR's aim was to create an ethnically heterogeneous imperial elite and to maximize integration. This was an empire with elements of autonomy which could not be tolerated in the totalitarian society engineered by Stalin.

Preoccupied with the power struggle in Moscow, Stalin to a degree left the policy intact until the Great Purge of 1936–1937. National communism was unpalatable to Stalin and chauvinist elements inside the party. In his quest for uniformity, Stalin began to roll the federalist policies back, replacing them with an imperialism rooted in Russian nationalism. The respite was over. The "historically inevitable" empire came back full force.

NATION BUILDING OPPOSED: THE STALINIST AND GREAT RUSSIAN CHAUVINIST REACTION (LATE 1920s–1937)

The policies of nation building and *korenizatsiya* resulted in numerous conflicts between the national communists (such as Georgians, Tatars and Ukrainians) and the Russians. Stalin and his apparatus left little leeway for these independent-minded elites.

Lenin and Stalin, standing at the cradle of the Soviet nationality policy, were acutely aware of the disintegration of the Austro-Hungarian empire. They made sure that all nationalist political parties were disbanded and their supporters encouraged to join the All-Union Communist Party (Bolsheviks).[60] National armed forces were demobilized or integrated into the Red Army.

The national communists, as early as 1920, made their grievances heard in Moscow. Led by a Kazakh, Turar Ryskulov, chairman of the Turkestani Central Executive Committee (VTsIK), the Central Asians demanded that the Central Committee (CC) in Moscow stop interfering in the internal affairs of Turkestan and withdraw the Red Army. When these demands were rejected, Ryskulov and his group resigned from all their posts. In retaliation, the whole Turkestani party *kraikom* (regional committee) was disbanded. The entire historical entity of Turkestan (after the revolution, the Autonomous Socialist Republic of Turkestan) was dismembered under Stalin's orders (1924).

Nevertheless, throughout the 1920s the major threat to the party's general line was considered to be Great Russian chauvinism, as confirmed by Stalin as late as June 1930.[61] However, the nationality policy now was depicted as a "battle on two fronts"—against non-Russian nationalism *and* Russian chauvinism.

Nation building encountered stiff resistance from the Russian-dominated party apparatus and Russian elites in the republics. Passive bureaucratic sabotage, or fake *(lipovyie)* reports hailing nonexisting achievements were regular phenomena. The first nationalist communist to be expelled from the party and arrested on charges of nationalism was Mir Said Sultan-Galiev, Stalin's assistant at the Commissariat for Nationalities and a leading theoretician of national communism. According to Sultan-Galiev, all classes of the oppressed Moslem society were to be labeled proletarian. Class struggle within formerly oppressed societies and fighting the national religions were proclaimed unnecessary.

National communism was influential in the 1920s in Ukraine, Georgia, and Tatarstan. Its adherents intended to de-Russify their republics as much as possible and develop true autonomy in cultural, economic and personnel policies. Republican party elites sought to transfer leadership tasks to the non-Russian intelligentsia and to stop Russian immigration. The Turks in the group also wanted to strengthen Islamic solidarity.

Stalin accused Sultan-Galiev of pan-Turkism and pan-Islamism. He also charged that Sultan-Galiev had ties to the Basmachi guerilla movement in Central Asia and connections to the Bashkir nationalist leader Validov, who had emigrated. But less than a year later, Sultan-Galiev was released without trial. He survived until 1928, plotting and preaching the creation of a sovereign socialist Republic of Turan which would encompass Turkestan, Tataria, Bashkiria, Azerbaijan, and the Northern Caucasus.

It is possible that Stalin instructed the Osoboye Glavnoye Politicheskoye Upravleniye (OGPU, the Main Political Directorate) to follow the Islamic revolutionary in order to uncover his contacts among the Soviet elites, to be picked up in the later purges, or that he was released as an OGPU informer.[62] The main difference between Sultan-Galiev and other national communists was the former's articulation of separatist goals, in addition to the territorial, party and army autonomy advocated by national communists.

The dismemberment of Turkestan (1924) was conducted against the will of prominent Central Asian and Moslem communists. The Turkic communists were frustrated by the dissolution of what they saw as the future Turkic socialist state. The creation of two union republics (Uzbekistan and Turkmenia) and two autonomous republics (Tajikistan and Karakirghiz) in its stead was unpopular. In 1929 Tajikistan was elevated to the status of a union republic. Kirghizia was promoted to that status in 1936. The millennium-old territorial entities of Khiva, Bukhara, and Kokand ceased to exist.

In 1928 Sultan-Galiev was sentenced to ten years at the Solovki camps, and he disappeared for good; a purge of the Tatar ASSR party apparatus began simultaneously with his trial.

The harshest blow to the Turkic communists was the arrest, trial, and execution of Veli Ibragimov, the Crimean Tatar leader, at the end of the 1920s. He was the first important official arrested while still in office and executed for nationalism after a short trial behind closed doors. Together with Ibragimov, 3,500 Crimean Tatars were executed, imprisoned or exiled from Crimea, the republic in which nation building had been the most successful. Another campaign took place in Uzbekistan. Numerous local leaders were arrested and jailed for nationalism and membership in the clandestine organizations.

The exposure of the nationalists opened the floodgates for the purge of intellectuals, especially in the educational apparatus.[63] The campaign against the "national communists" (approximately 1928–1937), led by the ethnic Russian members of VKP(b), targeted members of prerevolutionary socialist and reformist Islamic movements. As a result of that purge, the majority of educated elites of the Turkic Moslems were physically exterminated.

Kazakhstan suffered especially harsh treatment by the central authorities. Before 1914 immigration of the landless Russian and Ukrainian peasantry to the Kazakh steppes was encouraged by the Russian imperial government. After the revolution, the slogan of the Kazakh national communists, led by S. Sadvokasov and S. Khodzhanov, was "Kazakhstan to the Kazakhs." As part of this movement, some Russian settlers were driven out of their villages, and the lands were returned to the original owners.

The ensuing liquidation of *Alash Orda* followers coincided with the forced sedimentarization and collectivization of the pastoral nomads. The Kazakh nation was virtually subjected to genocide, in which one-third of the Kazakhs, including most of the intellectuals, perished.

The Orenburg region was returned to the Russian Federation's control, effectively cutting off the Tatar-Bashkir Volga Turkic lands from their coreligionists in Central Asia, ending the dream of a united Turkic state in the middle of Eurasia.[64]

The advances of Russian colonization in Kazakhstan indicate the continuity of tsarist and Soviet imperialist policies in Central Asia. While the tsarist administration established a significant Slavic minority in Kazakhstan, communist rulers reduced the Kazakh majority of 57 percent, versus 19.8 percent Russians in 1926, to a Kazakh minority under 50 percent in their own republic by 1939. While the Kazakh population was projected to increase by over 600,000, in the 1930s it actually decreased by 1.5 million due to famine, executions, and migration. The quest for land and natural resources, a traditional motive for imperialist expansion, have been the main reason for the Russian absorption of Kazakhstan. Slavic settlers, as in tsarist times, became "imperial agents" in the Russian colonization of the Kazakh steppe.

The Russian-led fight against Central Asian nationalism accelerated in 1933 and 1934. The purge was openly directed against former members of national communist, socialist, and SR groups—Sultan-Galievists, Mussavatists, Dashnaks, and *Alash Orda* members.

An extreme reversal of the fortunes of national communists occurred in Ukraine. The Ukrainian press and intelligentsia saw nation building as a legitimate endeavor throughout the 1920s, but by 1930 a pattern had been established by the GPU in which sham underground organizations were "uncovered" by the security apparatus. Thus, the League for the Liberation of Ukraine *(Spilka Vyzvolennia Ukraiiny)* was put on trial in 1930. In this show trial, forty-five prominent Ukrainian intellectuals were accused of having been in contact with Ukrainian emigré circles and planning to detach Ukraine from the USSR and reestablish a bourgeois order. Even earlier, Stalin personally attacked the Ukrainian People's Commissar of Education, A. Shumsky, the father of Ukrainian historiography, M. Hrushevsky, and the policies of Ukrainization. The wind in Moscow was shifting. Ukrainization was declared non grata with the "discovery" of another underground organization, the Ukrainian National Center.

By the end of 1932, the Ukrainian peasantry was suffering famine and unprecedented deprivation as a result of the Moscow-imposed collectivization. Anti-Russian feelings increased. On December 4, 1932, the VKP(b) Central Committee and the all-Union Council of People's Deputies (Stalin and Molotov) demanded an end to the "mechanical execution of Ukrainization."

On January 24, 1933, party secretaries were replaced in three out of seven Ukrainian regions *(oblasti)*. Three members of the Ukrainian Politburo and Secretariat were removed, and an ethnic Russian CC secretary was sent by Moscow to Kharkiv to serve as the Ukrainian Second Secretary.

In Ukraine, one might say, 1937 began in 1933. That year effectively signaled the end of Ukrainization. In November 1933, a resolution of the Ukrainian CC "acknowledged" that Ukrainian local nationalism, which was "closely associated with imperialist interventionists," was currently the main threat in the republic. This was the most extensive revision of the party's nationality policy since Lenin.

Now the whole country was repeating after Stalin that the main enemy was bourgeois nationalism. From 1936 on, there was no more mention of Great Russian chauvinism in the official media.

Simultaneously, a new mass mobilization tool was propagated by the Kremlin: Soviet patriotism. Its "declaration" in 1934 signaled another step in the strengthening of Stalin's totalitarian hold on power. The concept of "motherland" *(rodina)*, previously denounced as bourgeois, was reinstated. To provide a historical perspective to Soviet patriotism, the history of nations and states (as opposed to class struggle) was rehabilitated, and old heroes of the Russian tsarist past were taken out of the mothballs.

While Russian imperial history underwent a renaissance, the development of other peoples was increasingly distorted, appearing as the prehistory of integration into the Russian empire and the Soviet Union.[65]

Imperial ideology, though different from "orthodoxy, autocracy, *narodnost*" of the tsarist period was combination of the Stalinist version of Marxism-Leninism as dogma (orthodoxy), *vozhdizm* (cult of the leader)—as autocracy—and Soviet/Russian patriotism. Stalin was betting on ethnic Russians as the imperial *Volk*. He was also speeding up consolidation and centralization, making the USSR a highly integrated and homogeneous empire.

TOTALITARIAN EMPIRE: HIGH STALINISM (1937-1953)

The Great Purge

The Great Purge (1936–1939) not only decimated the Soviet ruling elites, it also severely affected the remnants of the non-Russian intelligentsia. Whole generations of pre-Stalinist national elites were physically eliminated under the slogan of struggle against "bourgeois nationalists" and "Trotskyite-Zinovievite fascist terrorists."

Stalin realized that it would take brutal repression to uproot the national assertiveness. He aimed at achieving the complete uniformity of a totalitarian empire, with Russian language and culture as its centerpieces.

In a dramatic shift, the national Latin alphabets (forcibly introduced in the 1920s) were replaced with Cyrillic. This measure, which ten years before would have been branded as Great Russian chauvinism, was now hailed as the acceleration of proficiency in Russian. Forty million people who had just acquired literacy became illiterate again.[66]

Stalin decided to return to Cyrillic in the spring of 1937. The introduction of Cyrillic contributed to the isolation of the Soviet Union, and separated the written languages of Soviet Uigurs, Kazakhs, Tajiks, Uzbeks, Azeris, and Rumanians from their counterparts living outside the USSR.

Intensive Russian instruction in the non-Russian schools was made compulsory. This was a signal to both Russian and non-Russian elites that an "imperial language" and a dominant imperial nation were being declared. The Russian language and the Russian nation once again occupied the position they had enjoyed in the Romanov empire.

Over the span of four years, *korenizatsiya* was transformed from being party dogma into a "bourgeois nationalist crime" punishable by death. Beria personally shot the allegedly nationalist secretary of the Armenian CC in his Tbilisi office on July 9, 1936.[67]

The wheel of terror turned several times before temporarily stopping in 1939, but only after hundreds of thousands of Soviet-era leaders and intellectuals had been annihilated.

In Ukraine, the chairman of the Council of People's Commissars, Panas Petrovich Lyubchenko, committed suicide in the summer of 1937 amidst allegations that Ukrainian nationalists were making attempts to detach the republic from the Soviet Union. His successors, Bondarenko and Chubar, lasted only a short time in office before disappearing forever. Neither was ever officially tried.

After the execution of Vlas Chubar (1938), the purges in Ukraine continued under Nikita Sergeyevich Khrushchev, former first secretary of the Moscow Party Committee, who enjoyed Stalin's confidence.

In Byelorussia, as in Ukraine, top officials were charged with nationalism and executed.

National communist elites were "merged" in the Moscow show trials with those Soviet leaders who were supportive of the federalist structure of the Soviet Union. This amounted to a Russian nationalist reaction against the *korenizatsiya* policy. Stalin, a quintessential empire builder, wanted nothing less than the physical elimination of the national semiautonomous, albeit socialist, elites. As Berdiayev put it in the fateful year of 1937:

Communist revolution in one country leads to nationalism. Only Trotsky remains an internationalist, maintains that communism in one country cannot be implemented. This is why he [Trotsky] was rejected, turned out to be useless, unfit to a constructive national period of communist revolution. The socialist motherland is the same old Russia. Stalin is a statist *(gosudarstvennik)* of the Eastern, Asiatic type.[68]

The Empire Strikes West

The "Asiatic statist" knew well the business of empire building inherited from his tsarist predecessors. In his policies, both the borders of the old Romanov empire and Russian aspirations vis-à-vis the Straits and Poland figured prominently.

In the aftermath of the Molotov-Ribbentrop pact, Stalin managed to recover for the Soviet Union almost all of the old Romanov patrimony. He definitely saw himself as heir to the old Russian realm. By the end of his rule, only Poland and Finland remained outside Soviet borders, although he dismembered the former and occupied parts of the latter in 1939–1940.

Lviv, Northern Bukovina, and Carpatho-Ukraine were annexed to the Soviet Union under the pretext of "reunification" of a Ukrainian homeland that had never before existed as a unitary state. The conquest of these territories also provided the opportunity for total suppression of the Ukrainian and Byelorussian nationalists who had operated under the Polish regime.

The USSR annexed the Polish territories it occupied as a result of its agreement with the Nazis. Arrests, mass deportations, and executions of citizens in the newly occupied areas followed.

The Baltic states were forcibly annexed by the USSR after twenty years of independence. According to the revised protocol of the Molotov-Ribbentrop pact of October 10, 1939, Lithuania was transferred from the German sphere of influence into the Russian one, in exchange for incorporation of Lublin and parts of the Warsaw province into the German sphere. That same day, the USSR forced a mutual assistance treaty upon Lithuania that placed Soviet garrisons in some strategic locations.

In June 1940, a Soviet ultimatum was presented to the Lithuanian government demanding the free entry of additional Soviet troops which proceeded to pour into the country. The president of Lithuania, A. Smetona, fled. On July 14, 1940, sham elections were staged and a communist victory was announced. The new Diet proclaimed Lithuania a Soviet republic, which was admitted into the Soviet Union on August 3, 1940.[69] Deportations of Lithuanian bourgeoisie, clergy, and intellectuals followed immediately.

Latvia, included in the Soviet zone of influence by the Molotov-Ribbentrop pact, faced the same predicament as Lithuania and was "admitted" into the Soviet Union on August 5, 1940.

Estonia was forced into a "pact of mutual assistance" on September 28, 1939. After Soviet garrisons were introduced upon Estonian soil, an ultimatum was delivered to the Estonian ambassador in Moscow on June 16, 1940. As in case of Latvia, Molotov told the Estonian ambassador that, if the ultimatum were not accepted, the Red Army would march in, suppressing any resistance by force. The invasion started the next day, and the occupation of Estonia was accomplished within two days, on June 18, 1940. On July 14, sham elections were staged to return a communist parliament. The president of the country, K. Päts, was deported to the Gulag and vanished. On August 6, 1940, Estonia was admitted into the Soviet Union.[70]

The Soviet annexation plan backfired in the case of Finland. The Soviet mutual assistance treaty was not signed, although the Finns were ready for a genuine compromise and prepared to make territorial concessions to their giant neighbor to the east. But Stalin and Molotov's plans were for total subjugation. On November 28, 1939, alleging Finnish attacks against Soviet targets, the Treaty of Nonaggression of 1932 was annulled and diplomatic relations were severed.

On November 30, 1939, Soviet troops invaded Finland and bombed Helsinki. However, the Red Army, weakened by the purges, could not defeat the highly maneuverable Finnish units, well trained for winter warfare. The League of Nations was convened, and the Soviet aggression was condemned. The USSR was expelled from the League, and the Western powers threatened to join the war on the Finnish side, a threat that made Stalin back off and eventually agree to Finland's ceding parts of its territory in exchange for continuing independence.

In all newly acquired territories, severe repression against political parties, labor unions, the market economy, and local elites was undertaken by the Narkomat Vnutrennikh Del (NKVD, the People's Commissariat of Internal Affairs) apparatus and communist leadership. For example, the November 28, 1940, directive of the Lithuanian NKVD prescribed mass deportation of members of all political parties, former government officials, officers, policemen, clergy, nobility, landowners, individuals with contacts abroad, and "esperantists and philatelists."[71] The total population loss (mostly elites) in the Baltic states due to deportations, executions, and drafts to the Soviet Army was estimated at over 300,000.

Similar measures were taken in the former Polish lands, with deportations primarily affecting over a million Poles and Jews, the majority among them gentry, entrepreneurs, and urban elites. The sharp decline in the standard of living, repression against religion, the executions of family members—all these caused hatred toward the Soviet power. In the Baltic states, the historic distrust of Germans was almost overnight replaced by hatred of all things Soviet and Russian.

In addition to local communists, tens of thousands of Russians and Ukrainians were imported to rule the newly occupied realms with their 23 million inhabitants. The historical position of the Russians as imperial administrators, relinquished in 1917, was reinstated with a vengeance under Stalin's leadership twenty years later.

Myths and Realities of Peoples' Friendship

During the Soviet military participation in World War II (1941–1945), the ideological focus shifted even farther from internationalism to Russian nationalism. Soviet patriotism was reinforced and acquired even more distinctively Great Russian overtones. Historic military leaders, such as princes Alexander Nevsky and Dmitrii Donskoy, generals such as Dimitrii Pozharsky, Alexander Suvorov, and Mikhail Kutuzov, and even the great conquering tsars Ivan the Terrible and Peter the Great were rehabilitated as part of the glorious past.

The boundaries between Russian and Soviet patriotism became increasingly blurry, with the Russian people elevated to the status of "elder brother." Stalin allowed the Russian Orthodox Church to partially resume its functions.

At the same time, there was a marked lack of similar patriotic development for the non-Russians, such as Tatars and Kazakhs, whose past national heroes had been freedom fighters against the Russians.

In the first phase of the war, while Stalin relied on Russian nationalism, both Russians and non-Russians enthusiastically greeted the Germans. Despite this, Nazi ideology prevented the Germans from taking full advantage of these offers of cooperation, as the conquered peoples were seen as *Untermenschen*.[72] Almost no serious political analysis of their national aspirations and goals was attempted at the decision-making level of the Third Reich due to its own severe ideological prejudices. Whatever was done occurred late in the war, when German defeat seemed inevitable.

Numerically, the greatest movement of cooperation with the Germans was General Vlasov's Russian Liberation Army (*Rossiyskaya Osvoboditel'naya Armi'ia*, or ROA) formed in November 1944. Vlasov, a general of impeccable Stalinist credentials, was abandoned by the Soviet High Command with his army in the swamps of northern Russia. He went to the German side to fight against Stalin. However, the Nazis denied Vlasov an opportunity to create a viable Russian opposition to the communist regime.

The Organization of Ukrainian Nationalists (OUN), which cooperated with the Germans prior to the war and itself had a fascist orientation, raised two elite units for the *Abwehr*, "Nightingale" and "Roland." The creation of the SS division *Halichina* (Galicia) from among western Ukrainians was widely supported by Ukrainian religious organizations.

One of the most favorable responses to Germany's appeals for collaboration occurred in the Baltic states. The Balts hoped, in vain, that their pre-1940 independence would be reestablished. The Lithuanian provisional government, based on the resistance organization Lithuanian Activist Front (*Lietuviu Aktivistu Frontas*), was ready, to an extent, to collaborate with the Germans. However, Hitler and his generals advocated "Germanization" of the Baltic lands without granting them independence. The provisional Lithuanian government was disbanded in August 1941.

Overall, relations with the German occupation regime remained correct, if not cordial. A great number of Balts took part in the genocide against the Jews, fought partisans, and collaborated on the republic levels as executive organs of the German occupation force.[73] Both the *Wehrmacht* and the *Waffen-SS*, received a flow of Baltic volunteers. Baltic units were so trusted that, despite direct orders from Hitler, they were deployed at the front. In Byelorussia, the nationalist forces were split between those who wanted "neither Russians nor Germans" and those who collaborated with the Nazis. Still, German brutalities in the republic made the efforts of collaborationists futile, and the sixty battalions they recruited in 1943 and 1944 were of no military significance and did not fight the returning Soviet army.

The numbers of Crimean Tatars, Kalmyks, and other southern peoples who collaborated with the Germans were proportionately considerable.

The Cossacks, who severely suffered from collectivization, were seen by the Germans as an autonomous nation and were not assigned *Untermensch* status. Many Cossacks and their families retreated with the invaders, later to be hunted down and severely punished by Stalin's NKVD.

The Germans also enlisted, often under threat of starvation, hundreds of thousands of Soviet POWs. The latter often were recruited into "national" battalions (about 1,000 men each) commanded by German officers. Fifty-three such battalions were organized in Poland: fourteen Turkestani, eight Azeri, seven northern Caucasian, eight Georgian, nine Armenian, and seven Volga Tatar. Their motivation was low, and frontline deployment was not possible.[74]

Overall, German nationality policy in the occupied territories was a fiasco. Under the blows of the *Wehrmacht*, the Soviet empire started to disintegrate. Twenty years of communist persecution had created strains in the system, which began to come apart at its ethnic seams. The lack of enthusiasm on the part of the minorities to defend Stalin's empire testifies to its oppressive character. But the Nazi leaders were unable to comprehend the phenomenon and formulate any viable policy. Had appropriate policies toward the non-Russians been implemented in time, the whole outcome of the war might have been different. However, as a captured Soviet official told the Germans, "between two tyrants the people will chose the one who speaks their language."[75]

The Empire's Punished Peoples

The deportations of "suspected peoples" in the USSR during World War II started with the Volga Germans in July 1941. However, Poles, Germans, and Finns, seen as enemy elements, were deported from the Western border areas as early as the mid-1930s. In 1937 tens of thousands of "unreliable elements" were massacred by NKVD troops near Vinnitsa.[76] In the Far East, Koreans and Chinese were exiled to Central Asia as potential Japanese agents. In this respect, Stalin followed the policies of the tsarist military administration, which exiled "hostile" Jews from the Western border areas in the face of the German advancement in 1915.

The policy of expulsions culminated during and after the war with the deportation of entire nations. In the case of the Crimean Tatars, fully one-third of the nation perished as a result.

Volga German families were given two hours to pack their belongings. The Germans of the Crimea were evacuated on August 20, 1941, and the Germans of the Caucasus followed suit in October. With the lifting of the siege of Leningrad, the Russian Germans of that city who had survived the famine were also deported to Siberia. From 650,000 to 700,000 people were deported. A Supreme Soviet resolution of September 7, 1941, retroactively eliminated the German ASSR on the Volga; the names of cities were changed to Russian ones. Reference to the Volga Germans in government publications became taboo.[77]

The deportations of the Crimean Tatars were based primarily on false reports to the Moscow HQ that all Crimean Tatars were collaborating with the Germans.[78] Contrary conclusions presented to Moscow by the underground Crimean Communist party, and later repudiation of their own reports by the authors themselves, were disregarded by the Kremlin. For decades, the Crimean Tatars continued to be reviled in their ancestral homeland by the Slavic settlers who took their place.

The traditional imperial practice of renaming occupied lands was applied in Crimea on a wide scale immediately after the deportation, and centuries-old Tatar-, Greek- and German-origin names were replaced by meaningless and falsely cheerful Russian titles.[79]

In the summer of 1942, autonomous republics and regions of the north Caucasus were occupied by the *Wehrmacht*. Kolkhozes were abolished, and a certain measure of self-rule was allowed. Mountainous people such as the Karachai were recruited to a collaborators' cavalry squadron.

In January 1943, the Soviet Army liberated the Karachai. In November 1943, the entire remaining Karachai population was brutally deported in cattle cars to NKVD-run settlements in Central Asia and Kazakhstan.[80] In the aftermath of the deportation, two counties (*rayons*) of the autonomous region were annexed to Georgia.

Prior to the outbreak of World War II, Chechnia was the scene of intense armed anti-Soviet struggle. The legacy of the antitsarist war of liberation and the decimation inflicted upon the republic by the collectivization and purges of the late 1930s all contributed to anti-Russian and anticommunist sentiments. Several anti-Soviet armed units were active. In 1940 a full-fledged rebellion and war of liberation, under the leadership of Khasan Izrailov, was proclaimed. During the war, containing rebellious Chechnia required that several Red Army units be removed from the front.

While many Chechens and Ingush fought bravely in the Soviet forces, others dodged the draft or deserted. Some fought against the Red Army in German-sponsored units.

In 1940 the Soviet General Staff warned the Kremlin that the whole population of the non-Russian northern Caucasus would present a security risk in case of war. "Special measures" were recommended to deal with the threat, but these were not implemented until after the Germans had been driven away.

The decision to deport the Chechens and Ingush was taken at a joint meeting of the Politburo and the Soviet High Command in February 1943—one year before the plan was executed. Stalin, Voroshilov, Kaganovich, Khrushchev, Kalinin, Beria, Molotov, Zhdanov, Voznesensky, Andreev, and Kosygin (then the premier of the RSFSR) participated in the historic meeting.[81]

The execution of deportations was particularly cruel. The Chechen men were invited to celebrate Soviet Army Day. They were then surrounded by troops, and deportation orders for "treason and collaboration with the enemy" were read. Many unarmed Chechens were shot on the spot or burned alive. In the meantime, the women and children were dragged out of their homes and loaded into trucks.

During their transport to Kazakhstan and Central Asia, almost half of the Chechen and Ingush succumbed to typhoid and malnutrition. Tens of thousands died shortly after arrival, as nothing awaited the deportees but the bare land in which they had to dig holes for shelter. Chechens from Dagestan and North Ossetia were also rounded up and shipped east.

To seal the fate of the republic, the Supreme Soviet of the USSR changed the names of Chechen villages and counties to Russian and Ossetian names. As in the case of Karachai, some of the *rayons* were transferred to North Ossetia and not returned to Ingushetia when the latter was reconstituted in 1956. In the autonomous capitals, all the republic ministers, members of the Presidium of the Supreme Soviet, and local Party and Komsomol committee members were arrested.[82]

Some of the Chechens escaped into the mountains and continued to hide from the NKVD troops until the early 1950s. The geographical dispersal of the deportees was vast: to Kirghizstan, northern Kazakhstan, the Sverdlovsk region in the Urals, and the camps of the Gulag in the Krasnoyarsk region in eastern Siberia. Without returning to their homeland, the Chechen and Ingush were doomed to slow extinction. Some Ingush and Chechen rebellions were reported; all of them were suppressed with great loss of life. To save the important oil-based economy of Grozny from collapsing, tens of thousands of Russians,

Ukrainians, and Caucasians were settled in Chechnia.

The Turkic Balkars did cooperate with the Nazis. Soviet propaganda made much of the white horse that was sent to Hitler as a present (at the suggestion of the local German authorities). Plans also were made to unite Balkaria with the ethnically close Karachai under the Turkish protectorate. This was an inducement for Turkish entrance into the war against the USSR.

When the Soviets regained the area, Kabardino-Balkaria was abolished replaced, without any formal announcement, by the Kabardinian ASSR (April 1944). The former leaders of Kabardino-Balkaria were purged. All of the Balkars and many of the Kabardines were deported.

The Kalmyks had a history of resistance to the Soviet power starting with the civil war and continuing throughout collectivization. The clan nobility and Buddhist lamas were especially affected by the purges. When the Germans arrived, the local population was impressed by promises of an independent Kalmyk state and the return of emigrés who actively collaborated with the Nazis.

Between December 27 and December 30, 1943, the returned Soviets loaded the entire Kalmyk people into cattle cars and shipped them to Siberia. All Kalmyk soldiers serving in the Soviet armed forces were discharged and assigned to labor battalions.[83]

The exiled nations often were made scapegoats for the inept performance of the Soviet military and political leadership during the war, but the policy of exile was continued beyond World War II.

Meskhetian Turks from the Caucasus, deported in 1945, and Greeks, exiled from the Crimea in 1944 and from the Black Sea towns of Georgia in 1949, were not officially accused of any collaboration with the Germans. Armenians deported from the Crimea also were not charged. Neither were the Kurds, the Armenian Moslems, nor the Khemshils (deported in 1947) exiled because they cooperated with the enemy. They were simply seen as unreliable elements in a strategically important territory (the Transcaucasus) at a sensitive time—war against Turkey was being weighed as a possibility.

As had Asiatic despots of the past, Stalin increasingly accepted the practice of exiling entire peoples, as witnessed by the deportation of masses of Ukrainians and Balts from the western border regions in the late 1940s and preparations for deportation of the Jews in 1953.

The practice of exile in the Soviet empire did not start with non-Russians, but with the Kulaks and others, exiled in the 1920s and early 1930s to Siberia. It had deep roots in Russian imperial history. The unreliable population of Novgorod was exiled in the fifteenth and sixteenth centuries. The mountaineers of the Caucasus and the Crimean Tatars were pushed out to Turkey in the nineteenth century. Jews were exiled from the western border regions during World War I.

The flip side of mass exiles was continued colonization. Reliable Russians and other Slavic settlers were introduced in newly depopulated territories. Strategically located settlements of ethnic Russians in the Königsberg (Kaliningrad) province, Sakhalin Island, the Kuriles, and islands in the Gulf of Finland performed primarily security functions. Under both the tsars and the Bolsheviks, Russians were encouraged to settle in Central Asia, the northern Caucasus, and the Baltics, where they performed leading economic and administrative roles. Thus, the Russian metropole from the Middle Ages until the mid-twentieth century had a clearly imperialist aspect.

After the War: Apotheosis of Russian Chauvinism

As World War II was winding down, the Soviet leadership determined that the western Ukrainians had not proved reliable. Hundreds of thousands of Nazi collaborators were hunted down and executed or arrested. Scores of party workers from the Russian federation and eastern Ukraine were assigned to administer Ukraine. The population that had survived the Nazi occupation had to be reeducated.

Khrushchev led the purge of alleged nationalists in the Ukrainian Writers' Union and on the staffs of several literary journals. When he told Stalin that cannibalism was occurring in the Odessa region as a result of the drought-induced famine of 1946 and asked for food assistance, the reply was, "You are a sissy, they are lying through their teeth to get your sympathy!" Khrushchev was then suspended for ten months from his post as Ukrainian party chief.[84]

Since the Russian reconquest of the Baltics in 1944, cattle cars had carried over 300,000 people to Siberia, including the elites. The deportation of about 340,000 peasants (kulaks) to Siberia included the separation of children and parents, incarceration of all able-bodied men in concentration camps, and multiple deaths in transit from disease and malnutrition. In place of the deported Balts, numerous Russian workers were brought in to work in industrial projects.[85]

By adding the northern part of former East Prussia and its capital Königsberg to the RSFSR, Russia effectively outflanked her Baltic acquisitions. In 1946 the USSR Supreme Soviet renamed Königsberg Kaliningrad, and the province became the Kaliningrad *Oblast* of the RSFSR. The Germans were ousted, and Russian and Byelorussian peasants were promptly brought in.

As a result of the war with Japan, Russia occupied the southern part of Sakhalin Island and the Kuriles. Prior to that, in 1944, Russia had annexed Tannu-Tuva, formerly an independent state. After World War II, the Soviet empire reached its geographical peak, similar to the tsarist empire at the end of the nineteenth and the beginning of the twentieth centuries.[86] The geopolitical limits of the empire were obvious: the North Atlantic Treaty Organization (NATO) block in the west, and the Pacific Ocean, China and Japan in the east. The remaining directions of contiguous expansion were the Middle East and Central Asia.

The renewed purge of nationalists was not limited to Ukraine—it spread to other republics. *Zhdanovshchina*, the heavy-handed intervention by the party into the most mundane aspects of cultural life, was an ideological steamroller presenting Russian as the dominant culture of the empire. All things Western, as well as Arabic and Persian influences in the northern Caucasus and Central Asia, were thoroughly expunged.

In September 1947, a crackdown against Armenian nationalism took place. A drawn-out campaign against nationalist tendencies in Kazakhstan raged throughout the mid- and late 1940s and early 1950s. The Russian bureaucracy also severely attacked Kirghiz writers and historians.[87]

After twenty-five years of severe persecution, the Russian Orthodox Church was rehabilitated after a meeting between Stalin and the head of the church, Metropolitan Sergii, in September 1943. The Holy Synod was restored. This was done despite the fact that, in the German-occupied territories, many priests and bishops had collaborated with the invaders.

It is conceivable that, under the pressure of the war, a concession to the strong devotion of the Russian people to its spiritual roots was made. Moreover, there was the Soviet program of postwar domination of the Balkans. The religion of the Bulgarians, Serbs, Rumanians, and Greeks could be exploited by the Soviets. There were also appeals to the racial solidarity of the Slavs: Czechs, Slovaks, Bulgarians, and others.[88] Third, when one examines the development of rituals, paraphernalia, as well as policies after 1937, one can distinguish a clear tendency of return to the images of Stalin's youth, a nostalgia for the symbols of the tsarist empire.

From the demands to rule the Straits to the celebration of the revanche over Japan in 1945, from the famous toast to the Russian people—the "elder brother"—to official anti-Semitism, Stalin's Russia increasingly looked like its previous incarnation. From the reintroduction of epaulets and officers' ranks in the army to separate-sex education and high school uniforms, Russia underwent a significant revival of the old imperial symbols. The opening lines of the USSR's new national anthem (1944), which glorified Great Rus' (*Velikaya Rus'*) was worthy of imperial tradition.

As heir to this tradition, Stalin bargained with Franklin Roosevelt in Yalta, demanding the return of the Eastern Chinese Railway in Manchuria, the southern part of Sakhalin, the Kurile Islands, and Port Arthur—everything tsarist Russia had lost in the "humiliation" of 1904–1905. Stalin was ready to sacrifice 300,000 soldiers to gain lands of questionable import. In the process, he also annulled the Russo-Japanese nonaggression treaty that had saved him in the autumn of 1941. "Forty years we, the people of the old generation, waited for this day," said the Generalissimo.[89] Stalin also won back from Roosevelt another imperial heirloom—Poland.

It was in the imperial tradition of the Roman emperors and the Persian shahs that reparations were meted out upon the vanquished. The industrial parks of Silesia and Saxony were reassembled in Russia. German rocket and nuclear scientists were hunted down and brought to Russia to work on supersecret military projects in Beria's scientific research prison camps.

By employing mass nationalization and collectivization of agriculture, the

Soviet/Russian empire was extended in Eastern Europe. Stalin also entered into a strategic alliance with the new communist colossus—China. However, the USSR did not pursue the global policies of either its Comintern past or its superpower future of the 1960s and 1970s. Instead, after 1945, xenophobia in Russia reached new heights, aggravated by a witch hunt for "rootless cosmopolitans" (Jews) and propagandist outbursts of Russian chauvinism.

Marrying a foreigner became a crime. Stringent secrecy laws were imposed. Soldiers who served abroad were forbidden to disclose information about the living standards of places they liberated. While life in the West was reviled, things Russian were glorified. It was announced to a somewhat skeptical West that the inventors of the airplane, radio, and steam engine were all Russians. Simultaneously, Western scientific achievements, from Einstein's theory of relativity to genetics, were severely denounced; the adherents of these heresies were mercilessly persecuted and sometimes executed.

Russian imperial expansion earned particular praise. Catherine the Great and the reactionary Nicholas I were hailed as "protectors" of the peoples of the Caucasus and Central Asia, while anti-Russian freedom fighters from those areas were castigated as British and Turkish stooges.[90]

A cult of the military and omnipresent secret police had been reestablished. The "apotheosis of imperial slavery, foretold by the prophets of the Russian Idea"[91] was born out of Lenin's dream and implemented by his heirs.

In the mid-1940s, Armenian and Georgian territorial claims against Turkey and Azeri calls for reunification with their brethren in Iran were revived. The Soviet occupation of Persian Azerbaijan in 1941–1946 involved some activities of nation building, not only among the Persian Azeris but also among the Kurds. In Tabriz, the capital of Persian Azerbaijan, an Azeri university and Azeri National Museum were opened. Parts of Persian Kurdistan were occupied by the Soviet army in 1941–1946. The Kurdish republic under Quazi Mohammed was nationalist, not Marxist, and existed for nine months. Nevertheless, the Kurdish Communist Party (PKK) received a big boost and remains active against Turkey to this day. Quazi Mohammed was hanged by the Persians in 1947. For years, Kurds decorated their walls with pictures of their Prime Minister—and of Stalin, who, they thought, had helped them achieve their short-lived independence.[92]

Between 1948 and 1953, a vicious anti-Semitic campaign raged throughout the USSR. Increasingly suspicious, Stalin viewed the Soviet Jews as Western agents, unreliable in case of a future war. The spontaneous demonstrations in Moscow that greeted the first Israeli ambassador to the USSR, Golda Meir, and her inept step of handing the Soviet government lists of volunteers for the Israeli War of Independence (1948) confirmed the dictator's fears. The answer was the roundup and execution of leading Soviet Jewish cultural figures, and thousands of ordinary Jews. The so-called Doctors' Plot was launched, and preparations took place for the mass exile of Jews to Siberia. The Doctors' Plot was a prologue to another purge that possibly would have engulfed some of Stalin's closest lieutenants.

The Generalissimo achieved an imperial feat that even Peter the Great and Catherine II could only have dreamed of: stationing armies of occupation in the heart of Germany and Austria and absolute rule over all of Eastern-Central Europe. Lenin and Trotsky had planned and plotted what Stalin was on the verge of achieving: control of all Europe. If not for the American presence and the policy of containment, Western Europe might have been overrun by the Soviet Army, and a totalitarian dictatorship, more durable than the Nazi nightmare, could have been imposed.

KHRUSHCHEV: BACK TO LENIN

The Empire Hesitates: Destalinization and Reform

With the death of Stalin in 1953 a chapter closed in the existence of the Soviet empire. It was understood by the more ambitious among Stalin's heirs (Beria, Khrushchev, and Malenkov) that support of the republican leaderships would be important to ensure their bids for the top position.

In June 1953, Beria presented the Central Committee with several memos decrying Stalin's policies of Russian domination in the republics. On June 12, 1953, the CC CPSU Presidium passed a resolution demanding a radical improvement of conditions in the republics and an end to "distortions in Soviet nationality policy." Education, advancement, and promotion of the indigenous cadres to leadership positions had to be bolstered. The members of the *nomenklatura* who did not speak local languages had to be recalled to Moscow for further placement. Administrations in national republics had to resume correspondence in local languages. The first party secretary in the republics from now on had to be from a titular nationality and not a Russian.[93]

Pronouncements in *Kommunist* in the summer of 1953 smacked of vintage *korenizatsiya*, hailing the flourishing *(rastsvet)* and continuous development of the national character of all the USSR socialist nations—operative language for national communism. The Russifying policies of merger *(sliyanie)* or drawing together *(sblizhenie)* were no longer mentioned. Local cadres and languages, traditions, education, and lifestyles became important once again. Tirades against Great Russian chauvinism, comparing this sin to local nationalism reappeared in the leading Soviet organs within weeks after Stalin's death.

Beria was removed from the CC Presidium in late June 1953, and with his downfall the Russian people reappeared in the press as "the leading nation," indicating the weakness of the internationalist faction.

Apparently, Beria advocated a rightist approach to the further course of the Soviet Union, presumably as a tactical respite after the paranoia and war hysteria of Stalin's last years. He had proposed a partial disengagement in Eastern Europe, and lightening the burden of exploitation of the peasants. His ally, Georgii Malenkov, promoted the development of light industry over the Stalinist preference for heavy industry. Accusations leveled against Beria by Khrushchev focused on these rightist policies.

Beria was accused of interfering with Party organizations in Ukraine, Byelorussia, and the Baltic republics, and of undermining Soviet unity by promoting national antagonisms. The December 1953 court sentence (presumably posthumous, as Beria apparently was executed in the summer of the same year) found him guilty of steps to "activate the remnants of bourgeois-nationalist elements in the Union republics, to spread animosity and dissent among the USSR's peoples and particularly to undermine the friendship of the USSR's peoples with the great Russian people.".[94] All these charges point to the possibility that Beria was prepared to tolerate, at least for a while, a return to some form of national communism. It is a different question whether (and how) he could have achieved this, taking into account his habitual reliance on secret police as a prime policy-execution tool.

The signs of Ukraine's new prominence as Khrushchev's old power base were abundant as early as 1954, when the 300th anniversary of the Reunification of Ukraine and Russia was celebrated with great pomp. The Ukrainians were promoted to the status of blood brothers of the leading imperial people—the Russians.[95] To celebrate the occasion, a princely gesture was made by Khrushchev: The Crimea, denuded of its original inhabitants, the Tatars, was "presented" to Ukraine, despite the fact that the majority of the population of the peninsula was Russian after the exile of tatars and other minorities.

Two of Khrushchev's defense ministers, R. Ya. Malinovsky and A.A. Grechko, were Ukrainian as was the head of the KGB, V.E. Semichastny. There were more Ukrainians (N.V. Podgornyi, D.S. Polyansky and P.E. Shelest) in Khrushchev's Central Committee Presidium than ever existed under Stalin.

In addition, Ukraine produced a number of key non-Ukrainian apparatchiki. They included future General Secretary L.I. Brezhnev, future Georgian First Secretary V.P. Mzhavanadze, Z.T. Serdiuk, I.D. Yakovlev, and A.I. Struyev.

In Khrushchev's attempts to undermine his former colleagues in the CC Presidium by speeding up decentralization, new powers were given to the republics. As part of his administrative reform (1954–1956), all-union ministries such as the coal mining, oil industry and education ministries, were converted into union-republic ministries, or dissolved. Other ministries, which dealt with transport, mineral resources and geology, metallurgy, and construction were also decentralized. Elites of the republics gained access to economic administration of their rich natural resources.

Further reform was undertaken with the Central Committee's introduction of regional economic councils *(sovnarkhozy)* on May 10, 1957, under the supervision of the respective Councils of Ministers, although certain key ministries, such as those involved in manufacturing weapons, remained under central control. Chairmen of the republican Councils of Ministers also sat on the Union Council of Ministers.

The Communist party general line at the Twentieth Congress in February 1956 further indicated a return to "Leninist norms" in the spirit of the 1920s.

It was stated that socialism does not eliminate national differences, but guarantees national development and flourishing. A major "rectification of wrongs" was the return of the exiled peoples of the Caucasus, and the alleviation of conditions for the Volga Germans and Crimean Tatars. Khrushchev's reforms did not question the fundamental premise of the Soviet state: Russia's domination of its periphery. They did not alter the political power monopoly of the Moscow-based Communist party's Central Committee, nor did they advance the republics to true autonomy and self-determination.

Khrushchev's Reconsolidation

Until the summer of 1957 and Khrushchev's victory over the anti-Party group, which consisted of Molotov, Malenkov, and Kaganovich, his nationality policies were similar to the *korenizatsiya* of the 1920s. With the consolidation of his leadership came a significant change, reflected in an article in *Kommunist* by former Tajik First Secretary Gafurov in August 1958. The Tajik criticized *mestnichestvo* (local patriotism) and the "local chauvinist trends" of individual republics. He also called for increasing usage of the Russian language and appealed for the "continued rapprochement and future merger" of Soviet peoples.[96] This article was followed by one by the Kazakh CC Secretary Dzhandildin, who attacked *korenizatzia*.

These articles were harbingers of purges in Turkmenistan, Uzbekistan, Azerbaijan, Latvia, Kirghizia, and Tajikistan. Khrushchev's style was different from Stalin's bloodbaths. This time people lost their positions, not their lives.

The recentralization of Khrushchev's rule also signified increasing Russification in the school system and renewed efforts to teach Russian to non-Russians. This trend was reflected in unpublished (i.e., secret) sections of the RSFSR education law of April 16, 1959, and secret normative acts of the RSFSR education ministry.[97]

The course toward maximum assimilation of the non-Russians was camouflaged with the rhetoric of a new historic community of people of various nationalities—the Soviet nation.

The consequence of this new approach was the center's renewed hostility to the patriotism of the non-Russians. Any glorification of their past was branded "bourgeois nationalism." Thus, official ideology remained imperialist in its essence, eradicating such terms as fatherland, homeland and patriotism from the vocabulary of the non-Russian nationalities, and reserving these concepts exclusively for Russia and the Soviet Union.[98]

In 1962 a Central Asian Economic Council was created and, in the mode of 1920s, Central Committee bureaus for Central Asia and the Transcaucasus were established. On March 13, 1963, the Supreme Economic Council of the USSR was created to supervise all economic activities of all the State Committees, the Central Planning Agency *(Gosplan)*, and the State Building Committee *(Gosstroy)*. The powers of the *sovnarkhozy* and of the republican Councils of

Ministers were significantly reduced.

Khrushchev attempted to balance republican autonomy and all-union centralization, but his attempts failed. Brezhnev and Kosygin embarked upon the road of unabashed consolidation of imperial controls, attempting to restore the Stalinist command-administrative system that was created in the 1930s. The Soviet empire could not tolerate any attempts to turn it into a federation, to strengthen and renew the assertiveness of the republics. The logic of the preservation of power dictated reconsolidation.

Khrushchev made the first halfhearted attempt to decentralize the Russian-Soviet empire that Stalin had built. The second such attempt was made by Gorbachev. It ended in another failure and the final demise of the empire.

BREZHNEV: IMPERIAL RECONSOLIDATION AND STAGNATION

After Khrushchev's ouster, the machinery of power employed by his heirs, Leonid Brezhnev and Alexei Kosygin, was neo-Stalinist, although without the excesses of the tyrant. The vocabulary and administrative style of the new leaders was Stalinist, too.

In 1966, for the first time, a central Ministry of Education was created. The republican ministries of education became union-republic ones. The Ministry of Justice, abolished in the mid-1950s, was restored in 1970. Moscow, and not republican supreme courts and legal commissions, as in Khrushchev's time, was back in the business of supervising legal administration, courts, lawyers, and notaries.

The all-union ministries assumed the majority of administrative responsibilities, and the *sovnarkhozy* were dissolved. The centralized vertical structure of economic management was put back in place. Administered by obedient first secretaries, the republics once again were reduced to the status of fictitious autonomies.

National relations under the Brezhnev era's "developed socialism" were described in Soviet literature as "flourishing" and "rapprochement." All discussion of "merger," with its implication of replacing the federal state with a unitary one, was abandoned during Brezhnev's consolidation of power (1964–1969).[99] In the meantime, the concept of "Soviet people" (*Sovetsky narod*), first advanced late in Khrushchev's rule, reappeared in the late 1960s. In 1970 Brezhnev spoke of "complete rapprochement," and in 1971 he revived Stalin's hail to the "Great Russian nation."[100]

Brezhnev's line on the Soviet people was contradictory (or should we say, dialectic) because, while speaking of the Soviet people as a "new historic community of people," he extolled the virtues of a very old community—the Russians. Soviet reality seemingly supported Brezhnev's stance: The number of nationalities in the USSR had decreased from 194 in 1926 to 92 in 1979.[101]

There was no full consensus among the top leadership in the Kremlin on the national issues. Debates between specialists in the media appeared in the early 1970s. Large-scale migrations of Russians to the Baltic republics and Central

Asia were encouraged under the guise of "selfless aid of the Great Russian people." Similar to Vladimir Zhirinovsky's position today, there were calls for the abolition of the autonomous structures of the non-Russian peoples of the union and "ethnic merging of nations and peoples in the foreseeable future."[102]

"Moderates" argued that socialist construction is a joint enterprise of all Soviet peoples and republics and that the important role of the Russian language does not deny the rights of national languages for development.[103]

Brezhnev appeared as an arbiter of the early 1970s debate, supporting assimilation and stressing in his speech at the celebration of the fiftieth anniversary of the creation of the Soviet Union (December 1972) the "heightened significance" of the Russian language.[104]

Throughout the Soviet era, the process of assimilation of the minorities into the Russian nation had been under way. The number of people assimilated into the Russian nation between 1926 and 1970 varies from at least 4 to as many as 17 million.

Ukrainians, Byelorussians, the Finno-Ugric peoples, Jews, and Germans were among the largest groups contributing to the Russian nation. In the autonomous republics, Russians made headway in the cities of Karelia, Komi, Udmurtia, and Chuvashia.

The Turkic peoples, with the exception of the non-Moslem Chuvash, showed remarkably low rates of Russification and assimilation. The Yakuts successfully absorbed small peoples of the north. Russians, as did members of imperial nations elsewhere, did not assimilate into other nationalities in the USSR.

In the economic sphere, Brezhnev's regime treated the Soviet economy as a "unified organism," denying economic diversification to the republics, but the RSFSR was granted preferential treatment in the development of natural resources, such as Siberian oil.

As under Stalin, every republic was supposed to develop an economic specialization. Economies of scale were to be realized by building huge enterprises, often in areas with poor infrastructures. Brezhnev's bureaucrats consciously created an interdependence among the republics that would increase the power of the imperial apparatus.

On the other hand, the appearance of a large cadre of educated non-Russians was *korenizatsiya* entering through the back door. The result was a conflict with the old Russian Soviet elite who had ruled in the republics since Stalin.

While under Stalin Russians came to dominate the leadership positions both on the union and the republic levels, under Khrushchev many non-Russians were brought into the inner sanctums of their republics, and some were promoted to all-union jobs.

Under Brezhnev, the process of Russification resulted in the Slavic domination of the union CC and Politburo. However, the Brezhnev leadership did allow non-Slavs to become increasingly involved in the affairs of their republics. The increase in the proportion of local nationalities in the political leadership of the republics was particularly obvious in Central Asia. It also took place in the

Baltic republics, Ukraine, and Azerbaijan. The top party posts dealing with culture and propaganda were in the hands of the locals, as were ministries of education, the Komsomol, and trade unions. Nevertheless, second party secretaries, chiefs of the republican KGBs, republican CC secretaries for construction, heads of the CC departments for organization and party work, and chairmen of the republican CC departments for construction were often Russians and Russified Ukrainians.[105]

Russian specialists and managers prevailed in Central Asian Moslem republics, especially in the technological sectors. On the other hand, the social sciences, the humanities, and health services increasingly became the domain of the non-Russians. This phenomenon could have been due to a dichotomy in the Central Asian education system. While health, the humanities, and social sciences were taught in the Turkic languages, natural sciences and technological subjects were taught in Russian.[106]

Brezhnev's pro-Russian policies, while enjoying the support of the Russians in the Central Committee and the Politburo, may have encountered growing resistance behind the scenes from among the non-Russian leaderships in the republics. This dissatisfaction might explain why Brezhnev took pains to extol the achievements of the nationalities after 1973. In his speech to the Twenty-fifth Party Congress (1976), in contrast to his address to the Twenty-third Party Congress (1971), the Russian people and Russian language were not mentioned at all.

While prosaic reasons for Brezhnev's change of heart are possible, such as new speechwriters on the nationality question, Thompson supposes that the debate over federalism and preparation of the Brezhnev Constitution were the main reasons for the softening of the Soviet leader's position on nationality issues.[107]

Preparation of a new Soviet constitution had started under Khrushchev. Brezhnev was resolute in pushing through a constitution with his hallmark. He first explicitly called for the adaptation of the new basic law in 1972, but the process of drafting was not completed before the Twenty-fifth Party Congress in 1976.

Republican party secretaries, in contrast to their position in 1972, were cool to Russification in 1977 and thereafter, as they were aware of the sentiments in their republics.[108] They also were opposed to the idea of replacing the union with a unitary state.

In May 1977, in a speech announcing the completion of the constitution draft, Brezhnev rejected the creation of a unitary state instead of a federated union and fully endorsed the continuation of the current structure. In October of the same year, Brezhnev criticized "some comrades" (a code word for factional differences) for attempts to limit the sovereignty of the union republics.

This hint of a recantation of his previous position raises questions about possible factional conflicts within the Soviet leadership in the mid-1970s, as evidenced by the political elimination of Politburo member Dimitrii Polyansky (1971), as well as the former Komsomol and KGB chief and Soviet trade union boss "Iron Shurik" Alexander Shelepin in 1976, who reportedly adhered to a more Russian-chauvinist position than Brezhnev. Very much a man of the status quo, Brezhnev attempted to preserve business as usual in the Soviet realm. But it would collapse less than ten years after his death.

THE GROWTH OF NATIONAL OPPOSITION

The Reemergence of Russian Nationalism

Russian nationalism influenced the Kremlin leadership throughout the existence of the Soviet Union. While some of these influences amounted to mere exploitation of Russian historical and religious symbols, since the beginning of the 1930s, ideas of Russian nationalism and Slavophilism received increasing support at the highest levels of the Soviet leadership.

Nevertheless, it was Khrushchev's thaw that provided the conditions for the renaissance of Russian nationalism and the "Russian idea" both in samizdat and in the official press. From the early 1960s, there were two trends in the nationalist movement—one part of the establishment, and the other dissident.

Simultaneously, a split occurred in the Russian dissident movement, active since the 1960s. A Westernizing liberal faction emerged, which concentrated primarily on the abysmal human rights record of the Soviet regime. Its counterpart was a nationalist faction, with its roots in the Slavophile currents of the nineteenth century and the Russian Orthodox Church. The nationalist dissident movement threatened to split the communist officialdom, which itself experienced a crisis of identity after Khrushchev's blows to Stalinism at the Twentieth and the Twenty-second Party Congresses.[109]

Liberal Russian nationalists of the 1960s often repeated word for word what their nineteenth-century predecessors had said. The Slavophiles despised parliamentary democracy and Western "decadence." They maintained that only through religious and spiritual freedom could true liberty for Russia be achieved, and that Russia would "save" the West from its moral degradation.

The Russian nationalists of the 1960s, similar to the Slavophiles in the nineteenth century, condemned the ruling absolutism. Ideological heirs of the Slavophiles, such as Alexander Solzhenitsyn, condemned "ideology" and the "black whirlwind from the West" (Marxism) as destroyers of the nation.[110] The nationalist painter Ilya Glazunov was in the same camp.[111] The movement in the 1970s called for the abandonment of Marxism-Leninism, for economic and administrative decentralization, a resurgence of the church, the decollectivization of agriculture, the introduction of a mixed economy, and withdrawal from foreign adventurism. The Russian Orthodox Church occupied a central place in the ideology of the nationalists.[112]

National Bolshevism, another branch of nationalist thought, was associated with the ruling elite (the so-called Russian Party) and had strong support in the army. It advocated a Russian nationalist dictatorship and was indifferent toward religion. The movement deified the state, called for strong leadership, advocated military and industrial might, and was hostile to the West. It appears that the eminence grise of the Brezhnev regime, Mikhail Suslov, was a supporter and protector of this faction since the mid-1970s.[113]

The National Bolshevik credo can be found in Sergei Semanov's collection of essays *Serdtse rodiny* (Heart of the Motherland), published in 1972.[114] Semanov, as other Russian nationalists, believed in the Jewish-Masonic conspiracy and viewed the anti-Russian West as being controlled by "Masonic and Zionist financial circles."[115]

If the National Bolshevik faction had come to power, the result would have been, in the words of Alain Besancon, "a pan-Russian police and military state."[116] One can find differences between the two camps on the questions of industrialization, urbanization, and Russian military might.[117] However, over the years, the boundaries between the two factions seem to have grown fuzzier, as was demonstrated by the support granted by the nationalist writers to the most reactionary elements in the agonizing Soviet regime prior to the putsch of 1991.

Russian chauvinism, however, failed to address the roots of Russia's cyclic stagnation vis-à-vis the West, or the inability of the Russian Idea to prevent the totalitarian reaction of the communists in 1917.

The CPSU attempted to fight the nationalists. In a special meeting of the Central Committee Secretariat, Brezhnev himself complained about "too much church bell ringing on the TV." A. Nikonov, chief editor of the leading nationalist journal, *Molodaya gvardiya*, was fired. However, another Russian nationalist, Anatoly Ivanov, Nikonov's deputy, was appointed editor in chief of *Molodaya gvardiya*. Moreover, a new nationalist journal emerged: *Nash sovremennik*, edited by Sergei Vikulov. *Molodaya gvardiya* even defended its positions, and was supported by the Stalinist *Ogonek* and *Moskva*. Open "factional struggle" was going on in Moscow's literary establishment, a struggle that reflected tensions higher up.

Molodaya gvardiya continued building bridges to the Stalinists by publishing a panegyric to Stalin's purges of 1937 (Sergei Semanov, "On Relative and Eternal Values"). According to Semanov, the purges marked the beginning of the "monolithic unity of our people" and got rid of "wreckers and nihilists."

Semanov's article caused dismay in the Propaganda Department of the CC. The party journal *Kommunist* unleashed a severe attack against *Molodaya gvardiya*. The acting head of the Propaganda Department of the Central Committee, Alexander N. Yakovlev, wrote a gigantic article, "Against Anti-Historicism," in *Literaturnaya gazeta*, in which Russophilism was attacked as an anti-Leninist, diversionary, and alien ideology. In retaliation, Yakovlev was exiled to Canada, as the Soviet ambassador, not to return until a decade later.

This turn of events indicates the very high level and breadth of support Russian nationalists enjoyed in the Soviet hierarchy. The halt on the attacks on nationalists and the flourishing of chauvinist magazines such as *Nash sovremennik* indicates that the Russian Party had not weakened.

In 1981–1982, the modernizing-internationalist group, led by KGB chief Yurii Andropov, was in ascendancy. Russophiles viewed this coalition of technocrats and international experts, bound on leading the USSR on the path of technological progress at all costs, with suspicion.

With the death of Mikhail Suslov, chief party ideologist and alleged protector of the Russian party and the organ of Russian nationalism, *Nash sovremennik*, in January 1982, an attack was launched on the chauvinist writers by the party flagships, *Kommunist* and *Pravda*. By 1982 the Andropovites had gathered enough forces to attempt a purge. Editors Seleznev and Ustinov were removed and five new, more reliable, members were added to the editorial board of *Nash sovremennik*.

In May 1982, Andropov was officially appointed secretary for ideology, and moved from Lubyanka to *Staraya Ploshchad'* (the CC headquarters).

In November 1982, Leonid Brezhnev died. Andropov assumed the mantle of general secretary. The period from 1983 to the first half of 1984 was characterized by attacks on Russian chauvinism. An onslaught against the nationalists was carried out by V. Oskotskii in *Pravda*.[118] In an article ominously titled, "In the Struggle with Anti-Historicism," the author revived the specter of Alexander Yakovlev's attack of 1972. Significantly, Yakovlev was back in Moscow, on his way to a new round in his spectacular career.

Thus, the 1970s debate between the proponents of the orthodox Marxist approach (i.e., the merger of the nationalities, as advocated by Andropov and Yakovlev) and the neo-Stalinist "Russia-firsters" played out again in the mid-1980s.

After the death of Andropov, the trend was reversed. In June 1984, the Russian Orthodox tribune Soloukhin was awarded the Order of the Red Banner of Labor. Other nationalists—village prose writers and even monarchists—also received awards.

Large parts of the nationalist movement rapidly degenerated into its chauvinist variation. Thus, the evolution of Slavophilism in the nineteenth century through the early twentieth century was repeated almost step by step by its contemporary incarnation. Some extremists even viewed both Stalin's and Hitler's regimes as embodiments of Slavic and Germanic principles opposing "international Jewry," and as historically inevitable and positive phenomena.[119] The chauvinists went so far as to propose the flogging, branding and forced sterilization of women who "gave themselves" to foreigners.[120]

It is only a logical culmination of the movement that the nationalist writers actively opposed Gorbachev's reforms. They even failed to support the decollectivization of agriculture, which could have helped their beloved Russian villages.

Preoccupied with the question of Russian Orthodoxy, the Russian party did not see how the merger between the Russian Orthodox Church and the Soviet state alienated all the non-Russians in the realm and contributed to the disintegration of the empire they were trying so desperately to preserve. In the putsch of August 1991, they supported the anti-reform forces. As usual, the Russian chauvinists were out of touch with the very people they were trying so vociferously to save.

Non-Russian Nationalism

National intellectuals—both in the establishment as well as opponents of the Soviet regime—criticized party nationality policies. Some of them ended up in the Gulag; others managed to remain free, presumably due to high-level support in their republics.

The creation of a nationally minded intelligentsia, which provided a basis for the future political class of the national republics, could have been reversed only through an application of terror that the post-Stalinist Soviet Union could not support.

Nationalism often expressed itself on the cultural front. Thus, the Baltic republics emphasized their music folklore festivals, Armenians stressed their anti-Turkish sentiments, and Central Asians cherished their Moslem family rituals. Often, the roots of these national traditions were incompatible with proletarian internationalism, be these sources Islamic, Catholic or Armenian nationalist, and Christian.

Historic continuity, which in the case of Central Asia involved links with the pre-Moslem Sogdian civilization and the Golden Age of the tenth century, was established, however tenuously. The Tatars assailed the imperialism of Ivan the Terrible and hailed the high development of the Kazan' khanate in the sixteenth and nineteenth centuries. Jadidism attracted the positive attention of intellectuals in the Moslem republics, while the stage had been set for rehabilitation of Sultan-Galiev and other national communists. The search for roots and reverence to Tatar heritage received the name of "Mirarism," and it was ignored by the central authorities.

The regime, ceding ground, tolerated publications that were unthinkable in the past. For example, a Georgian, Vladimir Machavariani, argued in *Literaturnaya Gruziya* for the Leninist national communist position. In fact, his criticism was primarily applied to the party's national and language policy as a whole.[121]

Two Ukrainians, Ivan Dzuba and Mikhaylo Braichevsky, achieved prominence with their works in the late 1960s. Dzuba's *Internationalism or Russification* was published in a classified edition in Ukraine under Shelest. Braichevsky's work *Prisoyedineniye ili Vossoyedineniye* (Annexation or Reunification) could be published only in the West. When his work appeared, Dzuba was sent to a labor camp despite his professed Leninist position.[122]

Attempted Ukrainization under Shelest (1963–1972) brought the percentage of Ukrainians in the republican Politburo to 93 percent. Ukrainians received preferential treatment in the party and national economy. The Shelest group fought with the central leadership in Moscow for a greater allocation of resources to develop the Ukrainian energy base. Premier Alexei Kosygin and *Gosplan* preferred to develop Siberia, thus benefiting the RSFSR.

From the late 1950s to the late 1960s, at least ten underground resistance groups were discovered in Ukraine. The Ukrainian National Front (1964–1967), a continuation of the wartime OUN, published a samizdat magazine *Volya i batkivshchina* (Liberty and Fatherland). The Alliance of Ukrainian Workers and Peasants was national-communist in its orientation and was headed at the time by one of today's most prominent Ukrainian politicians, a Lviv-based lawyer named Levko Lukyanenko. The political platform of the alliance was reminiscent of the Ukrainian Bolshevism of the 1920s: socialist in essence, nationalist in form. In 1971 Lukyanenko was put on trial and was meted out a death sentence, which was commuted to fifteen years of incarceration.

The opposition in the union republics attempted to cooperate when, in several capitals, local chapters of the Helsinki Committee were established. Committed to the observation of civil and human rights, intellectuals from Lithuania, Russia, Georgia, and Armenia collaborated in the Helsinki movement. The writer Mykola Rudenko, former secretary of the Ukrainian Writer's Union, was elected chairman of the Ukrainian Committee.

The Armenian Helsinki Committee drew heavily on the ideas and personnel of the opposition groups of the 1960s. In addition to civil rights, it promulgated Armenian national grievances. Territorial demands, such as the reunification of Eastern Anatolia, Nagorno-Karabagh, and Nakhichevan with Armenia, were also raised. In 1966 the most important underground Armenian group, the National United Party, was formed, with far-reaching territorial and national demands.

In a different pattern of development, the opposition movement in the Central Asian and Moslem autonomous republics of the northern Caucasus focused on the observation of religious and traditional rites and strengthening the Sufi brotherhoods (*Tariqat*).[123] The widespread and militant character of the Moslem brotherhoods in the northern Caucasus and elsewhere have contributed to the long-term systemic instability in the northern Caucasus and Central Asia.

Shelest's fall in May 1972 marked the start of a widespread purge in Ukraine, which soon developed into a campaign against writers, journalists, and historians in all republics. They were accused of "idealizing the past," "local chauvinism," "whitewashing bourgeois-nationalist ideologists," and other "doctrinal" crimes.

From the 1950s, mass movements of disaffected peoples had been protesting against the status quo. The Crimean Tatars submitted mass petitions to the Soviet leadership signed by hundreds of thousands of people. Over 200 Crimean Tatar activists were sentenced to long terms in the Gulag. Despite their resoluteness, the Tatars did not win their major demand—return to the Crimea. What they did achieve, for the first time in the history of the Soviet Union, was the cooperation and support of the Russian liberal-democratic movement. It is a bitter irony that, even after the collapse of communism, the Crimean Tatar autonomy is still waiting to be reinstated.

The policy of Russification, anti-Semitism, and denial of national identity led to the establishment of movements for emigration among two economically active and educated minorities: the Jews and the Germans. Both peoples were successful in attracting international support and publicity to their causes. The numbers of emigrés under Brezhnev and his successors varied according to the general climate of East-West relations. Both emigrations were a bargaining chip in Soviet-German and Soviet-American relations, as well as a safety valve to get rid of undesirables.

It is also significant that the Jewish emigration, at least in its earlier stages, assumed the form of a Zionist phenomenon, a bugaboo of the later Stalin era, as well as during Brezhnev's days. Due to the Soviet Union's history of jailing and executing Zionists (and Bundists), the 1967 Six-Day War placed many Soviet Jews and the Soviet state on two opposing sides of the Arab-Israeli conflict.

In 1968 the Lithuanian Catholics started a campaign to expand their religious freedoms. Soon, cooperation between the Catholics and nationalist supporters of self-determination developed, resulting in several politically motivated self-immolations (Romas Kalanta, 1972, was the most publicized one). The number of Lithuanians signing prodemocracy petitions increased almost tenfold from 1972 to 1979.

Numerous underground publications appeared in Lithuania, beginning with the *Chronicle of the Lithuanian Catholic Church* (1972), *Aushra*, and so on. Successful attempts were made to enlist the support of the Russian liberal democratic movement, as well as the nationally minded part of the Lithuanian apparat, to the cause of national resistance and independence.

The demands of the Estonians remained unswerving until independence was achieved in 1991: the withdrawal of Soviet troops, free elections, reinstitution of Estonian independence, and membership in the United Nations. The activists of the Estonian Democratic Movement received heavy sentences in October 1975. In October 1980, 1,000 Tartu workers went on strike—for the first time since the Soviet occupation began in 1940. Estonian First Secretary Karl Vaino blamed the strike on the influence of the Polish Solidarity movement, which was very popular in the Baltics.

The Latvian roots of post-Stalinist opposition date back to 1962, when members of the Baltic Federation group were sentenced to up to fifteen years in the camps for discussing Baltic independence. There were also remnants of the national communist tradition in the Latvian Communist party, as evidenced by a letter to the international communist movement, smuggled out of Latvia in 1971. After 1975 several proindependence groups sprang up. One of them maintained contacts with the Latvian Social Democratic Labor Party in Sweden. The members of that group were sentenced to up to fifteen years for espionage in 1981.

In 1975 Baltic opposition movements cooperated on a joint declaration asking for Western support against the Soviet occupation. They also cosponsored joint statements on the Molotov-Ribbentrop pact, the Soviet invasion of Afghanistan, and other issues.

Brezhnev's transitional heirs, Andropov and Chernenko, differed in their nationality policy. Andropov called for a scientifically based nationality policy in line with the 1977 constitution and orthodox Marxist analysis of the nationality question, including the controversial merger of peoples.

Chernenko, on the other hand, stressed the importance of the Russian language in communication and education, and he was close to the Russifying-assimilationist position advocated by Brezhnev in the early 1970s. Neither of the leaders lived long enough, however, to operationalize their views on this subject.[124] Under both, severe repression of nationalists and dissidents continued.

CONCLUSIONS

By 1917, Lenin and his comrades in the Bolshevik party had recognized the nationality problem as one of the central issues of the Russian empire. The White movement made a fatal mistake in unswervingly calling for "one and indivisible" Russia, thus denying itself support in Ukraine, Central Asia, and other borderlands. The minorities, which had initially opposed the communist takeover, felt alienated by the Russian anticommunist socialists, liberals, and monarchists advocating this Russian chauvinist line. Under the circumstances, the Bolshevik propagandists managed to split or at least to neutralize the non-Russian nationalists.

The Bolshevik's long-term preoccupation with the Austrian nationality question and dialectic maneuvering allowed them to conceal their unwillingness to dissolve the empire and grant the non-Russians *real* self-determination. Lenin's party pursued a more flexible (and devious) strategy, aimed at dissolution of the old state structure, while attempting to gain control over the geographic expanse of the Romanov empire. Lenin was willing to recognize the independence of Poland, Ukraine, and Finland—especially when the first two were under German occupation.

Once the military strength of the Bolsheviks was asserted, Lenin opted for forcible incorporation of the borderlands into the Soviet state. After the Soviet regime was installed by the power of the Red Army, Lenin was ready to grant the new republics cultural and economic autonomy, opting for communist federalism.

Lenin viewed the struggle with the outside world in social rather than national terms. Thus, the USSR was supposed to be a kernel of the future world communist federation, a bridgehead of the world revolution, not a socialist nation-state.

Stalin was the first Soviet leader to recognize that integration of the multinational empire was dependent upon the loyalty of the non-Russian elites. He strove to replace them with Russians or pro-Russian quislings.[125] The level of terror under Stalin was such that, after the mid-1930s, no active national opposition—be it Marxist-Leninist or otherwise—could survive.

The slow process of de-Stalinization in the national arena led to a revival of the political elites which had at least passively resisted Russification. Non-Russians began exerting pressure to assume increasing responsibilities in all areas of national life in their republics. The creation of these elites was caused by the spread of secondary and higher education initiated by the modernization demands of the Soviet state itself, thus planting the seeds of its own imperial demise. Modernization leading to national liberation was a phenomenon common to the Soviet Union and the Third World, which underwent decolonization in the 1950s and 1960s. As Hélène Carrère D'Encausse noted, "far from paving the way towards integration, this modernization serves as a framework for a nationalism that is being asserted more than ever before and above all more knowingly."[126]

Thus the union was caught between two clashing tendencies—Russification and nationalization—that blocked imperial homogenization. The conflicting prescriptions offered by the Soviet leadership—the glorification of the elder brother, side by side with the veneration of the Soviet people—demonstrated the inability of the Soviet empire to solve the nationality problem:

In sixty years, the Soviet regime has considerably transformed its society. But one thing is clear: of all problems facing Moscow, the most urgent and the most stubborn is the one raised by the national minorities. And like the empire that it succeeded, the Soviet State seems incapable of extricating itself from the nationality impasse.[127]

As a result of the nationalities' desire for greater cultural, economic, and state sovereignty, diverse national opposition movements sprang up in the Baltics, Ukraine, Armenia, and to a lesser degree Georgia, Azerbaijan, and the Central Asian republics. These groups, often connected to religious and traditional roots, were symptomatic of the deep systemic crisis the empire was undergoing. However, in retrospect, one can say that in Central Asia the noncommunist polity had not developed enough to provide a viable alternative to the communist apparatus.[128]

The emigration movements of Soviet Jews, Germans, and Armenians were also characteristic of the deep discontent with conditions in the USSR. The suppression of peoples attempting to return to their historic homelands—Crimean Tatars, Volga Germans, and Meskhetian Turks—was characteristic of an imperial dictatorship.

The increasing disenchantment of Russians with the Marxist-Leninist experiment and with the corrupt and pompous Brezhnev government resulted in rejection by them of the sacrifices demanded in the name of Soviet internationalist duties; the costs of empire. A "Russia first" attitude grew within and outside the party.

The processes of modernization, started under Lenin, continued, despite the terror, under Stalin, and during the reigns of Brezhnev, Andropov, and Chernenko. They resulted in the development of dissident and nationally minded elites, and, to follow Nederveen Pieterse's model, created bases for future emancipation. The empire, held together by force, was waiting for the hour of liberation.

NOTES

1. V.I. Lenin "The National Question in Our Programme," in his *On Proletarian Internationalism* (Moscow: Progress Publishers, 1976), pp. 17–18.

2. Joseph Stalin, *Works*, vol. 2, pp. 52–53, quoted in Samad Shaheen, *The Communist (Bolshevik) Theory of National Self-Determination* (The Hague: W. Van Hoeve, 1956), p. 53.

3. V.I. Lenin, "The Right of Nations to Self-Determination," *Prosveshcheniye*, nos. 4, 5, 6, 1914.

4. V.I. Lenin, "On the National Pride of the Great Russians," in his *On Proletarian Internationalism*, p. 110.

5. V.I. Lenin, "The Socialist Revolution and the Right of Nations to Self-Determination," quoted in Shaheen, *Communist Theory*, p. 127 [italics mine].

6. See documents of the Third Congress of the SR party (May 1917) and the Menshevik paper *Rabochaya Tribuna* of June 1917, cited in *Revolutzia i natzional'nyi vopros*, vol. 3, pp. 88, 95; quoted in G.P. Makarova, *Osushchestvleniye Leninskoy natzional'noy politiki v pervyiye gody sovetskoy vlasti*,(Moscow, FSU: Nauka, 1969), p. 20.

7. Jan Librach, *The Rise of the Soviet Empire* (London: Pall Mall Press, 1964), pp. 138–39. On the indignant reaction of the Russian ruling parties to the First Ukrainian Universal, see Makarova, *Osushchestvleniye Leninskoy natzional'noy politiki*, p. 24.

8. Librach, *The Rise of the Soviet Empire*, p. 141.

9. Ibid., pp. 141–42, 152.

10. Chantal Lemercier-Quelquejay, "Muslim National Minorities in Revolution and Civil War," in S. Enders Wimbush, ed., *Soviet Nationalities in Strategic Perspective* (London: Routledge, 1989), p. 38.

11. Georg von Rauch, *A History of Soviet Russia* (New York: Praeger, 1957), pp. 78–79.

12. Ibid., pp. 79–80.

13. V.I. Lenin, "The Tasks of the Proletariat in Our Revolution" (April 10, 1917), quoted in Shaheen, *Communist Theory*, p. 134.

14. Shaheen, *Communist Theory*, pp. 140–41.

15. V.I. Lenin, "Resolution on the National Question," adopted at the Seventh All-Russian (April) Conference of RSDLP(b), quoted in Shaheen, *Communist Theory*, pp. 141–43.

16. "Declaration of Rights of Peoples of Russia," in *Sbornik dokumentov i materialov po istorii SSSR sovetskogo perioda* (Moscow: Izdatel'stvo Moskovskogo Universiteta, 1966), pp. 53–54.

17. Victor S. Mamatey, *Soviet Russian Imperialism* (Princeton, N.J.: Van Nostrand, 1964), p. 30.

18. Von Rauch, *A History of Soviet Russia*, p. 80.

19. V.I. Lenin, "Speech at the First All-Russia Congress of the Navy," in his *On Proletarian Internationalism*, p. 201.

20. "Resolution of the First All-Ukrainian Congress of Soviets on Organization of the Soviet Power in the Ukraine," in *Sbornik dokumentov*, p. 63.

21. Librach, *The Rise of the Soviet Empire*, pp. 139–40.

22. Lemercier-Quelquejay, "Muslim National Minorities," in Wimbush, *Soviet Nationalities in Strategic Perspective*, p. 40.

23. Ibid., pp. 40–42.

24. Ibid., pp. 47–49, 57.

25. Compare with the 1994–1995 war in Chechnia. The Chechen liberation struggle in 1920–1921 was supported by the Georgian Mensheviks, who rightly feared the deployment of the Red Army troops in Dagestan, threatening independent Georgia. The Soviet invasion of Georgia came only months after the suppression of the Chechen rebellion, in the spring of 1921. An alliance developed between Georgia under President Gamsakhurdia and the Chechens against the pro-Russian Ossetians, and indirectly against Russia in autumn 1991.

26. Lemercier-Quelquejay, "Muslim National Minorities," in Wimbush, *Soviet Nationalities in Strategic Perspective*, pp. 50–52. Parallels to the war in Afghanistan are obvious, as far as the ferocity of the Moslem warriors is concerned, but the results are remarkably different: Dagestan and Chechnia are geographically smaller. The uprising of 1920–1921 had no outside support. The Red Army had just emerged victorious from the bloody civil war and it was highly motivated and apparently well led. This was not the case in Afghanistan.

27. Walter Kolarz, *Russia and Her Colonies* (London: George Philip and Son, 1953), pp. 183–84.

28. Quoted in Librach, *The Rise of the Soviet Empire*, p. 143.

29. "The Constituent Assembly proclaims freedom of self-determination for Armenia." V.I. Lenin, "Declaration of Rights of the Working and Exploited People," in his *On Proletarian Internationalism*, p. 203.

30. Librach, *The Rise of the Soviet Empire*, p. 144.

31. Ibid., p. 145.

32. With the Japanese evacuation of the coastal areas in autumn 1922, the need for a buffer state disappeared.

33. Von Rauch, *A History of Soviet Russia*, p. 123.

34. Ibid., p. 121.

35. Ibid., pp. 83–84.

36. Lenin, "Report on the Party Program," quoted in von Rauch, *A History of Soviet Russia*, p. 255.

37. V.I. Lenin, "To the Communists of Turkestan," in *On Proletarian Internationalism*, p. 254. The *Turkomissia* (Turkestan Commission) was created under VTsIK and *Sovnarkom*. None of the members was a Turkic Moslem. Its role was to "rectify the mistakes" the local communists caused by alienating the local population. It also was to evaluate the military situation in the region vis-à-vis the Basmachi rebellion, as well as the possible future confrontation with the British in the direction of Afghanistan and India.

38. Von Rauch, *A History of Soviet Russia*, p. 135.

39. Kolarz, *Russia and Her Colonies*, p. 229.

40. "Rezolutsia kavkazskogo buro TsK RKP(b) o Federatsii Zakavkazskikh Respublik," *Sbornik dokumentov*, pp. 203–4.

41. "Iz protokola soglasheniya mezhdu RSFSR i Azerbaidzhanom, Armeniyey, Belorussiyey, Bukharoy, Gruziyey, Dal'nevostochnoy Respublikoy, Ukrainoy i Khorezmom o peredache RSFSR predstavitel'stva oznachennykh respublik na Genuezskoy Konferentsii,"

22 February 1922, in *Sbornik dokumentov*, p. 204.

42. I.V. Stalin, "Draft Resolution on the Relations between RSFSR and Independent Republics," August 11, 1922, in *Izvestia TsK KPSS*, no. 9, p. 192, quoted in Lowry Wyman, "Soviet Constitutional Law: Towards a New Federalism," paper presented at the AAASS annual convention, Washington, D.C., October 1990, p. 4.

43. Wyman, "Soviet Constitutional Law", p. 5.

44. Ibid., p. 6. Wyman points out that dissidents in the Brezhnev era were imprisoned for committing "formalism"—"attempting to put content and substance back into words from which they had been removed."

45. Ibid., p. 8.

46. Ibid.

47. Letter to Lenin and members of Politburo, September 27, 1922, published in *Osteuropa*, XXII, 1972, pp. A 808–A 810, quoted in Gerhard Simon, *Nationalism and Policy toward the Nationalities in the Soviet Union* (Boulder, Colo.: Westview Studies on the Soviet Union and Eastern Europe, Westview Press, 1987), p. 22. Stalin's quest for power and Lenin's illness had a great deal to do with the developing clash.

48. "Soyuznyi dogovor zakavkazskikh Sovetskikh Sotsialisticheskikh Respublik," in *Sbornik dokumentov*, p. 205.

49. "Deklaratsia sed'mogo vseukrainskogo s'yezda sovetov," "Deklaratsia VII vseukrainskogo s'yezda sovetov," and "Iz postanovleniya IV vsebelorusskogo s'yezda sovetov ob obrazovanii Soyuza Sotsialisticheskikh Sovietskikh Respublik," in *Sbornik dokumentov*, pp. 207-208.

50. "Postanovleniye X vsserossiiskogo s'yezda sovetov ob obrazovanii SSSR," in *Sbornik documentov*, p. 208.

51. V.I. Lenin, "The Question of Nationalities or 'Autonomization'," in his *On Proletarian Internationalism*, p. 329, first published in *Kommunist*, no. 9, 1956. It should be noted here that the article was suppressed in the USSR until deStalinization, and it corresponds in time to the Testament (December 25, 1922), and the Codicil to the Testament (January 4, 1923), in which Lenin demands Stalin's ouster.

52. Lenin, "The Question of Nationalities or 'Autonomization',"in *On Proletarian Internationalism*, pp. 329–35.

53. See Stalin's article in *Pravda*, October 10, 1920; resolution on the nationalities of the Tenth Party Congress (March 1921), and the confirmation of the latter by the Twelfth Party Congress (April 1923), quoted in Simon, *Nationalism and Policy*, p. 24.

54. Simon, *Nationalism and Policy*, p. 31.

55. Ibid., pp. 37–38, based on *Natsional'naya politika VKP(b) v tsifrakh* (Moscow, 1930), pp. 44–47, 199, and a study conducted by the Commissar of Workers' and Peasants' Inspection (1931) confirmed the numbers and described the situation as "scandalous." It should be noted that after Stalin's death, the trend was reversed, and the numbers of non-Russians in local administration increased.

56. Simon, *Nationalism and Policy*, pp. 38–40.

57. Ibid., pp. 29–30.

58. Ibid., pp. 43–44.

59. Ibid., pp. 44–45.

60. This is the English translation. The party was called the Vsesouyuznaya Kommunisticheskaya Partiya (bolshevikov), or VKP(b).

61. Report to the Sixteenth Congress of the Party, quoted in Simon, *Nationalism and Policy*, p. 73.

62. Simon, *Nationalism and Policy*, p. 79. Simon claims that Turar Ryskulov (vice chairman of the RSFSR Council of People's Commissars until 1937), Veli Ibragimov (chairman of the Crimean Tatar CEC, executed in 1928), and possibly the *Jadid* Faizullah Khodzhayev (chairman of the Uzbek Council of People's Commissars, executed in 1938) maintained links with Sultan-Galiev's conspiratorial organization. No sources for this claim are quoted.

63. See Alexander Bennigsen and Marie Bruxup, *The Islamic Threat to the Soviet Union* (London: Croom Helm, 1983), pp. 77–80, 90–93; and Hélène Carrère d'Encausse, *Islam and the Russian Empire* (New York: Newsweek Book, 1988), p. 62ff and esp. ch. 6, "Era of Secret Societies."

64. Kolarz, *Russia and Her Colonies*, pp. 263-264.

65. Simon, *Nationalism and Policy*, p. 88.

66. Particularly ironic was the plight of those nations who used Cyrillic prior to 1917, had to learn the Latin alphabet, and after 1937 were forcibly switched back to Cyrillic. This was the case of the Finnish peoples of the northern Soviet Union, the Udmurts and Komi, as well as the Ossetians, and the Yakuts in eastern Siberia. Simon, *Nationalism and Policy*, p. 154.

67. *Pravda* article, August 19, 1936, "Killing of Khandzhian"—quoted in Medwedew, *Die Wahrheit ist unsere Starke: Gesichichte und Folgen des Stalinismus* (Frankfurt, 1973), p. 230; both quoted in Simon, *Nationalism and Policy*, p. 158.

68. Nikolay Berdiayev, *Istoki i Smysl Russkogo Kommunizma* (Paris: YMCA Press, 1955); reprinted (Moscow: Izdatel'stvo Nauka, 1990), pp. 118, 120.

69. Ibid., p. 150.

70. Ibid., p. 152.

71. Ibid., p. 179.

72. Alexander A. Alexiev, "Soviet Nationalities under Attack," in Wimbush, *Soviet Nationalities in Strategic Perspective*, pp. 60–62.

73. Simon, *Nationalism and Policy*, pp. 194–195.

74. Ibid., pp. 196–198. Alexiev, however, stresses the overwhelming response of Turkic Moslems to German calls to enlist in "Eastern Legions" and maintains that some nationalities had higher representation in the German forces than in the Red Army. Alexiev, "Soviet Nationalities under Attack," in Wimbush, *Soviet Nationalities in Strategic Perspective*, p. 72.

75. Theodor Oberlander, "Bundnis oder Ausbeutung," June 22, 1943, p. 130, r6/70, Bundesarchiv, Koblenz; quoted in Alexiev, "Soviet Nationalities Under Attack," in Wimbush, *Soviet Nationalities in Strategic Perspective*, p. 73.

76. Simon, *Nationalism and Policy*, p. 200.

77. Ibid.

78. Aleksandr M. Nekrich, *The Punished Peoples: Deportation and Fate of Soviet Minorities at the End of the Second World War* (New York: W.W. Norton, 1974), p. 26. Nekrich quotes a memo written by the commanders of the Crimean partisan movement, A.N. Mokrousov and A.V. Martynov, to Marshal S.M. Budennyi, commander of the southwestern front.

79. See the October 20, 1944, resolution of the Crimean regional party committee; August 21, 1944, decree of the Presidium of the RSFSR Supreme Soviet, quoted in Nekrich, *Punished Peoples*, p. 34.

80. Robert Conquest, *The Nation Killers: The Soviet Deportation of Nationalities* (New York, Macmillan, 1970), p. 101; Nekrich, *Punished Peoples*, p. 42.

81. Conquest, *Nation Killers*, pp. 99–100.

82. Ibid., p. 102.

83. Ibid., pp. 76–83.

84. Nikita Khrushchev, *Khrushchev Remembers*, quoted in Simon, *Nationalism and Policy*, p. 205.

85. Between 1945 and 1959, 400,000 Russians and 100,000 other non-Latvians immigrated to Latvia. In 1945–1947 alone 180,000 Russians settled in Estonia. Due to parallel deportation of the indigenous population, the proportion of the titular nationalities in Latvia and Estonia plummeted to approximately 50 percent over the first twenty-five years of the Soviet occupation. Simon, *Nationalism and Policy*, p. 218.

86. The point is even more obvious if one counts the "informal" empire in Eastern Europe. Never before had Russia expanded so deeply into Eastern and Central Europe. This imperial apogee lasted from around 1948 to 1990.

87. Simon, *Nationalism and Policy*, p. 206.

88. Isaac Deutscher, *Stalin* (London: Oxford University Press, 1967), pp. 491–92.

89. Stalin's speech celebrating the victory over Japan, published in *Bolshevik*, no. 16, August 1945, quoted in Deutscher, *Stalin*, p. 528. Ironically, "people of the old generation," who wished for Russian revenge upon Japan, were the monarchists and the old Russian right. At the time of the 1904 defeat, the Bolsheviks, Mensheviks, and the Russian liberals celebrated the blow the hated Romanov dynasty suffered.

90. Ibid., p. 603.

91. Alexander L. Yanov, *The Russian Challenge and the Year 2000* (New York: Basil Blackwell, 1987), p. 68. For a detailed description of the vision of the future by the Russian ultranationalists, see Sergei F. Sharapov's novel *Cherez Polveka* (After a half-century), written in 1901, and summarized in Yanov, *The Russian Challenge*, pp. 40–41.

92. Kolarz, *Russia and Her Colonies*, pp. 250–52.

93. Unpublished CC resolution quoted in Simon, *Nationalism and Policy*, pp. 228–29, footnotes 2–3.

94. *Pravda*, December 24, 1953, quoted in Simon, *Nationalism and Policy*, p. 230.

95. Simon, *Nationalism and Policy*, p. 233.

96. B. Gafurov, "Uspekhi natsional'noi politiki KPSS i nekotoryie voprosy internatsional'nogo vospitaniya," *Kommunist*, no. 11, 1958, pp. 10–24.

97. Simon, *Nationalism and Policy*, pp. 249–50.

98. Michael Bruchis, *The USSR: Language and Realities. Nations, Leaders and Scholars* (Boulder, Colo.: Westview East European Monographs, 1988), pp. 22–23.

99. Editorial in *Kommunist*, no. 13, 1969, p. 10.

100. Terry L. Thompson, *Ideology and Policy: The Political Uses of Doctrine in the Soviet Union* (Boulder, Colo.: Westview Special Studies on the Soviet Union and Eastern Europe, 1989), p. 77.

101. Yulii Bromlei, E. Bagramov, M. Guboglo, and M. Kulichenko, eds., *Razvitiye Natzional'nykh otnoshenii v SSSR v svete reshenii XXVI s'yezda KPSS* (Moscow, 1982), p. 279.

102. Michael Bruchis, *The USSR: Language and Realities. Nations, Leaders and Scholars* (Boulder, Colo.: Westview East European Monographs, 1988), pp. 28–29, 136.

103. Ibid., p. 190.

104. A detailed program to increase Russification was presented to an educational conference in Tashkent (1975). K. Khanazarov, *Resheniye natzional'no-yazykovoy problemy v SSSR*, 2d ed., p. 24, quoted in Bruchis, *Language and Realities*, p. 270.

105. Bruchis, *Language and Realities*, pp. 274–77.

106. Ibid., p. 272.

107. Thompson, *Ideology and Policy*, p. 84.

108. See, for example, Shevardnadze's handling of student demonstrations in Tbilisi in 1978, when the Georgians managed to preserve the definition of their language under the Georgian constitution as the "state" language of the republic.

109. Yanov, *The Russian Challenge*, pp. xi–1.

110. Alexander Solzhenitsyn, *Pis'mo k vozhdyam Sovetskogo Soyuza* (Letter to the leaders of the Soviet Union), quoted in Yanov, *The Russian Challenge*, p. 22.

111. Yanov, *The Russian Challenge*, pp. 88–89.

112. Ibid., p. 89.

113. Ibid., p. 13. Suslov appeared to protect Il'ya Glazunov's art exhibitions in Moscow and Leningrad, the writer Vl. Soloukhin, and Gennadii Shimanov's Samizdat almanac *Mnogaia Leta*.

114. Sergei Semanov, *Serdtse rodiny* (Moscow: Moskovskii Rabochii, 1977).

115. John B. Dunlop, *The New Russian Nationalism* (Washington, D.C.: Washington Papers; Praeger, 1985), p. 91. Nikolay Yakovlev's "August 1, 1914" was mentioned by the late Marshal Sergei Akhromeyev, during his visit to the United States, as "containing an explanation of why we [who—the Soviet Army?—AC] lost World War I." Yakovlev's book "explains" that World War I was the result of a Jewish-Masonic conspiracy against Russia.

116. Dunlop, *The New Russian Nationalism*, p. 90.

117. Ibid., pp. 91–92.

118. V. Oskotskii, "V bor'be s anti-istorizmom," *Pravda*, May 6, 1984, p. 2.

119. Yanov, *The Russian Challenge*, p. 83.

120. Suggested by a Moscow Komsomol leader, Valeriy Skurlatov, who also called for "orienting our youth toward the mortal struggle" connected to the "cosmic mission of our people"—quoted in Yanov, *The Russian Challenge*, p. 83.

121. Vladimir Machavariani, "Natzia, ee kul'tura i yazyk," *Literaturnaya Gruziya*, no. 7, 1971, p. 79.

122. "Natsional'ny vopros v SSSR," in *Sbornik dokumentov*, pp. 62–132.

123. For a lengthy study of the phenomenon, please see Bennigsen and Bruxup, *The Islamic Threat to the Soviet Union*, pp. 73–77. See also other articles written by A. Bennigsen on sufism in the former Soviet Union.

124. Thompson, *Ideology and Policy*, p. 152.

125. Simon, *Nationalism and Policy*, p. 265.

126. Hélène Carrère d'Encausse, *Decline of an Empire: Soviet Socialist Republics in Revolt* (New York: Newsweek Books, 1979), p. 266.

127. Ibid., p. 274.

128. Ukraine is a special case, dominated by the former apparatus, but also allowing for a large degree of political freedom.

4

Perestroika and the End of Empire

IMPERIAL COLLAPSE: IDEOLOGICAL CRISIS

In April 1985 the last Cold War general secretary, K.U. Chernenko, died. The torch had to pass to a new generation, and Mikhail Sergeyevich Gorbachev was elected general secretary. The top Soviet leaders were aware that the old system was inadequate to meet the challenges of the latter half of the twentieth century. In a 1992 article, Gorbachev recalled:

It is possible that with repressions and political maneuvers the inevitable collapse could have been postponed. It would have ended in an explosion; the consequences would have been even more horrendous—domestic and international.

The choice had to be made. It had to be made by those who by will of fate were at the top of power. And the choice was made, I think, the only correct one. It would be a great exaggeration to say that from the beginning we imagined the scope and the difficulties of *perestroika*. Moreover, its starting designs did not go beyond the framework of the system, neither ideologically, nor politically. For us it was then improvement of the existing society, "forcing the system to work."[1]

The ideological justification for empire had collapsed at the pinnacle of power. The high priests were the ones who had lost their faith.

In the beginning of *perestroika*, French journalists wrote that the center of counterrevolution was the general staff of communism, the CC of the CPSU. According to Alexander Tsipko, former consultant to the International Department of the CPSU Central Committee, this was close to the truth:

While working in CC as a consultant I found to my surprise that the attitudes among those in the topmost positions of the hierarchy were not different from the attitudes in the Academy of Sciences and humanitarian institutes. It was clear that only a complete hypocrite could believe in the advantages of socialism over capitalism. It was also clear that the socialist experiment had suffered a defeat. Everyone who had preserved self-respect and had not lost, despite everything, an ability for independent thought, was abandoning Marxism. Without this there would have been no *perestroika*, nor the liberation that followed it.[2]

The role of Alexander N. Yakovlev, chief ideologist of *perestroika*, in bringing about the process of reforms is controversial. On one hand, his track record as a persecutor of dissidents and "screen-writer" for the Siniavsky-Daniel and other show trials of the 1960s is well known. However, his struggle in the 1970s against Russian chauvinists is also on record.

By the second half of the 1980s, Yakovlev, who had returned from his Canadian exile, was secretary of the CC and chief of the Department of Ideology, and later, of the International Department of the CC, a member of the Politburo, and one of the brains behind Gorbachev's reforms. He consistently broadened the framework of permissible discussion, introduced non-Marxist categories and terms, and attacked the dogma and hypocrisy of the Soviet social sciences.

By 1985–1986, Gorbachev, Yakovlev, and other leaders of *perestroika* believed that, while theoretically correct, due to the atmosphere of censorial omnipotence, persecution of dissidents, spiritual despotism, and far-reaching moral corruption, Marxism suffered from a lack of truthful analysis.

In a television interview, Eduard Shevardnadze, former first secretary of the Georgian Communist party, recalled talking to Gorbachev on the Black Sea beach—just before the latter's nomination to the highest post—about the "penetrating rot" of the system. Both agreed that fundamental changes were necessary. The guardians of the empire were becoming increasingly aware of their inability to continue to rule the realm in the old way.

According to Yakovlev, during the Khrushchev and Brezhnev period, control of the party apparatus had been transformed into the rule of institutional and local interests over those of the party. Directors of the military-industrial enterprises and local military commanders often overruled party secretaries. The CC CPSU "reigned but did not rule," inefficient and ever dependent on information provided by government ministries and offices, hardly affecting even personnel decisions.[3]

A complementary and different view of economic management in the pre-*perestroika* Soviet Union is provided by former USSR Chairman of the Council of Ministers, Nikolay I. Ryzhkov. He spent the better part of his career as first deputy chairman of *Gosplan*, CC secretary in charge of economics under Andropov, and prime minister under Gorbachev (1985–1990). Ryzhkov claims that the Central Committee managed the economy without having any professional knowledge of the subject and without bearing any responsibility for the results. He decries the ubiquitous presence of ideology that stonewalled any attempt to reform the economy: "The Party directed everything, the instrument of direction was the Central Committee".[4] Despite his titular position as Chairman of the Council of Ministers, the prime minister did not have authority over his deputy in charge of the military-industrial complex, nor over the ministers of defense or foreign affairs or the chairman of the KGB, who were all formal members of the Council.[5]

According to Yakovlev, the party apparatchiki in the central organs were increasingly replaced by specialists, industrial hacks (*khoziaystvennyi aktiv*) who lacked ideological spark and were primarily motivated by their career interests and a thirst for personal graft. Since the mid-1960s, the principal means of control the party apparatus could exert on these economic *aktiv* was blackmail, threats of prosecution for real or imagined breaches of a myriad of bureaucratic instructions, and "laws." The results of this system were increasing corruption and the growing influence of ministerial and industrial interests in the party central apparatus.

The *perestroika* team began to coalesce inside the Andropov administration. It was very much a next-generation group, with Gorbachev being the undisputed leader. In addition to Ryzhkov and Yakovlev, the team included former first secretary of the Tomsk *oblast* Party Committee, Yegor Kuz'mich Ligachev; former Georgian minister of the interior and first secretary Eduard Amvrosiyevich Shevardnadze; and Vitaly Vorotnikov, former ambassador to Cuba, who became prime minister of the Russian Federation.

In 1983 Andropov brought Ligachev from Siberia to become the head of the Organizational and Party Work (*orgpartrabota*) Department of the CC. Ryzhkov characterized the man as being phenomenally active, tough, having the "undefeatable purposefulness of a mighty tank," and notes that he was an irreplaceable ally of the "stealthily becoming more powerful" Gorbachev. These "tank" qualities were crucial for strengthening the Gorbachev team not only in the center, but also on the *oblast* level, where the old generation was respectably retired, preserving most of the perks of office and status. New people, loyal to Gorbachev, the future CC plenum's crucial majority, were put in place.[6] Ryzhkov intimates that Ligachev was critical in forging the Politburo coalition that unanimously voted Gorbachev in upon Chernenko's death.

The majority of the top CPSU leadership believed in the necessity for reform. Yakovlev even advocated splitting the CPSU into two parties that would compete in elections. The aim was to encourage renewal and improve and democratize socialism.[7] "The belief in improvement of socialism was dominant in the ruling apex *(verkhushka)* of the Party and leadership."[8]

Gorbachev's *perestroika* (restructuring) was supposed to take the form of *uskoreniye*—"acceleration of science-technical and socio-economic progress." *Uskoreniye* failed, and it had been abandoned by 1987. Its real achievement was to demonstrate to the Soviet political class that the improvement of socialism was totally insufficient to solve the problems facing the society. It lacked the mechanisms to translate the considerable potential of Soviet science and engineering (primarily in the military-industrial sphere) into any meaningful improvement of the standard of living of the masses.

The more visible facet of Gorbachev's reforms was *glasnost*, the weakening of censorship and the opening up of formerly unmentionable topics for discussion. *Glasnost* was later proclaimed the more successful of Gorbachev's reforms by both Russian democrats and Western political analysts. It was the interaction of these two facets, the successful and the unsuccessful, that characterized the

USSR's travel along the road of change, ending with the drama of imperial disintegration in 1991. As attempts to modernize socialism failed, more comprehension developed among the elites that nothing short of the total rejection of socialism and the imperial principle of the Soviet state was necessary.

Yakovlev notes that as *perestroika* began, the economy, ideology, and state and societal structures all proceeded to crumble. To save socialism, it would have been necessary to restore pre-*perestroika* conditions, in all their conservative and reactionary facets.[9]

Yakovlev has shown that six years of *perestroika* did not succeed in sufficiently neutralizing the old Soviet structures such that they would allow political and economic reforms to take place. The communist-dominated forces emasculated the democratic process, rejected the transition to market economy, and were hostile to liberty and free creative activity. After the defeat of the August 1991 counterrevolution, they not only cling to the past and struggle for survival, but have managed to stage a seemingly impossible comeback.[10]

Ryzhkov also recognizes that *perestroika* failed. He testifies that it was conceived as the improvement and preservation of socialism and of the Soviet state.[11]

Upon his election, Gorbachev moved quickly to consolidate his power in the Politburo. The enterprise directors, anxious to attain more power, were among the supporters of the group he led. In the academic realm, the reformers drew upon the expertise of Abel Aganbegyan, Georgii Arbatov, Oleg Bogomolov, Tatyana Zaslavskaya, Leonid Abalkin, and Nikolay Petrakov, to mention a few. Thus, a broad coalition for *perestroika* was put together among the Soviet political class. Effectively, this group of "establishment reformers" produced a result similar to that of their Constitutional Democrat *(kadet)* predecessors in 1917—the collapse of the Russian/Soviet empire.

IMPERIAL COLLAPSE: CRISIS IN THE CENTER

The policies of *glasnost* and *perestroika* also brought to the surface new nationalist political players. Faced with this challenge, the central Communist party apparatus exhibited its inability to continue administering the country it had ruled for seventy years. A survey of formerly secret documents in the CC CPSU archives reveals how completely inadequate the regime's responses to the new conditions actually were.

The first severe ethnic crisis of the Gorbachev era was the Azeri-Armenian conflict over Karabakh, which escalated in 1988. The Politburo prepared a Supreme Soviet decree allowing law enforcement organs to exercise administrative detention for up to thirty days for instigating national hatred or provoking the violation of public order.[12] However, the Politburo disregarded the fact that the law enforcers themselves had already begun taking sides with the nationalists in both camps and were effectively out of central control.

The ideological department was tasked with "measures to improve coverage of inter-ethnic questions in the central press and local organs of mass media of the Armenian and Azerbaijani SSR." Simultaneously, the *Glavlit* (the main censorship body) was directed to strengthen the censorship services of Armenia and Azerbaijan and to effect a "temporary" introduction of "censorship on publications in local media."[13]

Finally, in anticipation of widespread disorder, and prompted by the Karabakh events, the Politburo, as early as December 1988, adopted a resolution to develop the legal regulation of emergency rule in the whole country or parts thereof within one month.[14] The whole Politburo voted in favor of these measures. However, the crisis was proceeding so fast, and was so deep, that no emergency rule could salvage the agonizing empire.

For years, the communists of Russia had been denied a party of their own, while their colleagues in the union republics were organized in their own parties. Any demand to create a separate Russian Communist party would have been severely punished in earlier decades.[15] Under Gorbachev, the Russian apparatchiki, feeling threatened by the appearance of "national communists," pressed for the establishment of an RSFSR party structure. The satisfaction of this demand would have given these elites a tool to assert Russian national interests as *they* understood them—witness Boris Yeltsin's success in doing the same with the Russian Supreme Soviet. If the Russian Communist party had been established earlier (circa 1987-1988), taking into account the extremely hard-line character of its membership, Russia might have been able to thwart attempts to dissolve the Soviet Union more effectively. The orthodox Russian communists would have resisted any attempts on the part of the republics to break away, and they could have provided an organizational basis for fighting the reforms. Under these circumstances, the events of the August 1991 putsch might have developed quite differently.

Gorbachev had resisted the call for a Russian party for a long time, but the issue was finally taken up at a June 1990 meeting of the Politburo and CC secretaries.[16] There it was suggested that the all-Russian Party conference would constitute a constituent party congress. The meeting recommended prolonging the establishment procedure of the Russian party, presumably to ensure central control over it. As it turned out, the Russian Communist party, under the leadership of Ivan Polozkov, emerged as the most conservative element in the Soviet political scene, inimical to *perestroika* and its leaders. However, it was too late to brake the reform process effectively.

As far as the USSR's future was concerned, Gorbachev was seeking a transition to a more manageable nine-plus-one federation model, in which more powers would be allocated to the union republics. But centrifugal processes inside the Soviet Union CPSU had gone too far.

The Central Committee lost control over the USSR's legislative body, the Supreme Soviet, chaired first by Gorbachev and later by his close associate, Anatoly Lukyanov. In April 1991, the Supreme Soviet adopted a law on the

Rehabilitation of Repressed Peoples and corresponding regulations. This law called for the reconstitution of the republics that had been wiped off the map by Stalin's deportations. In June 1991, the Central Committee deliberated on "some problems connected with the rehabilitation of repressed peoples,"[17] and took issue with the law, as it allegedly discriminated against the Russian-speaking population living in the areas formerly occupied by these "punished peoples." The internal papers of the Central Committee clearly reflect the disagreements that plagued the work of the central Soviet organs toward the end of the existence of the USSR.[18] For example, the activities of the state commission on Soviet Germans was defended against the attacks of more liberal people's deputies, despite the fact that the commission did everything possible to leave the Germans in Kazakhstan and prevent their return to the Volga region.

Formerly, the Supreme Soviet had merely rubberstamped CC decisions, and it did not lead in the political process—it appeared that now the "tail" was wagging the "dog."

As the union slowly disintegrated, the Central Committee Secretariat, once an omnipotent executive body, lost its control over popular resistance in the republics against the Soviet military. Inability to ensure law and order and a lack of efficient control in the periphery are characteristics of an empire in the process of disintegration.

To counter this trend, the CC passed a decree On Urgent Measures in Connection with the Strengthening of Anti-Army Manifestations in a Series of Regions of the Country, which adopted, in general, the recommendations of the CC commission on party-military policy.[19] The commission complained about "anti-military campaigns" in the Baltic republics, Transcaucasia, western Ukraine, and Moldova. The authors of the decree protested discrimination (*proizvol*) aimed at Soviet army officers and their families by the local governments. Instances of refusal to hire officers' wives (who did not speak the local languages), as well as denials of medical treatment, education, child care, and *propiska* (housing permits) were cited.[20] The commission was concerned with victims among the officer core—97 killed and 150 severely wounded in 1989 and 1990—as well as about draft dodging and desertions from the ranks of the Soviet army. The authors protested "anti-military propaganda" in the media and calls for the formation of territorial army units in the republics within or outside the Soviet army structure, along with pacifism, insufficient knowledge of the Russian language, criminal activities, and drug abuse among the recruits.[21] Nevertheless, the CC failed to resurrect Soviet military power, which had become unreliable as far as protection of the state and party structures was concerned. The events of August 1991 showed that the party's control of the military had become tenuous at best.

In attempting to address the situation, the commission failed to offer realistic and concrete policy options, calling instead for the "taking of urgent measures by state organs, as well as the CC CPSU, CCs of republican party committees, republican, *kray* (region) and *oblast* party committees." Party committees were called upon to analyze the implementation of the Twenty-seventh Party Congress resolution on party military policy, to give "principled assessments" of the negative phenomena in relation to the Soviet military, to define measures directed toward boosting military authority, to increase the prestige of military service and defense of its honor, and to improve the life and health of servicemen.[22] The commission further called for

repelling of destructive forces, giving aggressive [*nastupatel'nye*] character to the local party organs' propaganda activities aimed at an explanation of the Party military policy. It is important to attract to this work communist people's deputies, veterans of the party and armed forces, all party and propaganda *aktiv*. Patriotic education of the population demands serious improvement, energetic Party measures to ensure the autumn draft of youths are needed. We deem it useful to cover implementation of such measures in the mass media.[23]

This amounted to a lot of bureaucratic hot air, and very little concrete action.

One of the harshest Secretariat resolutions was that on the Baltic states. It adopted a report and recommendations written by future coup plotter, hard-line CC secretary Oleg Shenin. Returning from an inspection tour of Lithuania, he submitted a lengthy account severely criticizing the nationalist Lithuanian leadership led by Vitautas Landsbergis.[24]

In his report, Shenin termed the "week of Europe in Lithuania" (a series of events designed to highlight Lithuania's solidarity with Europe) a "nationalist psychotic action," organized to distract the attention of the Lithuanian people from their deteriorating situation. The report contained a thinly veiled attack on communist reformers. "Harsh criticism" (without attribution) was reportedly directed by the local rank and file against "the CC CPSU, Presidential Council, Council of Ministers, and personally comrades Gorbachev M. S., Ryzhkov N. I., Yakovlev A. N., Medvedev V. A., Bakatin V. V. for the situation in the Baltics, and for not fulfilling many promises given while visiting the Lithuanian SSR."[25]

Shenin's recommendation, adopted by the Secretariat, included a ten-point agenda aimed at strengthening the Soviet delegation charged with negotiating with the Lithuanians, "re-establishment of application of the Soviet and Lithuanian SSR constitution," confirmation of Soviet and CPSU property rights, and the preparation of a Politburo statement to support Lithuanian "healthy forces." Especially ominous was a recommendation to the state and law department of the CPSU Central Committee to have "the communists—leaders of law-and-order organs" of the country prepare criminal and administrative prosecution of "leaders of different nationalist and anti-Soviet organizations, extremists and deserters who have broken Soviet laws. For this purpose, the activities of the USSR *Prokuratura*, Ministerstvo Vnutrennikh Del (MVD, the Ministry of Internal Affairs), KGB and USSR Supreme Court should be coordinated and an 'operational-investigative fast reaction group' [*operativno-sledstvennaya gruppa bystrogo reagirovanya*] should be sent to Lithuania."[26]

Shenin also suggested allowing members of a "military unit formed from the ranks of KGB employees" to join the Lithuanian Communist party.[27] Thus, Shenin, Kriuchkov, and other Politburo "visitors" to the Baltic states are to blame for the bloodshed inflicted by the Soviet army and special forces in Riga and Vilnius in the winter of 1991. Despite the use of force, the CC had lost control over the republic and over the situation in the Baltics in general. Disregarding quite concrete suggestions offered in Shenin's memo, its later resolution, On the Situation in the Baltic Republics,[28] adopted already familiar language, calling for solutions by "lawful means" (which looks like complete hypocrisy after the brutal slaughter by the OMON[29] of thirteen Lithuanians in January 1991).

The Central Committee was also concerned with the increasingly proindependence mood in western Ukraine. On August 21, 1990, the Secretariat passed a resolution "on the socio-political situation in Western *oblasts* of the Ukraine" in which the "concrete measures" called for by the local party leaders boil down to sending CC CPSU and CC CPU (Communist Party of Ukraine) cadres to assist local party organizations, issuing directives to the Ukrainian minister of interior to ensure law and order, and launching a propaganda campaign against the Popular Movement of Ukraine for *Perestroika* (Rukh) and other Ukrainian nationalist organizations. Finally, the CC decided to ask the Supreme Soviet to ensure legal norms protecting registered political parties and their property—a uniquely weak response in the face of collapsing imperial control and nationalist challenge.[30]

The center was increasingly faced with a dilemma: whether to act as a *Russian* body or an *all-union* organ. The leaders of the union often seemed confused about their own national identity and the policies they formulated. It is safe to assume that the majority of them under Gorbachev could be characterized as Russian imperialist. In the conflict between the Uniates (the Ukrainian Greek Catholics) and the Moscow-controlled Orthodox Christians in western Ukraine, the center was squarely on the side of the Orthodoxy. Former chairman of the USSR Supreme Soviet Anatoly Lukyanov reported to the Central Committee on his appeal to the Orthodox bishops:

I want to stress once again that our attitude to the Russian Orthodox Church has not changed. It has proved, with all its activity, especially in the war and post-war years, that we can cooperate well together. There is no other way. This position of ours is very firm. Everything that occurs here [in western Ukraine] is connected to the situation in the country, with the weakening of power. Nationalism [coming] from the bottom of the soul results in the support of Eastern Catholics.[31]

The crisis of the union was reaching its peak in early 1991. In the face of events, a resolution of the CC Secretariat, On the Telegram of the President of Azerbaijani SSR, First Secretary of the Azerbaijani CC, Comrade Mutalibov, A. N., seems totally inadequate. After quoting Mutalibov's dire warnings about the National Front of Azerbaijan coming to power and the escalation of war with Armenia, all that the resolution suggests is a meeting of the Council of the Federation to "discuss the whole circle of questions."[32]

The March referendum produced a majority of votes in support of continuing the union, and the Politburo passed a decision on the Political Results of the USSR Referendum and the Tasks of Party Organizations. The Central Committee Secretariat then developed its Plan of Action on the Realization of Tasks resulting from the above-mentioned Politburo decision.[33] The plan included the following:

organization and control of discussions to achieve multi-faceted realization and propaganda of the referendum results, paying special attention to implementation of urgent measures in the economic sphere, connected to reestablishment of economic ties, increase of production of goods, strengthening of order and undertaking of other stabilization measures. Reports should be made to the CC regarding work undertaken to implement tasks put forward by the Politburo.[34]

This vague verbiage was merely an attempt to cover up impotence and the lack of realistic solutions to save the empire, which was speedily being disassembled by the republican leaderships.

As the republics increasingly asserted their rights, the center attempted to cling to the old levers of control, such as key cadre nominations. In the Central Committee decision, On Some Suggestions on Change of Order regarding Nominations of Procurators and Chairmen of the KGB of the Union Republics, the Politburo pushed to retain the authority of the USSR procurator general and the KGB Chairman to nominate their respective functionaries. Thus, central Union control would have been retained. The threat came from the republican Supreme Soviets striving to assume authority for the these nominations.[35] But even when the center had nominated its supposed loyalists to the republics, they often switched allegiances and went over to the powerful republic leaderships. Thus, even without controlling all cadre nominations, the republics had asserted their independence by the summer of 1991, prompting the unsuccessful August coup.

A top secret Politburo resolution regarding the Central Committee memo calling for a fight against the international links of the emerging anticommunist opposition proved equally toothless.[36] Among the targeted forces were the Lithuanian Sajudis movement, the Estonian Popular Front, the Latvian Popular Front, and Western broadcasters to the Soviet Union. Russian activists from the *Demokraticheskaya Perestroika* Club were also attacked.

Noted are attempts to turn the growing and healthy movement for the development of democracy, *glasnost* and socialist pluralism in the direction of confrontation with authorities, fanning of nationalism, moods alien to socialism, discrediting of the CPSU line for *perestroika* and renewal of Soviet society. Such anti-social, destructive activity of extremist elements aspiring to leadership in informal movements of workers receives not only the moral support of reactionary circles abroad.[37]

What followed was the regular Soviet fare on Western "special services" and "ideological diversion centers" attempting to utilize "some" informal leaders for the purpose of undermining socialism and destroying the Soviet Union. The CC instructed the State and Law Department and the International and Ideological Departments, as well as the KGB, MVD, and Foreign Ministry, to present suggestions regarding political, legal, organizational, and propaganda measures, directed at stopping any attempts to use the "growing potential of social groups" against the goals of *perestroika* and socialism."[38]

The Central Committee was involved in an "ideological struggle," which demonstrates its unreformed nature, until the very end of the empire. However, its activities were of little consequence. It fought against Western broadcasts to the Soviet Union, and the utilization of these broadcasts by representatives of the "Yeltsin circle" and other opponents.[39] It attacked representatives of the "Democratic Platform" and warned about possible property claims against the party estate by this and other groups.[40]

Roused by increasing calls for the return of party property to the people, the CC Secretariat, in a secret decision, established a commission to provide expert appraisals of the party's assets. Evidently, the party did not have an updated property register. The head of the commission was CC secretary (and later putschist) Oleg S. Shenin and his deputy, Nikolay E. Kruchina, manager of the CC CPSU, who reportedly committed suicide after the collapse of the August coup.[41] There are rumors in Moscow that Kruchina's suicide was connected with attempts to squirrel away CPSU funds.

In the spring of 1991, the CC's deputy head of the Organizational Division, Yu. Ryzhov, attempted to launch a severe attack on a reformist faction known as Communists for Democracy, led by the Afghan war hero Alexander V. Rutskoi, future vice president of the Russian Federation. The old Leninist principles of democratic centralism, forbidding factionalism in the party, were dragged out of the mothballs. Calls for vigilance and unity "in the face of danger of splitting and destruction of the party" were heard once again. Deputy CC General Secretary Vladimir Ivashko and CC secretaries Luchinsky and Girenko somewhat softened the blow, with Ivashko calling for discussion at the Secretariat and working meetings between the CC secretaries and representatives of some factions and "streams."[42]

IMPERIAL COLLAPSE: MULTIPLE CRISES IN THE PERIPHERY

Kazakhstan

Within one year of Gorbachev's ascendancy to power, the first widespread ethnic unrest shattered the republic of Kazakhstan, formerly under the control of Brezhnevite First Party Secretary Dinmukhammed Kunayev.

The turnover of cadres in the Kazakh capital of Almaty had begun in the days of Andropov. With the new reformist general secretary established in Moscow, a campaign was launched attacking the local party officials. Many senior party and Soviet apparatchiks were dismissed. Gorbachev, aware of the widespread corruption and nepotism of the Kunayev regime, as well as of abuses in Tashkent, Frunze, and Ashkhabad, attempted to reintroduce Moscow's control of personnel and to rotate cadres into Central Asia from the other republics. With the denunciations of the previous Central Asian regimes and the removal of the Tajik, Turkmen, and Kirghiz first secretaries, it was only a matter of time before full Politburo member Kunayev would follow suit.[43]

Despite his reelection at the Kazakhstani party congress of 1986, Kunayev became the target of a campaign orchestrated from Moscow. He was blamed for the economic slowdown in the republic, and toward the end of 1986 his retirement from the republican post and the USSR Politburo was announced. Gorbachev and Ligachev decided to replace the Kazakh with an ethnic Russian, the Ulyanovsk *oblast* party first secretary Gennadii Kolbin. Upon his assumption of office, however, three days of demonstrations orchestrated by Kazakh officials erupted. Kazakh university students were used by the organizers as "extras", university professors provided the intellectual inspiration for the riots. Kolbin called in the troops, and the unrest was quelled. Participants were expelled from the universities and in some cases prosecuted.

In the aftermath of the Kazakh riots, Kolbin established a council for work with cadres within the Kazakh CC. The council's goal, officially, was to promote ethnic Kazakhs. Kolbin himself remained at the helm of the Kazakh party apparatus almost until the end, when he was replaced as first secretary by Nursultan Nazarbayev, Kunayev's chairman of the Council of Ministers.[44] Moreover, Kolbin had became a voice *for* Kazakhstan, advancing its cause more forcefully than his ethnically "pure" predecessor. This Moscow-appointed first secretary turning local patriot was a sign of the changing times, and it indicated the end of centralized control.[45]

Gorbachev, only a year earlier, at the Twenty-seventh Party Congress (February 1986) had stated that nationality issues would be secondary to economic concerns. The subordination of republican and regional economic interests to those of the USSR as a whole was declared. Yegor Ligachev was even more explicit, calling for repudiation of the long-standing practice of appointing representatives of titular nationalities to the top posts in their republics.[46]

After the Alma-Ata riots, however, in his January 1987 report to the CC plenum, Gorbachev conceded that national feelings deserved "respect" and "special tact and care." He confirmed the principle of proportional representation of ethnic groups at the republican and all-union level, and he indicated that ethnic interests were to be taken into account in the policy-making process. A year later he even "promoted" the status of ethnic interests to "vital."[47]

The incident in Kazakhstan showed other non-Russian political elites of the union that, although Moscow still reacted with some amount of force (which was restricted when compared with former Soviet practices), the political instrument of mass demonstrations now offered a road to gain unprecedented concessions. The Soviet empire had started on the painful—and sometimes violent—road to unraveling.

The Baltic States: National Renaissance

It took over two years for *glasnost* to take root in the most politically developed area of the Soviet Union—the Baltic states. By the summer of 1987, Latvians were openly commemorating the 1941 deportations at the Independence Monument in Riga. In August, all three republics observed the anniversary of the Molotov-Ribbentrop pact of 1939. For the first time, open attempts to commemorate the independence days of the prewar states took place. The celebrations in Riga were disrupted by the authorities, but the ceremonies in Vilnius and Tallinn were carried out without interference.[48]

On April 1–2, 1988, the plenum of Estonian creative societies passed a resolution calling for sweeping changes within the republic and in its relationship with the center. In fact, the Estonians wanted far-reaching economic and political autonomy. The plenum also called for a no-confidence vote against the republic's Russian-born first secretary, Karl Vaino. Two weeks later, a popular front was launched, to support all-union *perestroika* and to implement the changes called for in the resolution. In the same month, similar fronts were launched in Latvia and Lithuania (the Restructuring Movement, or Sajudis).[49]

The Baltic states were engulfed in mass demonstrations that numbered in the hundreds of thousands. While the stated goal was autonomy, or in Soviet political language, "sovereignty," the content of the demands was tantamount to nothing less than independence. The symbols of prewar independence—the flags, the anthems and the street names—were all returned to use.

The popular movements, with large numbers of Communist party members participating in them, profoundly influenced inner-party politics in the Baltics. Antireform Estonian first secretary Vaino was ousted and replaced by Vaino Valjas in June 1988. In October 1988 Lithuanian proreform Central Committee Secretary Algirdas Brazauskas replaced the unpopular Ringaudas-Bronislovas Songaila. The conservative Latvian first secretary, Boris Pugo, was promoted to head the Party Control Commission (a post that had been occupied in the Brezhnev regime by Pugo's mentor, Arvidas Pelshe).[50] His replacement by the more conservative Janis Vagris, the Supreme Soviet chairman, seems to indicate that Pugo had a say in the nomination of his successor. It also positioned the secretary for ideology, Anatolijs Gorbunovs, for his future role as the proindependence Latvian leader as Gorbunovs moved into Vargis's job.

In the fall of 1988, a constitutional crisis ensued, as the Estonian legislature proclaimed "sovereignty" and veto power over any central Soviet decision making affecting the republic. This was a serious challenge. Political elites in all the republics, even faraway Kirghizstan, watched with great attention.[51] The USSR Supreme Soviet declared the Estonian decision unconstitutional and summoned the leadership for consultations. Despite the reluctance of the Latvian and Lithuanian legislatures to follow suit, there was massive pressure in both republics to emulate Estonia's example.

It was clear that what would have brought about massive sanctions previously, including deportations and lengthy imprisonments, was now going to go unpunished. The regime was in the process of divesting itself of the control mechanism with which it had held the empire together since the days of Lenin and the tsars: the use of force.

1989 signaled even further liberalization of political life, with the prewar parties resurrected and political pluralism being tolerated by the communists. The Lithuanian and Estonian Communist parties went to great lengths to distance themselves from the Russian-dominated center, a process that culminated, in December 1989, in the Lithuanian Communist party declaring itself independent from the CPSU. The republic komsomol had been independent since the summer of the same year. Thus, centralism in the USSR was coming to an end.

Most telling were the elections held in the republic legislatures. In the spring of 1989, proindependence Sajudis carried thirty-six out of forty-two seats. Brazauskas and his deputy ran unopposed by Sajudis. In Estonia, the proindependence Popular Front won thirty-one out of a contested thirty-six seats. In Latvia, two-thirds of the seats were carried by candidates supported by the Popular Front.

In May 1989, the Supreme Soviet of Lithuania adopted a sovereignty declaration similar to that of Estonia. In June 1989, the Latvians passed one of their own. Brazauskas was almost as adamant as the spokesmen of Sajudis in demanding independence. The Baltic delegations led the attacks on conservative forces in the USSR's Supreme Soviet. They singled out Prime Minister Nikolay Ryzhkov, who opposed the devolution of economic control to the republican level. The Balts staged impressive walkouts from Supreme Soviet proceedings that were televised countrywide. In fact, the republics were "walking out" of the Soviet Union.

In August 1989, a human chain of over one million people was formed, stretching across the three republics, from Vilnius to Tallinn, commemorating the fiftieth anniversary of the Molotov-Ribbentrop pact. Moscow reacted with denunciations of Baltic nationalism and separatism. The Politburo added vague threats to the very existence of the Baltic nations. However, these were perceived as empty insults.

Glasnost had allowed the nationalist elites of the Baltic states, which had always felt themselves a part of the Scandinavian and Western European political universe, to organize into popular fronts. These ostensibly supported *perestroika*, but differed in their ideology and social makeup from the local communist parties. Popular fronts sprang up in other republics, with the exception of Central Asia.

The fronts collaborated with the local communists against the center. There was a correlation of interests: The local authorities could co-opt the opposition, while the opposition gained legitimacy and resources unthinkable in early Soviet periods. The proreform wing of the Communist party could demonstrate to ordinary citizens that involvement in public affairs was possible, while the fronts mobilized hundreds of thousands of citizens in support of causes that seemed worthwhile to the reform wing of the party. The latter assumed that, by providing leadership to popular fronts, it would remain in control of the situation. However, it was not long before the front leaderships felt that the support of hundreds of thousands put them on an equal footing with the communist leadership.[52]

Throughout 1988, the fronts, with the toleration and, in many instances, the "aiding and abetting" of local authorities, advanced demands for language and cultural concessions. These calls soon turned into strong political mobilization tools that could organize supporters of nationalist causes. As during the *korenizatsiya* of the 1920s and 1930s, the advancement of native language and cultural demands by the local party meant valuable commodities for its supporters: jobs, promotions, housing, and greater control of national resources.[53] Those who dreamt about sovereignty and independence without yet verbalizing their demands were among the leading activists of the fronts.

Soon the Supreme Soviets of the Baltic republics declared their respective tongues the official state languages. Despite the resistance of the Russian-speaking population and their support from Russian imperialist circles (first and foremost, the military) the Balts won.

The Baltic quest for independence played an important role in the Russian Federation's assertiveness in the face of the center crackdown of late 1990 and early 1991, led by KGB Chief Vladimir Kriuchkov and Minister of Defense Marshal Dimitrii Yazov, future perpetrators of the August 1991 coup. The killing of thirteen Lithuanians at the Vilnius television station and the deaths of six Latvians in the center of Riga at the hands of the Soviet military and OMON forces in January 1991 led to widespread denunciations by Russian reformers.

Yeltsin and his allies, attempting to gain power by removing Gorbachev and dismantling the imperial center, articulated democratic Russian national interests which differed from Soviet imperial aspirations. These included the recognition of Baltic independence and a demand not to use force against the prodemocracy leaders in Vilnius, Riga, and Tallinn.

Mikhail Gorbachev failed to denounce the killings. The Soviet president remained noncommittal and even justified the crackdown, trying to prevent further moves by the hard-liners against himself, not fully comprehending the importance of the republics in the imperial endgame.

The incident prompted Boris Yeltsin to fly to Riga and Tallinn to meet with the Latvian and Estonian leaders. Yeltsin promised the support of the Russian democratic movement to the Balts. This bold move turned out to be, in retrospect, an important point in rallying democratic support behind the Russian Supreme Soviet Chairman, which contributed to the victory of the pro-reform forces in August 1991.

Ukraine Plods Toward Independence

With the emergence of the policies of *glasnost*, the cultural elite of Ukraine revived the campaigns of the 1920s and 1960s for protection of the Ukrainian language. Demands emerged for "Ukrainization" of the educational system and granting Ukrainian official national language status, and the republic's Supreme Soviet started to work on a constitutional amendment to this effect. In February 1989, the Taras Shevchenko Ukrainian Language Society was founded.[54]

The move for the revival of the Ukrainian language and culture developed despite the reign of Brezhnevite Ukrainian Communist party First Secretary Volodymyr Shcherbitsky, who was opposed to Ukrainian nationalism. Shcherbitsky, an archetypical Soviet imperial governor, had full control of the republic's party organization after the purge of Petro Shelest in the 1960s. This explains his reelection as first secretary in February 1986 and his survival in the Politburo until September 1989. The Chernobyl nuclear disaster (1986) and the emergence of the Rukh weakened Shcherbitsky's power and paved the road for the end of imperial rule of Ukraine by Moscow.

In 1988 mass demonstrations took place in Lviv, traditionally a hotbed of anti-Russian nationalism. The Helsinki movement, led by former political prisoner Levko Lukyanenko, as well as a number of historical and cultural societies were particularly active in that city. The Lviv nationalists and Kyiv intellectuals were the founding fathers of the Rukh, which was launched almost simultaneously with the disappearance of the last Soviet overseer from the political scene in Kyiv.

The Rukh started out by declaring full civil rights for Russians, Jews, and other non-Ukrainians residing in the republic. It was instrumental in revealing the truth about the famine caused by Stalin and the horrors of collectivization in 1932 and 1933, as well as in promoting the rehabilitation of central figures of Ukrainian history.

The Ukrainian Catholic (Uniate) Church, while not an active participant in politics, enjoyed an unprecedented revival due to the staunch support of the Vatican and Gorbachev's quest for international acceptance and recognition for the USSR. Several petitions made by underground Ukrainian Catholic bishops and clergy, meetings between Soviet leaders and Vatican Secretary of State Cardinal Casaroli and the pope's envoy Cardinal Willebrands, and finally the meeting between Gorbachev and the pope (December 1, 1989) paved the road to legalization of the Uniate Church.[55]

Despite these activities, on the eve of Soviet imperial disintegration, the level of social activism in Ukraine was lower than that in Russia. The idea of a national renaissance, with its anti-imperialist potential, was the dominating motif of Ukrainian political life. In the Supreme Soviet of the republic, the majority faction, called "239," represented the interests of the central and local *nomenklatura*. The democratic and nationalist opposition, the People's Council (*Narodna Rada*) numbered from 115 to 125 members. The latter was a coalition that developed from the bloc of democratic forces in the summer of 1990. The democratic opposition included the Rukh, the Democratic Party of Ukraine (DPU), the Ukrainian Republican Party (URP), and the social-democratic Party of Democratic Renaissance of Ukraine (PDVU) (formerly the Democratic Platform of the Ukrainian Communist party).

Relations within both the coalition and the opposition were not easy. The Ukrainian Communist party faced the real possibility of a split between a nationalist (left) and an internationalist (right) wing, while the PDVU was considering leaving the *Narodna Rada*, as it was in favor of signing the revised union treaty. However, the question of the treaty became moot with the putsch in Moscow and the subsequent disintegration of the union. In turn, the URP and the DPU were involved in a conflict over control of the Rukh. Eventually, the more radical URP won, ensuring the election of Mykola Goryn' as deputy chairman of the movement. As a result, the Rukh withdrew its support from collaboration with the proindependence elements of the Ukrainian Communist party.[56]

While the absolute majority of Rukh membership was ethnic Ukrainian, the majority of the PDVU was Russian speaking. The PDVU represented the lower-level Ukrainian Communist party *nomenklatura*, the eastern Russified provinces, major city intelligentsia, and highly skilled workers. Despite the PDVU's communist past, the party supported Ukrainian independence and the introduction of private property.

The communists, for their part, were also split. The more "progressive" sector of the apparatus had adopted, though belatedly, the Ukrainian national idea. Paying obligatory lip service to Ukrainian independence, the *nomenklatura* supported the state's controlling role in industry and agriculture, "socialist values," a high level of state involvement in property control, and the rejection of individual and human rights. The independence-oriented policy of the Ukrainian Communist party leadership caused proimperial Russian-speaking forces in the Donbass region, the Crimea, and Novorossia to call for autonomy from Kyiv. "Internationalist" communists in western Ukraine, representing the Soviet regime, and fully dependent on Moscow, also rejected the national communist policy of the Ukrainian Communist party leadership.

The radical nationalists were united in the All-Ukrainian Interparty Assembly (VMA), which conducted its first session on June 30–July 1, 1990, in Kyiv. The Ukrainian National-Democratic Party, the Ukrainian National Party, the Republican Party of Ukraine, and other organizations were all represented. The assembly created a National Council (*Rada*), and committees to build a national army, to elect a Congress to replace the Supreme Soviet, and to write a new constitution for the republic. The assembly also accused liberal democrats from the Rukh of collaborating with the "occupation regime" and of being tainted with communist ideology.

The second session of the VMA, which took place on October 8–10, 1990, called for the creation of a Ukrainian state "with the help of the Cossack sabre."

The assembly called for the establishment of parallel structures, such as citizens' committees to liquidate and replace Soviets and expropriate state property; 850,000 people joined VMA.[57]

The Ukrainian position in favor of independence became abundantly clear during the March 1991 referendum on preservation of the Soviet Union. While voting "yes" on the USSR's continuation (70.2 percent), over 80.2 percent in a seemingly contradictory vote favored the declaration of Ukrainian sovereignty. Separatist tendencies, which were escalating in the eastern *oblasti*, especially in the Crimea, did not express themselves at the voting booth. First Secretary Leonid Kravchuk utilized this vote to reinforce his position toward Moscow. He ignored the Novo-Ogarevo negotiations for an accord to renew the union. While playing a cautious game during the coup, Kravchuk steered Ukraine toward independence.

After the prosovereignty vote and despite grim prognoses, Ukraine avoided a territorial split between the Russified left bank and the nationalist right bank, as well as the civil strife, unrest, and violence predicted by the Russian opponents of its independence.[58] Staunchly nationalist western Ukraine did not vote to separate from collaborationist Kyiv. No attempts were made to tear off the Donbass, Crimea, or Russian borderlands from Ukraine and attach them to Russia (despite Alexander Solzhenitsyn's calls for a referendum on Ukrainian independence by *oblast*).[59]

In the December 1, 1991 referendum, many regions with a Russian-speaking majority, such as the Crimea and Donbass, voted overwhelmingly in favor of Ukrainian independence. Much was said about a Kyiv-based "thousand-year" Eastern Slavic state, which has as much historical legitimacy as a Moscow-based one.[60] Without a doubt, Kyivan Rus' has a romantic, mystical appeal and commands loyalty from ethnic Ukrainians and Russians alike. It seems, however, that the ancient Slavic state was not the reason for the overwhelming proindependence vote. The basis for Russian speakers voting for Ukrainian independence was probably more prosaic: There were expectations of better economic performance and a higher standard of living in independent Ukraine. Ninety percent of the referendum vote favored independence, whereas only 72 percent of the republic's population at the time of the referendum were ethnic Ukrainians.

On the other hand, Great Russians, despite all efforts to the contrary on the part of the Yeltsin-led democratic movement,[61] had psychological difficulty adjusting to the idea of Ukrainian independence. While paying tribute to the "normalization" and "de-Sovietization" of Russo-Ukrainian relations, many Russians, such as philosopher Alexander Tsipko and leaders of the Constitutional Democrats and Russian Christian Democrats, believed in a future Russian-Ukrainian union.

Gorbachev fought Ukrainian sovereignty tooth and nail, calling Ukraine an "irreplaceable factor in the building of our Union."[62] He also termed Kharkiv, the Donbass, and the Crimea "Russian."[63] For the leader of *perestroika* there always was a conceptual confusion between Russia and the USSR, and he was famous for slips of the tongue, such as calling the USSR "Russia" while on a visit to Kyiv.[64]

Gorbachev had awakened forces he did not foresee and could not, and presumably did not want to, control by the old Russian and Soviet imperial means of coercion. Thus the question of the "unity and indivisibility" of Russia (*yedinaya i nedelimaya Rossiya*), the official slogan of the White movement seventy years earlier, and the de facto banner of the Bolsheviks, became once again, through the Ukrainian quest for independence, a pivotal question for the fate of Russia—and its empire.

The Caucasus: On the Warpath

Glasnost in Armenia resulted in the appearance of a nationalist movement preoccupied with the reunification of the Nagorno-Karabakh Autonomous *Oblast* (NKAO) and the Azerbaijani Nakhichevan enclave with Armenia. Nagorno-Karabakh, a region populated by a large majority of Armenians (85 percent in 1959, 75 percent in 1979) lay within Azerbaijan due to a compromise with Turkey and Azerbaijan worked out by communist Russia in 1921. The Karabakh Armenians had been complaining to Moscow about discrimination by the Azeri authorities since the 1960s.

The advent of *glasnost* allowed the Karabakh Armenians to petition the Gorbachev government, demanding reunification with Armenia. Hundreds of thousands of signatures were collected and delivered to Moscow in August 1987. Violence erupted, albeit sporadically, against Armenians in Karabakh. In October 1987, Geidar Aliev, longtime Azeri communist party first secretary and Politburo member, was removed from the central leadership in Moscow, signaling a diminishing Azeri influence in the center. Simultaneously, the Karabakh movement was gaining strength in Yerevan.

On February 13, 1988, the Karabakh Armenians began a series of demonstrations demanding incorporation into Armenia. Gorbachev offered to hold a special session of the USSR Central Committee to discuss state policy toward the nationalities. In an unprecedented move, the Karabakh local Soviet (usually a rubberstamp body) voted to demand that the USSR Supreme Soviet transfer the area to Armenian control.[65] During the end of February 1988, the beleaguered Soviet leadership had to face hundreds of thousands marching in Yerevan in support of this demand.

When Azerbaijanis began fleeing Karabakh, a brutal pogrom of Armenians occurred in the Azeri industrial town of Sumgait. While the Soviet Army stood passively by, hundreds of people were severely beaten and over thirty men, women and children were murdered. The Azeri leadership denounced the pogroms.

Instead of offering a clear-cut solution, Gorbachev deplored the Armenian demonstrations, promised more economic development for Karabakh, and insisted that no administrative changes would take place. Against Moscow's will, the Armenian Supreme Soviet voted to incorporate the area into the republic, while the Azerbaijani Supreme Soviet vetoed the proposal. Once again, Moscow's response seemed limp. The imperial center had demonstrated that it could not effectively wield power. It was a clear sign for the peripheral actors to start taking events into their own hands.

Renewed Armenian demonstrations started in early July 1988. A general strike was called, and the Yerevan airport was shut down. Soviet troops were called in, and in attempting to control the situation, one demonstrator was killed. At his funeral, the Armenians erupted in anti-Russian and anti-Soviet demonstrations. Other nationalities joined the fray, with hundreds of thousands demonstrating in Vilnius in support of the Armenians. The call for national self-determination was a propaganda ploy many a time utilized by the Soviet empire beyond its own borders as part of subversion. This time its vassals were practicing what the empire preached.

On July 18, 1988, the Presidium of the Supreme Soviet of the USSR, under the chairmanship of Gorbachev, finally took up the Karabakh issue. The decision not to change the area's status made the Armenians feel betrayed. The region was placed under the direct rule of an emergency commission chaired by Arkady I. Volsky. The violence escalated, with anti-Armenian pogroms taking place in Nakhichevan and Kirovabad. Tens of thousands of Armenians began leaving Azerbaijan, while the Azerbaijanis, afraid of retaliation, were in turn leaving Armenia. On December 7, 1988, while Gorbachev was in triumph at the United Nations, a giant earthquake destroyed Kirovakan and Leninakan, the second and the third largest cities in the Armenian republic.

During the winter of 1988 and the spring of 1989, the Volsky commission demonstrated itself incapable of resolving the issue. The situation was sliding toward civil war. Not since the strife of 1917–1921 had the republics been so close to outright violent conflict. The National Front of Azerbaijan (NFA), formed to counter the "docile" line of Communist party First Secretary Ayaz Mutalibov, declared a general strike against the Soviet government throughout the republic, and a boycott of Armenia. Railways were cut off, and energy supplies and trade with the rest of the union and the world were at stake.[66]

In January 1990, the Soviet army attempted to establish military rule in Baku. Tanks were moved into the city, and special forces (*spetsnaz*) troops, commanded by generals Alexander Lebed and Viktor Achalov, shot and killed about 100 people. Amidst the prospects of further violence and a campaign by mothers of Russian soldiers against sending their children to "pacify" another Moslem region after the fiasco in Afghanistan, an assessment was made in Moscow that the price of maintaining an imperial presence in Azerbaijan was too high. Military rule was called off, and Azerbaijan was abandoned politically. Thus, Russian national interests, which in some cases called for discarding parts of empire, began to appear in the imperial calculus of the center.

At the beginning of the confrontation in the propaganda war, the Azeris were outmaneuvered by the Armenians, who had traditional ties with the Russian intelligentsia and the Armenian diaspora. Eventually, the Azeris established connections based on their ethnic ties with Turkey and solidarity with other Moslem Turkic republics in the Soviet Union and Moslem states abroad.[67] In the following years, despite losses in the battlefield, the Azeris proved to be skillful fighters in the battle for hearts and minds in Russia and beyond.[68]

The Karabakh conflict demonstrated that, by 1989, the Soviet imperial leadership had lost control over one of its important outlying provinces, which had been in Russian hands for almost two centuries. The only solution the leadership had in the long run was to cut its losses and pull out its troops. Yet another section of the Russian/Soviet empire was drifting away, becoming part of the northern rim of an unstable Middle East rather than part of a relatively stable Russian- and communist-dominated Eurasia.

While there was outright war between Armenia and Azerbaijan, Georgia plunged into civil war. On April 9, 1989, Soviet interior troops *(vnutrenniye voyska)* were used to crush a peaceful demonstration and hunger strike in the central square of Tbilisi. The demonstrations, which had been held on and off since 1988, were led by the Chavchavadze Society, headed by the late Zviad Gamsakhurdia, a prominent dissident writer.

The troops, primarily Slavs, in addition to using a strong poisonous gas (so-called *Cheremukha*), employed sapper's spades to crush the skulls and bones of Georgian demonstrators. Over twenty protesters, including women and youths, were killed. Tbilisi was in shock, and nationalistic Georgians were forever lost to the cause of the union.

The Georgian and Soviet leaderships were quick to lay the blame on each other's shoulders. The commander of the Transcaucasus military district, General Igor Rodionov, claimed that he had not wished to introduce troops into the Georgian capital, and he had done so only after the Georgian Communist party (GCP) Central Committee, headed by First Secretary Dzhumber Patiashvili, had insisted upon their deployment. Patiashvili, however, claimed, at the USSR's Congress of People's Deputies, that he had found out from Rodionov that the decision had been taken *in Moscow*. According to the Georgian, the Soviet first deputy minister of defense had been in Tbilisi without the Georgians' knowledge, and it had been the Politburo, allegedly chaired in this crucial meeting by Yegor Ligachev, that had given the order.[69]

The Georgian leadership, said Patiashvili, had retroactively endorsed Moscow's decision. It seems that Rodionov was lying, as in the Soviet Union, military district commanders took orders from the Ministry of Defense and the Politburo only.[70]

As a result of the massacre, Patiashvili was fired, and a new first secretary, Georgian KGB chief Givi Gumbaridze, was nominated in his stead. Gorbachev, as usual, denied any advance knowledge of the events. Moscow's handling of the crisis in Tbilisi demonstrated a willingness to use force in the face of a perceived threat to the empire's integrity. While this had been the case in 1989, and the outcry in Russia was tolerable, later events in Baku and the Baltic states demonstrated that the Soviet leadership's grip on the reigns of power were slipping.

In October 1990, in the first multiparty elections held in Georgia in seventy years, a coalition of seven nationalist parties defeated the incumbent communists. The GCP was sent to opposition. But its new platform called for Georgian independence from the Soviet Union, and thus its position was similar to that of the majority of political organizations in Georgia. Parties and groups throughout the republic maintained armed militias, Lebanon style, contributing to the fragility of the situation.

The Roundtable/Free Georgia coalition, headed by Gamsakhurdia, was openly in favor of independence. It moved quickly to consolidate power by replacing the minister of the interior and the republican KGB chairman. The parliament created its own National Guard. The local Soviets were suspended, in order to "dismantle Soviet power structures." New executive committees were elected in March 1991.[71]

Attempting to utilize the internal weakness of the Georgian state, the legislature of the South Ossetian Autonomous *oblast* in the town of Tskhinvali voted to secede from Georgia and join the Russian Federation, which already included the North Ossetian Autonomous *oblast*. The Georgian parliament overruled the Ossetian legislation and denied its bid for autonomy. In January 1991, a war broke out that claimed thousands of lives. The militias of both warring sides, as well as Soviet interior troops, were involved. Georgia seemed to be falling apart at the seams.

The conflict in the Autonomous Republic of Abkhazia had been brewing for over a decade. The Soviet government had rejected the appeals of the Abkhazs (who were a minority in their own republic) to join the Russian Federation. The Abkhazian parliament then voted in August 1990 to elevate the republic to the status of a union republic and to assert the supremacy of its laws over those of Georgia and the USSR. The Communist-dominated parliament of the Georgian SSR rejected the Abkhazian demand.[72] With the ascendancy of Moslem mountaineers in the Caucasus, and the creation of the Confederation of the Peoples of Caucasus, the Abkhaz could receive aid from Moslem organizations and the Confederation. As the Soviet Union was collapsing, Moslem and Russian volunteers joined the Abkhazian forces to fight the Georgians.[73]

THE RUSSIAN CHOICE: REJECTING THE EMPIRE?

During the collapse of the Soviet Union, the attitudes of the Russians toward national self-determination were complex and inextricably tied to the question of imperial preservation. In the eyes of many Russians, the USSR *was* the Russian state. Mikhail Gorbachev, sermonizing against the disintegration of the union, warned against the collapse of the "state that was built for hundreds of years by our forefathers," identifying himself with the tsarist realm even more than with Lenin's and Stalin's creation.

The conflicts between ethnic Russian (*russkii*) and Russian state (*rossiiskii*) identity, between all-union and RSFSR perspectives, and between the communist power as an instrument of Russian statism and anticommunism were all entangled. The questions of empire and nation-state had not been solved before, during or after the 1917 revolution, nor had they been clearly resolved in the late 1980s. The contradictions had been suppressed throughout the Soviet period. With the lifting of suppression, the conflicts flared up once again.

While for the Russians living in the non-Russian republics, preservation of the union could be a question of continuing prosperity and privilege, many Russians living in the Russian Federation thought that the costs of maintaining the union, with its extravagant attributes of a superpower—foreign aid, a gigantic army, a far-flung intelligence apparatus and mighty bureaucracy to administer them all—were too expensive. As S. Enders Wimbush has pointed out, "Multi-ethnicity is an ongoing cost of empire, and for the political accountant ethnic unrest is an inflated cost at any given time."[74]

Other costs of Soviet imperialism included Russia's rule over ethnic groups split by national borders, such as Azeris, Turkmen, Kirghiz/Uygur, and to a lesser degree Poles, Lithuanians, and Ukrainians, which could result in cultural, nationalist, and religious spillovers from abroad. Whether an Islamic, Catholic, or pro-Chinese influence, it was not welcomed by Moscow. Dominion over restive nationalities served as a brake on Russian imperial designs against Turkey and Iran—the fiercely independent north Caucasians who sustained protracted wars against Russia/USSR being a case in point. Further, Russians, with their low demographic growth, would in the future have to compete against the Moslem Turks for scarce investment resources, resulting in yet another unacceptably high cost of empire.

In addition, the rise of Russian imperial consciousness was in itself a cost of empire,[75] distracting attention from more peaceful economic pursuits and turning the Russians into a communist version of the master race. The drain on national resources for imperial administration and away from productive engagements was becoming a policy issue widely discussed in the metropolitan media. Other Russians resented resource allocations to support republican cultural autonomy, as well as the role of titular nationalities in managing the institutions that came to express it.[76]

Russians in the RSFSR deplored the fact that they, as the *narod-patron* (the patron nation), lacked the institutions taken for granted by residents of the other republics, such as academies of science and the arts, a party organization, and a Central Committee of their own. Many even came to see Moscow as paying the price of being a union capital *instead* of being the capital of Russia. With the republics assuming independent political roles, there was a growing sense that Russian national interests were blurred with those of the union. The emergence of marginal groups, such as *Pamyat*, should not obfuscate the fact that Russian nationalism began to be espoused by a considerable part of the population. It expressed itself in the renaissance of the Russian Orthodox Church, the movement to restore architectural and artistic treasures, and a growing appreciation of prerevolutionary Russian art and culture.

Russians in the republics were definitely imperial agents, similar to the Ottoman Turks, Austrian Germans, and the French in North Africa. They tended to view the republics in which they resided as part of the Russian patrimony. However, they, as a minority, developed a behavior vis-à-vis their host republics similar to that of the non-Russians toward the Moscow metropole. Russians in the Baltic states, for example, to a great degree came to behave as a political bloc forcing a set of ethnically based demands upon republic leaderships. In addition, the Russian activist organizations in the republics enhanced ethnically assertive Russian behavior in Russia proper. Ties were created between "Russians abroad" and ultranationalists in the metropole, and chauvinist slogans and demands were promulgated. More sophisticated republic leaderships, such as those in the Baltic states, succeeded in splitting the Russian speakers into reform-oriented supporters of the local popular fronts and hard-line adherents of pro-Moscow internationalist fronts.

The union leadership was caught on the horns of a dilemma: If the Russian "interfronts" (hard-line communist) were openly supported, for example in the Baltics, this could have caused a nationalist backlash and the rush for independence that Gorbachev was trying to avoid. However, if they had been cut loose, they probably would have become even more radical,[77] as they eventually did both in the Baltics and in the Trans-Dniester region.

Moscow, as an imperial capital, had supported preservation of the union. After all, the centers of imperial control, such as the CC CPSU, the General Staff, and the KGB, all resided in Moscow. However, Moscow had also remained the capital of Russia, regardless of extremist nationalist claims that its national character had been subverted by the *kosmopolity* and obliterated. The center was staffed by ethnic Russians, many of whom had developed a split identity, being loyal to Russia and the USSR simultaneously, which led to an imperialist mindset. Others in the bureaucracy were connected to the pro-Yeltsin circles by familial, professional, and personal ties.

As time went on, the all-union structures increasingly demonstrated their inability to find a way out of the multiple crises the USSR had plunged into since the beginning of the reforms. Increasingly, the self-awareness of union Moscow-based elites had become that of *Russian* elites, as the growing support of Boris Yeltsin, who expressed a "Russia-first" approach, indicated. This support was best measured in the elections of June 1991, when Yeltsin gained 57 percent of the vote against candidates of the center such as Nikolay Ryzhkov and Vadim Bakatin, as well as against the imperialist Vladimir Zhirinovsky. Violence and direct rule was tried (in Tbilisi, Baku, and Vilnius) but proved inefficient and was forsaken. The leadership never did manage to muster the political tools of institutional innovation, social agenda setting, domination of the media, and economic resource allocation[78] required to seize the initiative and reverse the process of disintegration. Gorbachev and the Soviet leadership were running out of imperial options (a fact that the putschists failed to understand). With the renunciation of violence and having demonstrated its inability to use it effectively, the center proved that it could not use the only tool it might have had to reestablish the empire.

It seemed to many that the Soviet empire had reached a fork in the road: The choice ostensibly was either to crack down or to fall down. The majority of Sovietologists could not conceive of the latter, but they strongly hesitated to justify the former. As late as the fall of 1990, Stephen P. Cohen of Princeton University was proclaiming that "democratic forces will never take control over Russia" and that the union would not disintegrate. He further stated that Russia was inherently conservative, with the Communist party firmly in control.[79] Millions of Russian anticommunist demonstrators and scores of Russian voters proved otherwise. Others declared that "the first apocalypse—the disintegration of the USSR—remains just as unlikely as it was in the past."[80]

Russian nationalism manifested itself in a variety of ways, from the more enlightened approach espoused by Academician Dmitrii Likhachev, to the darkest expressions, complete with black shirts and stylized swastikas. With the advent of democratization, it became clear that the nascent Russian nationalism was not assuming exclusively chauvinistic forms. In Leningrad, an ultranationalist *Pamyat* organization candidate running for election in a working-class district was soundly defeated by a democratic opponent.[81] And as with every broad social movement, postcommunist Russian nationalism could not fully crystallize in the relatively short period of Gorbachev's rule. From its modest beginnings in the Brezhnev era, it is still growing and developing today. Its postcommunist incarnation deserves separate treatment.

IMPERIAL COLLAPSE: THE PUTSCH AND ITS AFTERMATH

Frightened by the loss of control over nationalist popular politics, Gorbachev attempted to "tighten the screws" beginning in the fall of 1990. He pushed decrees on vastly expanded presidential powers through the complacent Congress of People's Deputies. He ousted the relatively liberal interior minister, Vadim Bakatin, replaced him with former Latvian KGB chief Boris Pugo,[82] and installed hard-liner General Boris Gromov, commander of the Soviet withdrawal from Afghanistan and a Gorbachev critic, as deputy minister of the interior.[83] The objective of this creeping counterrevolution was to save the Soviet empire.

In October 1990, paratroops were brought to Moscow and paraded around the city. When asked about the purpose of their presence, their dire reply was, "*Manevry*" (maneuvers). The army commanders stated that the troops (fully equipped with helmets and submachine guns) had come to harvest potatoes.

In December 1990, the Soviet chief of the General Staff, the deputy minister of defense, the commander of the navy, and the head of the interior ministry troops called upon the USSR's president to initiate a countrywide crackdown.[84]

On December 27, 1990, after issuing his famous warning about the coming of a dictatorship, Eduard Shevardnadze dramatically resigned as foreign minister. He was replaced by the more pliable Alexander Bessmertnykh. Finally, when Nikolay Ryzhkov was dropped as prime minister—a move long demanded by the liberals—he was replaced by the even more orthodox Valentin Pavlov.[85] Relatively liberally-minded ideologues, such as Yakovlev and Medvedev, came under attack. But although the last Gorbachev "team" consisted of people loyal to the Soviet idea, including the general secretary himself, it was too inept to save it.

The communist hard-liners in the leadership were becoming increasingly bold. The attacks in Vilnius and Riga were easily seen as a rehearsal for what might later occur in Russia. On January 13, 1991, Pavlov initiated a de facto expropriation of the Soviet population's savings by cancelling large-denomination ruble banknotes, a step that added to popular discontent. On March 28, 1991, a "banned" mass demonstration in Moscow in support of Boris Yeltsin was tolerated by the authorities, demonstrating their weakness, but a full takeover by the hard-liners did not occur.

Gorbachev, vacillating, abandoned his hard-line allies, and he attempted to strike a deal with the heads of the republics. An agreement was announced on April 23, 1991,[86] and the so-called Novo-Ogarevo agreement, or nine-plus-one formula was signed on June 28, 1991. This was the last attempt to reform the empire and turn it into a federation, with a greatly reduced center and power devolving to the republican leaderships. Yeltsin, Kravchuk, and Nazarbayev were poised to become the strongest leaders of the proposed Union of Sovereign States. The agreement was to be formally signed in Moscow after Gorbachev's return from vacation on August 23, 1991.

In June 1991, Boris Yeltsin, running on a reformist "anticenter" platform, was elected to the Russian presidency, convincingly defeating hard-liners Nikolay Ryzhkov and General Albert Makashov; ultranationalist Vladimir Zhirinovsky; and "moderate" Gorbachevite, Vadim Bakatin.

Future putschists Prime Minister Pavlov, Defense Minister Marshal Yazov, Interior Minister Boris Pugo, and KGB Chairman Vladimir Kriuchkov had twice attacked Gorbachev in the Supreme Soviet, calling for the introduction of emergency rule and warning against Western spies. Simultaneously, planning was under way in the CC apparatus to overthrow Gorbachev as general secretary of the CPSU. Moscow was full of dire hints. *Ogonyok*, a reformist weekly, prominently published a description of Khrushchev's ouster. *Samoubiytsa* (A Suicide), a play describing postcoup Russia gripped by a civil war in 1992, was a hit on the Moscow stage. However, the self-confident Gorbachev did not take any measures against his detractors, and brushed aside warnings from inside and outside Russia about a coming coup.

The coup leaders, top apparatchiki and heads of the imperial (central) structures, were trying to salvage the crumbling empire. The coup committee (GKChP)[87] consisted of Gennady Yanayev, former Komsomol and trade union chief and Gorbachev's then vice president; Prime Minister Valentin Pavlov; Minister of Defense Dmitrii Yazov; KGB chief Vladimir Kriuchkov; Minister of the Interior Boris Pugo; Alexander Tiziyakov, from the defense industry; and Vasiliy Starodubtsev, the agriculture chief, supported by Marshal Sergei Akhromeev, a hard-line former Soviet armed forces chief of staff.[88] They counted on a lack of political reaction in the country, with troops following orders and citizens being cowed. They were apparently confident of meeting a weak opposition, as had been the case in Khrushchev's ouster in 1964. However, they failed to understand that whatever vestiges of legitimacy the regime had left resided with the very man they were trying to depose—the unpopular Mikhail Sergeyevich Gorbachev.

The coup leaders, though presiding over a machine that had a lot of experience with the seizure of power (from 1917 in Russia through 1979 in Afghanistan), did an unprofessional job. Instead of moving on a Friday or Saturday, when bureaucrats around the world are not in their offices and Russians are out of town at their *dachas* and can be easily arrested, they began the coup on a Monday. They failed to arrest or kill Yeltsin, Yakovlev, and their supporters. They did not secure the Russian parliament building. They did not seize control of the means of communication, including telephone and fax links with the West. They neither shut down the Western media nor introduced full censorship.[89]

The Muscovites who turned out to save Russian democracy were the real heroes of the botched coup. With careful courtship of the military and the KGB, Yeltsin had managed to split these structures before August 1991. He and his supporters, such as Mayor Anatoly Sobchak of St. Petersburg, were careful to countermand every order by a counterorder from a high-ranking general officer, paralyzing the movements of the army. With a hand-held megaphone and a batch of hand-written decrees, Boris Yeltsin defeated the plotters—and, at least temporarily, Russian communism—providing the leadership that Alexander Kerensky and the Provisional Government had sorely lacked in 1917. A throng of 100,000 people was a small one for a city of 8 million, which Moscow is, but this shows that revolutions are more often than not made by active minorities in the face of passive majorities. Following his seventy-two hour detention in a luxurious villa in Foros, Crimea, Gorbachev returned to Moscow where crowds were dismantling the towering statue of Dzerzhinsky on Lubyanka Square. He was still talking about "people making the socialist choice" and preserving the Communist party and the Soviet Union. He was unpopular, irrelevant, and pitiable.

IMPERIAL COLLAPSE: CONCLUSIONS

Why did the Soviet empire collapse? According to Paul B. Henze, Russians at most levels in Soviet society were increasingly aware of the pain and cost of operating a multinational empire. Like all imperial peoples, they found that benevolent treatment of subject nations does not produce gratitude. Even if they thought that the non-Russians were raised by them to a higher level of economic development, and new social and intellectual horizons were opening up for them, this did not necessarily make the relationships easier. Some Russians reacted to the burdens of empire with scorn and resentment, some with open hostility, some with patience and a dedication to principle, many with indifference.

The Russians never did develop a successful formula for turning non-Russians into Russians. Officially, they continued to deny that they were trying to do so at all. While the New Soviet Man proved elusive, national feelings overcame myths about "proletarian internationalism," among Russians as well as non-Russians.[90] The proimperial Soviet leadership, which staged the abortive coup, was abandoned by the Russian elites. As in the case of the Ottoman empire, Russians found themselves neglecting their heartland, facing disproportionate demands, and making great sacrifices to maintain an imperial structure that had declining relevance to their needs as a nation.[91] This frustration was utilized by Russian nationalists of all stripes.

An elegant political science explanation is offered by Motyl:

What totalitarian states cannot do well, however, is persist under conditions of normality. Indeed, left to their own devices, totalitarian states come to be afflicted with a number of degenerative pathologies of their own making. The root of the problem is the state itself—hypercentralization, bureaucratic extensiveness, and monopoly of resources. Decay begins with the fact that extreme centralization produces horizontal bureaucratic fragmentation. Because regional officials are exclusively dependent on the center both for their material existence and for policy directives, the horizontal ties binding them with one another progressively erode and come to be replaced with vertical ties binding them only to the center. After all, as rational actors themselves, regional bureaucrats are best able to pursue their centrally mandated tasks by keeping their gaze focused on the center, the giver of bread and data.[92]

The totalitarian state structure creates an information glut in the center, a glut that it is not possible to process. Without adequate information management, regional bureaucrats assume increasing independence from the center, pursue their own interests, and assume their own identity. Thus, central overload, corrosion of the centralized structure, and disintegration into its integral parts is an inherent quality of the totalitarian state.[93] Hypercentralization, therefore, causes horizontal as well as vertical fragmentation, which allows regional officials to engage in a sort of political feudalism that could be termed "localized empire building." The result of such disruption is the "dual sovereignty" evidenced so clearly during the "terminal stage" of the Soviet Union. Under such conditions, "decision making is incoherent, resources are squandered," and the state decays.[94]

NOTES

1. Mikhail S. Gorbachev, "Mir na perelome" (World at a breaking point), *Svobodnaya mysl* (Moscow) no. 16, November 1992, p. 10.

2. Alexander Tsipko, "Pravda nikogda ne opazdyvayet" (Truth is never late), preface to Alexander N. Yakovlev, *Predislovie. Obval. Posleslovie.* (Preface. Collapse. Conclusion.) (Moscow: Novosti, 1992), p. 5.

3. Ibid., p. 135.

4. Nikolay Ivanovich Ryzhkov, *Perestroika: istoriia predatel'stv* (*Perestroika*: History of betrayals) (Moscow: Novosti, 1992), p. 63. Also see pp. 34–35, 38–45.

5. In addition, the ministers of defense and of foreign affairs, the first deputy chairman of the council of ministers in charge of the military-industrial complex, and the chairman of the KGB were all Politburo members, and in this respect, equal to the prime minister.

6. Ryzhkov, *Perestroika*, p. 78.

7. The idea of two left-wing parties competing in elections, and recognition of the value of a quasi-democratic process (in that case, a putative party of intellectuals set up by Gorky) was uttered by another communist right-winger, Nikolay Ivanovich Bukharin, during his conversations with Boris Nikolaevsky in Paris, in 1936. See Robert C. Tucker, "On the 'Letter of an Old Bolshevik' as an Historical Document," *Slavic Review*, volume 51, no. 4, Winter 1992, pp. 783–84.

8. Yakovlev, *Predislovie. Obval. Posleslovie.*, p. 128.

9. Ibid., p. 133.

10. Ibid., p. 131.

11. Ryzhkov, *Perestroika*, p. 80.

12. Politburo TsK KPSS, "O neotlozhnykh merakh po navedeniyu obshchestvennogo poriadka v Azerbaijanskoy SSR i Armianskoy SSR" (Politburo CC CPSU, On urgent measures to install public order in the Azerbaijani SSR and Armenian SSR). Secret (No. P 141/56, Moscow) November 23, 1988, fond 4, opis 102, d. 1058, ll. 22–26.

13. Postanovleniye Politburo TsK KPSS, "O pervoocherednykh meropriyatiyakh po uluchsheniyu osveshcheniya voprosov mezhnatsional'nykh otnoshenii v tsentral'noy pechati i mestnykh organov massovoy informatsii Azerbaijanskoy i Armianskoy SSR" (Resolution of the Politburo CC CPSU, On high-priority measures to improve coverage of inter-nationality relations in the central press and local media). Top Secret (No. P143/2, Moscow) December 2, 1990, fond 3, opis 102, d. 1065, ll. 120–122.

14. Politburo TsK KPSS, "O pravovom regulirovanii rezhima chrezvychainogo polozheniya, obyavlennogo v otdel'nykh mestnostiakh ili po vsey strane s vremmenym vvedeniyem pri neobkhodimosti osobykh form upravleniya" (Politburo CC CPSU, On legal regulation of the regime of emergency rule, declared in some areas or countrywide, with temporary introduction if a need arises, of special forms of rule). Secret (No. 144-35, Moscow), December 9, 1988. Source: materials, declassified for the CPSU trial, available in *Tsentr Khranenia Sovremennykh Documentov*. There is no fond or opis indication in this or in some other documents used in this research.

15. Witness the famous Leningrad affair of 1948. Stalin, understanding the unique role of Russians as the "imperial" nation, resisted a separate RSFSR party.

16. Postanovleniye TsK KPSS, "K voprosu o sozdanii Kommunisticheskoi Partii Rossii" (Resolution of CC CPSU, On the question of the creation of a communist party of Russia). Top Secret (No. 187-115, Moscow), June 8, 1990.

17. Postanovleniye TsK KPSS, "O nekotorykh problemakh, svyazabnnykh s reabilitatsiyey repressirovannykh narodov" (Resolution of CC CPSU, On some problems connected with the rehabilitation of repressed peoples). (Moscow), June 13, 1991. This decree was prepared by the Nationality Policy Department of the CC CPSU, no. St-30/7g.

18. "K zapiske otdela natsional'nykh otnoshenii TsK KPSS 'O situatsii vokrug problemy sovetskikh nemtsev'" (On the Memorandum of the department of national relations of the CC CPSU "On the Situation around the Problem of Soviet Germans") (No. ST-6/36 g, Moscow), October 5, 1990.

19. Postanovleniye Sekretariata TsK KPSS, "O neotlozhnykh merakh v sviazi s usilenieyem antiarmeyskhikh proyavleniy v ryade regionov strany (Resolution of Secretariat CC CPSU, On urgent measures in connection with the increase of anti-military manifestations in a number of regions of the country) (No. St-11/17g) November 15, 1990, and appendix. The report of the party's military policy commission.

20. Ibid. pp. 1–2.

21. Ibid., p. 3.

22. Ibid., pp. 3–4. Among the authors of this rather toothless resolution were the future putsch participants: CC Secretary Oleg Baklanov; General V. Achalov, USSR deputy defense minister and later head of Ruslan Khasbulatov's "analytical center" in the Russian Supreme Soviet; and former chief of the General Staff of the Soviet Army General Mikhail Moiseev. Marshals Kulikov and Shaposhnikov were also among the signatories.

23. Ibid., p. 4.

24. Postanovleniye TsK KPSS, "Ob itogakh vstrech i besed s pariynym aktivom, kommunistami i trudiashchimisia Litovskoy SSR" (Resolution of CC CPSU, On results of meetings and talks with party *aktiv*, communists and workers of the Lithuanian SSR). Secret (No. St-4/5, Moscow) August 29, 1990.

25. Ibid., p. 4.

26. Ibid.

27. Ibid., p. 6.

28. Postanovleniye TsK KPSS, "O situatsii v baltiiskikh respublikakh" (Resolution of CC CPSU, On the situation in the Baltic Republics). Secret (No. St-16/3, Moscow), February 7, 1991.

29. OMON—*otriad militsii osobogo naznachenia*—police special forces often used for riot control.

30. Postanovleniye TsK KPSS, "Ob obshchestvenno-politicheskoy obstanovke v zapadnykh oblastyakh Ukrainy" (Resolution of CC CPSU, On the socio-political situation in the western oblasts of Ukraine) (Moscow), August 28, 1990.

31. TsK KPSS "Zapis' osnovnogo soderzhaniya besedy A.I. Lukyanova s iyerarkhami Russkoy Pravoslavnoy Tserkvi 1 fevralya 1990 goda" (CC CPSU, Transcript of basic content of talk of Anatoly Ivanovich Lukyanov with hierarchs of the Russian Orthodox Church 1 February 1990) (Iskh. No. 131-AL, Moscow), 1990.

32. Postanovleniye Sekretariata TsK KPSS, "O telegramme Prezidenta Azerbaijanskoy SSR, pervogo sekretarya TsK kompartii Azerbaijana t. Mutalibova A.N." (Resolution of the Secretariat of CC CPSU, On the telegram of the president of the Azerbaijani SSR, First Secretary of the Azerbaijani CC Comrade Mutalibov, A.N.) (No. St-15/1g, Moscow) January 17, 1991, p. 3, fond 4, opis 42, d. 55, ll. 2–4, 16.

33. Plan deystvii Secretariata TsK KPSS po realizatsii zadach, vytekayushchikh iz postanovleniya Politburo TsK KPSS "Politicheskiye itogi referenduma SSSR i Zadachi Partiynykh Organizatsii" (Plan of Action of the Secretariat CC CPSU on the realization of tasks resulting from the Politburo decision on "Political Outcomes of the USSR Referendum and the Tasks of Party Organizations"). Secret (No. St-21/2, Moscow), April 10, 1991.

34. Ibid., p. 1.

35. Postanovlenye TsK KPSS, "O nekotorykh predlozheniyakh po izmeneniyu poryadka naznacheniya prokurorov i predsedateley KGB souyuznykh respublik" (Resolution of CC CPSU, On some suggestions on change of order regarding nominations of procurators and chairmen of the KGB of the Union Republics). Secret (No. 164-103, Moscow), August 10, 1989, fond 3, opis 102, d. 1226, ll. 56, 57, 59–62.

36. TsK KPSS, "O negativnom aspekte mezhdunrodnykh sviazey nekotorykh samodeyatel'nykh obshchestvennykh obyedineniy" (CC CPSU, "On negative aspects of international connections of some informal social groups"). CC memorandum and Politburo resolution concerning it. Top Secret (No. P147/8, Moscow), January 29, 1989, fond 3, opis 102., d. 1102, ll. 90–98. This CC memorandum was authored by A. Pavlov, director of the State and Law Department, R. Fedorov, deputy director of the International Department, and A. Degtiarev, deputy director of the Ideological Department. It was dated January 14, 1989 and voted upon by the Politburo on January 25, 1989.

37. Ibid.

38. Ibid., pp. 5–9.

39. TsK KPSS, "O nekotorykh merakh protivodeystviya podstrekatel'skoy deyatel'nosti zapadnykh radiostantsii", Zapiska 15 Marta 1991 (CC CPSU, "On some measures of counteraction against inciteful activity of Western radios) authored by A. Degtyarev, head of the Ideological Department, and V. Rykin, deputy head of the International Department (Moscow) 1991.

40. Postanovleniye Sekretariata TsK, "O rekommendatsiyakh partiinym komitetam v sviazi s trebovaniyami predstaviteley Demokraticheskoy platformy" (Resolution of the Secretariat of CC CPSU, "On recommendations to party committees in connection with demands by representatives of democratic platform"). Secret (No. St-4/61g, Moscow) August 27, 1990.

41. Postanovleniye Sekretariata TsK KPSS, "Ob obrazovanii i organizatsii raboty kommisii po ekspertnoy otsenke obyektov sobstvennosti KPSS" (Resolution of the Secretariat CC CPSU, Regarding the creation and organization of commissions on special evaluation of CPSU property objects). Secret (No. St-12/1g, Moscow), 1990.

42. TsK KPSS, "O fraktzii "Kommunisty za demokratiyu" (CC CPSU, On the faction 'Communists for Democracy'). (No. St-0996). April 15, 1991. Also see CC secretaries' discussion and Ivashko's note of May 29, 1991.

43. Martha Brill Olcott, "Central Asia: The Reformers Challenge a Traditional Society," in Lubomyr Hajda and Mark Beissinger, eds., The Nationalities Factor in Soviet Politics and Society (Boulder, Colo.: Westview Press, 1989) pp. 260–61.

44. Steven S. Burg "Nationality Elites and Political Change in the Soviet Union," in Hajda and Beissinger, The Nationalities Factor, pp. 30–31. Nazarbayev is currently the president of Kazakhstan.

45. Paul Goble, "Ethnic Politics in the USSR," Problems of Communism, July–August 1989, p. 2.

46. *Pravda*, February 28, 1986, quoted in Burg, "Nationality Elites," in Hajda and Beissinger, *The Nationalities Factor*, pp. 26–27.

47. *Pravda*, June 26, 1987, in FBIS June 26, 1987, p. R5; *Pravda*, February 19, 1988, in FBIS February 19, 1988, p. 49, quoted in Burg, "Nationalities Elites," in Hajda and Beissinger, *The Nationalities Factor*, pp. 30–31.

48. Romuald J. Misiunas, "The Baltic Republics: Stagnation and Striving for Independence," in Hajda and Beissinger, *The Nationalities Factor*, p. 209.

49. Ibid., p. 210.

50. Boris Pugo was further promoted when he replaced the relatively liberal Vadim Bakatin as the last Soviet interior minister. Pugo reportedly committed suicide after taking part in the failed coup of August 1991.

51. As evidenced by a Western traveler to Bishkek, the Kirghizs people were saying, "If they [Moscow] swallow the Estonian challenge, we will follow suit, and so will the other republics." "Situation in Kirghizia," field report to Radio Free Europe, Radio Liberty Media and Opinion Research (MOR), fall 1988 (unpublished).

52. Goble, "Ethnic Politics in the USSR", p. 9.

53. Alexander J. Motyl, *Sovietology, Rationality, Nationality*, (New York: Columbia University Press, 1991), pp. 180–81.

54. Roman Solchanyk, "Ukraine, Belorussia and Moldavia: Imperial Integration, Russification and the Struggle for National Survival," in Hajda and Beissinger, *The Nationalities Factor*, pp. 190–91.

55. Ibid., pp. 196-197.

56. Maksim Pavlov, "Ukraina: Natsional'naya Ideya Tsenoy Territorial'nogo Raspada" (Ukraine: national idea at the cost of territorial disintegration), *Vek XX i Mir*, no. 3, 1991, pp. 9–10.

57. Ibid., pp. 13–15.

58. Ibid., p. 15.

59. Alexander Solzhenitsyn, appeal in *Trud*, October 31, 1991. Also see "Kak nam obustroit' Rossiyu" (How we should restructure Russia), *Literaturnaya Gazeta* and *Komsomolskaya Pravda*, September 18, 1990.

60. Mykola Rybchuk, "Two Ukraines?," *East European Reporter*, July–August 1992, p. 20.

61. See the Declaration of the Principles of Interstate Relations between Ukraine and RSFSR based on the Declarations of State Sovereignty, signed in August 1990 between representatives of the Ukrainian *Narodna Rada* and "Democratic Russia." Quoted in Roman Solchanyk, "Ukraine and Russia: Before and after the Coup", *Report on the USSR*, vol. 3, September 27, 1991, p. 15.

62. Roman Solchanyk, "Ukraine, the (Former) Center, Russia and 'Russia'," *Studies in Comparative Communism*, Vol. 25, no. 1, March 1992, p. 32.

63. *Pravda*, January 12, 1990, quoted in Solchanyk, "Ukraine and Russia," p. 14.

64. Solchanyk, "Ukraine and Russia," p. 35.

65. Ronald Grigor Suny, "Transcaucasia: Cultural Cohesion and Ethnic Revival in a Multinational Society," in Hajda and Beissinger, *The Nationalities Factor*, p. 245.

66. Ibid., pp. 247-248. Mutalibov was finally ousted after the collapse of the Soviet Union and replaced by the National Front of Azerbaijan's leader, Abulfaz Elchibey, a moderate Islamic scholar of pro-Turkish orientation. In summer 1993, Elchibey was overthrown by a local warlord, Surat Guseinov, and the seemingly indestructible Geidar

Aliev once again took over the government in Baku.

67. Paul Goble, "Ethnic Politics in the USSR," p. 9.

68. Witness the dispatch of Afghani *mujahedeen* to Azerbaijan in the fall of 1993.

69. Personal interviews in Moscow with Russian ethnic experts, August 1992.

70. Yurii Afanasyev, "Tekst nesostoyavshegosia vystuplenia na sjezde narodnykh deputatov," (Text of the presentation that did not occur at the Congress of People's Deputies), *Russkaya mysl*, September 15, 1989, p. 5.

71. Daniel Abele, "Recent Developments in Soviet Georgia," *Newsletter of American Association for the Advancement of Slavic Studies*, vol. 31, no. 2, pp. 1–2, March 1991.

72. Ibid.

73. In 1992 and 1993 the Abkhas also received support from Russian imperialists in the army and in the Congress of People's Deputies, intent upon removing Shevardnadze and bolstering those who were willing to join the post-Soviet Russian federation and thus contribute to the restoration of the Russian empire.

74. S. Enders Wimbush, "Introduction: The Ethnic Cost of Empire," in his *Soviet Nationalities in Strategic Perspective*, (London: Routledge, 1989), p. xxv.

75. Ibid., pp. xxvi–xxvii.

76. Paul B. Henze, "The Spectre and Implications of Internal Nationalist Dissent," in Wimbush, *Soviet Nationalities*, p. 26.

77. For an excellent analysis of the issue, see Goble, "Ethnic Politics in the USSR", pp. 11–12.

78. Goble, "Ethnic Politics in the USSR," p. 12.

79. Stephen P. Cohen, remarks made at the American Association for the Advancement of Slavic Studies (AAASS) annual convention, Washington, D.C., September 1990.

80. Goble, "Ethnic Politics in the USSR," p. 12.

81. *Leningradskaya pravda* (Leningrad), February 2, 1989, quoted in Goble, "Ethnic Politics in the USSR," p. 3.

82. See Misiunas, "The Baltic Republics: Stagnation and Striving for Independence," in Hajda and Beissinger, *The Nationalities Factor*, p. 208.

83. John B. Dunlop, "Crackdown," *The National Interest*, Spring 1991, p. 24.

84. Ibid., p. 28.

85. Former tax collector and Soviet finance minister, Pavlov (nicknamed in Russian *svino-yezhik*, swine-hedgehog, for his corpulent physique and short haircut) was famous for his incompetence and constant inebriety.

86. "Gorbachev Yields on Sharing Power and Cuts in Prices," *New York Times*, April 25, 1991, pp. A1, A8.

87. GKChP—*Gosudarstvennyi Komitet Chrezvychainogo Polozhenia*—the State Committee on the State of Emergency was announced on Monday, August 19, 1991. At their famous press conference, Yanayev's hands were visibly shaking, while Pavlov was absent due to another bout of inebriation.

88. Interviews with former Soviet General Staff officers in Moscow, in August 1992, and in Washington, D.C., in October 1992.

89. Melor Sturua, "The Real Coup," *Foreign Policy*, Winter 1991/1992, pp. 64–65.

90. Henze, "The Spectre and Implications of Internal Nationalist Dissent," in Wimbush, *Soviet Nationalities*, p. 27.

91. Ibid., p. 31.

92. Motyl, *Sovietology, Rationality, Nationality*, p. 64.

93. Karl W. Deutsch, "Cracks in the Monolith," quoted by Motyl in *Sovietology, Rationality, Nationality*, p. 65.

94. Motyl, *Sovietology, Rationality, Nationality*, p. 65.

5

Conclusions

RUSSIA/THE USSR AS AN EMPIRE

The disintegration of the Soviet Union into fifteen ethnically based successor states underscores the multinational, multiethnic nature of the Russian-dominated realm. According to most of the definitions discussed in Chapter One, the Soviet Union *was* indeed an empire, with one ethnic group (the Russians) dominating the others,[1] simultaneously drawing on non-Russian elites as a reservoir of imperial servants.

The Russian and Soviet imperial ventures were successful attempts to subjugate peoples with the intention of ruling them for an indefinite period[2]; however, some of the ideological aspects differed radically. Messianic communism, especially during its first twenty years, effectively concealed the imperial nature of the old Romanov state's communist reincarnation.

In its early stages, the Moscow principality came to dominate and effectively deny sovereignty to other political societies, such as the Tatar khanates and Russian principalities. This process continued into the eighteenth and nineteenth centuries, when major expansion occurred in the west, south, and east. At that point, such relatively developed states as the Baltic lands, Poland, the Crimean khanate, Finland, Khiva, and Bukhara came under the domination of the Russian crown.

After the empire collapsed in 1917, as a result of Russia's defeat in World War I, and the attempts of the dominions to achieve self-determination had been quashed, Lenin and the Bolsheviks, reflecting the Russian political consensus of the time ("Russia one and indivisible"), proceeded to put "the other sick man of Europe" back together again.

Despite borders almost identical to those of the Romanov realm, the USSR was rarely termed an empire, and its policies were only occasionally labeled "imperialist." This was because, even in Western political science literature, the term "imperialist" had become a pejorative reserved almost exclusively for the overseas empires of England, France, and other traditional European colonial powers, and for the trade and investment domination of the United States. Thus, the interpretation of "imperialist" and "imperialism" spread from the left in general and Marxist-Leninist terminology in particular to popular Western terminology, coloring the use of terms which initially denoted the qualities of *any* empire.

THE METROCENTRIC APPROACHES

Historically, imperial structures predated industrial capitalism; and analyses of such structures are applicable to the multiethnic, Russian-dominated Romanov and Soviet empires. The modern examination of empires began with the study of imperial centers and their ruling classes. It is proper, therefore, to examine the imperial history of Russia from the point of view of Schumpeter's "military elite."[3] However, tsarist Russia's imperial elites went beyond the military cast, influential as it was. The circles intent on imperial plunder and aggrandizement included bureaucrats seeking lush offices and provinces to rule, clergy bound on attracting converts to the "true faith," trade classes looking for new markets, and (in the nineteenth century) political philosophers and military geographers advancing their pet theories on Russia's "God-chosen special missions"—fighting the British empire, opposing the German bid for domination, or saving the West from the "yellow peril."

Expanding Lenin's and Hobson's focus on special interests that support an imperial order,[4] one might say that Russia before and after 1917 had its share of influential imperial "lobbyists." These advocated a host of geopolitical arguments in favor of conquering a warm port on the Indian Ocean, liberating Constantinople, stirring up revolution in China and India, or just ensuring a steady supply of Uzbek cotton for soldiers' uniforms, Azeri oil to fuel the tank engines, or Yakut diamonds to pay for the Comintern's revolutionary plots.

It is ironic that Lenin's anti-imperialist tirades could have easily been applied by the Turkestanis or Ukrainians to their sorry fate. Communist domination, just as its capitalist counterpart, brought with it exploitative coal mining in the Ukraine, a cotton monoculture in Central Asia, and droves of blue- and white-collar colonizers.[5] In Russian colonies, as in their Western counterparts, brilliant careers were made, environments ruined, locals divided and exploited, and imperial power strengthened. The Soviet experience meets some criteria that were formulated in the Marxist and neo-Marxist analysis of imperialism as "unequal economic relations." As in other cases of imperial domination, economic development of a sort also took place, with both the Russian and non-Russian areas being used as natural resource cornucopias. Capital investment flowed from the imperial center (Moscow) to the Kazakh steppes or Ukrainian and Baltic industrial zones.

As in other cases of colonial or postcolonial economic dependency, raw material production and less advanced manufacturing were relegated to the periphery, thus resulting in low incomes. Dependence rendered economic growth and social change in the periphery vulnerable to the restrictions emanating from the metropolis. This happened because the prices, technologies, capital, and patterns of consumption generated therein shaped the development of the periphery without it being able to exercise control over these external forces.[6] The Soviet experience therefore demonstrated that such a mode of development is characteristic of *any* colonial domination, not only a capitalist one, thus placing in question the validity of Marxist analysis.

The Bolshevik Weltanschauung was formed in the nineteenth and early twentieth centuries, the era of empires. The Bolsheviks were influenced by the imperialist views prevalent at the time among the lower and lower-middle classes.[7] Anticipating large-scale military clashes of continental or even hemispheric blocks, their views justified the maintenance of great states, regardless of the ideology otherwise professed by their proponents.

It is typical that, during the Russian Revolution, all political parties, including even the most left-wing (Communists, Mensheviks, SRs) were all de facto in favor of the slogan "Russia one and indivisible." Lenin and the communists used the slogan of national self-determination as a tactical weapon to split the anti-Red coalition and to build alliances in the civil war.[8] When all was said and done, the Russian-dominated Romanov empire was "reopened under new management."

Bolshevik ideology favored the creation of a global communist state as the *programme-maximum*, with a continent-wide communist superstate that would include a communized Western Europe. When this idea failed, Russia was supposed to merge with Bolshevized India and China. Trotsky's adage about the road to Paris and London lying through India and China was taken seriously. After the Bolshevik takeover, Russia was ruled by an elite that, for awhile, officially could not conceive the possibility of development as a nation-state. But effectively it was building a Russian-dominated empire which was in many respects a continuation of its tsarist predecessor.

Comparative Approaches

It can be convincingly argued that Russia/the Soviet Union possessed many characteristics of a universal empire striving for world domination, as described by Robert Wesson.[9] Sprawling for many thousands of square miles, Russia, and later the USSR, was a "world unto itself." However, unlike closed China, Russia alternately resisted and assimilated foreign influences and ideologies, especially those from the West.

As other universal empires, the Russian state arose on the periphery of an older civilization—Byzantium. Russia learned the arts of war and administration from Constantinople and, after the Mongol invasion, from the Golden Horde. Russia's major achievement, as with other great empires, was the creation of a war machine adequate to one of the greatest territorial aggrandizements in history. Resistance to the Russian expansion was stiff. While the Finno-Ugric tribes were subjugated rather easily, the conquests of the Tatar khanates and Baltic states entailed major warfare and extensive bloodshed. In fact, the early empire built by Ivan the Terrible practically collapsed in the beginning of the seventeenth century (the so-called Time of Troubles), and the conquest of the

Baltics was delayed by more than a century.

The expansion continued with the annexation of the Crimea and Poland in the eighteenth century and conquests in the Caucasus and Central Asia in the nineteenth century. Russia masterfully exploited Christian-Moslem tensions in the Caucasus in the cases of Georgia and Armenia, the weakness of the elected Polish monarchy, and the deterioration of the Ottoman empire.

In Soviet times, after World War II, the formal empire was augmented by an informal one in Eastern Europe. Cuba, Mongolia, Vietnam, and, for a short period of time, Angola, Mozambique, Afghanistan, and South Yemen became overseas colonies of the USSR. However, as with other empires, after the conquests conservatism, material and intellectual poverty, institutional rigidity, and apathy set in. In the Soviet case, the period of stagnation of the late 1970s to the early 1980s is an obvious example.

After reaching the limits of their expansion, empires settle into a pattern of balance-of-power politics, attempting to protect what is already considered theirs, and closing their borders to guard against undue influence and temptation from the outside world. The Iron Curtain, in fact, was installed as early as 1929, with Stalin's consolidation of the Soviet empire, not in 1946, the year of Winston Churchill's speech given in Fulton, Missouri.

According to Wesson, the foreign economic relations of empires, from ancient China, to Rome, to the USSR, are limited. Even inside the "socialist camp," trade and the freedom of movement were restricted compared with the more liberal Western practices.

Russian and Soviet history fit the pattern of political institutions described by Wesson as typical for a universal empire: the elevation of an autocrat (the "cult of personality" in Soviet parlance), a ban on any and all political parties, and the army as a power broker. Empires, including the USSR, were characterized by the prevalence of ideology, a fearsome secret police, and sprawling networks of internal spies. Stalin's USSR demonstrated all of these totalitarian elements.

Empires, as a rule, are established by forceful dictators who command awe from their followers. Both those who fear them and those who do not are often eliminated in bloody, irrational purges. Lenin and Stalin are typical in this respect. They fall into the category of imperial founding fathers. Their heirs are representative of the imperial pattern of development as well. In due course, the personality of the leader becomes less and less powerful, as the political class, fearing for its life and influence, elevates nonentities it hopes to control. The sequence "Lenin, Stalin, Khrushchev, Brezhnev" reflects this tendency as much as a list of Roman emperors from the first to the fourth centuries A.D. Without representative government and consent of the ruled, the leaders have to coerce the bureaucrats and the subjects into submission and play one faction off against the other. In the absence of the rule of law and separation of powers, one of the ways in which the competing factions are kept in check is by the supreme arbiter.[10]

Universal empires for eons justified waging war in the name of universal peace, prosperity, or some other equally appealing ideology. From *Pax Romana* to the "struggle for peace," converts and dupes have fought for imperial causes. Those who refused to convert or be duped were bought or killed.

If the Soviet empire was the epitome of strong controls and an assertive foreign policy, how and why did it collapse, and why did the implosion occur so quickly?

Conservatism and resistance to change are two of the major issues at stake. Social concepts, technology, and even the arts have stagnated in every case of a universal empire going under. With the profit motive absent and economy, science, and technology bureaucratized, there is no incentive for innovation and change. The USSR, once a world leader in nuclear research and space exploration, became the laughingstock of the industrial world. Believing in its own propaganda about capitalist encirclement, the USSR overstretched itself, allocating an extremely high percentage of its gross domestic product to the military and security forces. But with production plummeting under the burden of inept economic management, there was less and less money even for the military. The complaints of officers' families concerning living standards were widespread before and during the Soviet debacle in Afghanistan.

The symptoms demonstrated by the USSR both in its aggressive stage and during its stagnation and decline fit the description found in Wesson's study of the Chinese, Indian, Incan, and other empires. As with many other imperial state formations, after the decline and breakup often comes the creation of several states instead of the old conglomerate. This is the development we have witnessed to date in the case of the former Soviet Union.

A comparative approach allowed Geoffrey Parker to distill a concept of imperial expansion and disintegration common to Spain, Austria, France, Germany, and Ottoman Turkey.[11] Similarly to all these powers, which developed at the periphery of more advanced civilizations, the Russian principalities grew on the border of what used to be the Byzantine civilization, with Slavic and Finno-Ugric tribes that roamed from the Dnieper to the Urals. The center of the new expansionist state was located in convenient proximity to a number of waterways (the Moskva, the Oka, and close to the Volga), but was protected enough to prevent constant invasions from the Tatars.

Inspired by the Tatar example, the Moscow principality (termed by Parker a "dominant state") grew into a centralized monarchy, characterized in its initial stages by a high degree of ethnic homogeneity. As increasingly vast tracts of territory were captured, peasants from the Slavic hinterland colonized formerly Finno-Ugric and Tatar territories, creating a fluid frontier moving east and south. Simultaneously, the ideology of Orthodox expansionism was developing in Moscow, culminating with the declaration of Moscow as the Third Rome, the last and only center of true Christianity. Orthodoxy was imposed on the newly conquered realms.

The expansion (stage one of Parker's theory) went on for centuries, until the natural borders were reached. In the sixteenth and seventeenth centuries, the border began to move west as well. Those peoples and states that could not resist the power of Russian arms were crushed. Only by the end of the nineteenth century did Russia reach what proved to be the historical borders of the empire: Germany in the west; Turkey, Iran, and the British empire domains in the south; and China, Japan, and the Pacific Ocean in the east.

Russia contested Austria-Hungary in the Balkans, aspiring to reestablish herself as the new patron of the Christian Orthodox cultural sphere, and dreaming of returning (in accordance with stage two of Parker's theory) to the very heart of "her" original cultural area—Constantinople. At this stage, cultural homogenization and Russification constituted the dominant cultural policy. Moscow and St. Petersburg enhanced their status, turning into ever more important transportation hubs and cultural centers.

Stage three was reached after World War II, when the USSR established its control over Eastern Europe. Uniformity was imposed with a great degree of coercion, as Soviet-type regimes were installed, to last for almost half a century. Ideological purity was enforced by the Kremlin's agents in Eastern Europe. However, full absorption of the Eastern European acquisitions into the Russian/Soviet empire seemed difficult even for Stalin, and so an informal imperial model was pursued.

According to Parker, the dissolution of empires comes about as the result of countervailing efforts by a state or a group of states. The geopolitical factor plays a great role, as the dominant state finds itself expanding into realms it knows little about, and which are geographically very remote from the imperial core. This was the case of the Soviet Union's involvement in Afghanistan, Angola, Vietnam, and Nicaragua. In these areas, local populations resisted the Soviet invaders (Afghanistan) or their collaborators (Nicaragua, Angola) with the assistance of a countervailing coalition led by the United States. Vast resources were spent by the USSR in its attempts to win these colonial wars. Domestically, more stringent political and ideological controls were imposed, and long-needed reforms were postponed, further delaying a necessary economic overhaul.

An insupportable status quo began to deteriorate. Parts of the USSR's empire started to break away: first, Eastern Europe; second, the "inner tier," the union republics; and finally, the imperial core, Russia itself, turned nationalist and temporarily anti-imperialist, as evidenced by Boris Yeltsin's challenge to the imperial center in the Kremlin. Yeltsin's course in 1989–1990 was supported by a large faction of the Russian political elite, which recognized the obsolete character of the Soviet empire.[12] Imperial unity was undermined, and the unstable equilibrium, through which the Soviet empire had been sustained, finally collapsed.

THE PERICENTRIC APPROACHES

The pericentric approaches of Gallagher and Robinson,[13] and others, are applicable to understanding Russian and Soviet imperial development and decline.

The causes of Russian territorial growth from the fourteenth through the nineteenth centuries, and the Soviet reestablishment of the empire in the twentieth century did not lie in Moscow and St. Petersburg alone. While, in many cases, lands were conquered in open battle, both before and after the war a series of unequal bargains were drawn, which sometimes satisfied the political elites of subjugated lands and states. Thus, in addition to military conquest and imperial geopolitics, relationships both within the periphery and between the periphery and the metropolis represent an important explanatory tool of imperialist behavior.

The concept of the turbulent frontier, applied to a territory plagued by instability into which an imperial power moves under the guise of "restoration of law and order," is particularly suitable to the Ukrainian case of the seventeenth century. Almost uniformly, from Poland to Ukraine and Kazakhstan, one can find splits in the local elites. Some were more inclined than others to fight for independence. Those who did usually were destroyed by the Russians and their local supporters. An examination of the institutions and personnel of the colonial players, from Cossack adventurers to the corrupt and incompetent emirs of Khorezm and Bukhara, still awaits its scholars in the tradition of Gallagher and Robinson.

After the 1917 revolution, Bolshevik parties and organizations, in what would become the Soviet republics, representing mostly Russian working class and lumpen interests,[14] supported Moscow's domination. In those areas where Bolsheviks were almost nonexistent, such as Central Asia, they temporarily tolerated local elites (the Jadids, for example) who deemed alliance with Moscow to be in their strategic interests. Later, these elites were physically exterminated.

Imperial domination created Russia's forced economic bridgeheads in the former Soviet Union. The republican economies were tied with that of Russia, often serving as her raw materials appendices. Ukraine supplied Russia with coal for over a century. Kazakhstan provided ferrous and nonferrous metals. Russian light industry flourished on the Uzbek cotton it received at a fraction of world prices. Azerbaijan's oil reserves were exploited by its northern neighbor for a century. The economic planners of *Gosplan* intentionally created myriad links of dependency between the republics and Moscow, so that republics would not dare consider independence or would not be able to survive it. Russia currently is surviving the collapse of her empire better than the peripheries, which are detached from their most important sources of components, finished goods, and energy resources.

A periphery-centered analysis is particularly helpful when one examines the imperial decline of the USSR. By the time Gorbachev took over, Eastern Europe and most of the Soviet republics had developed local leadership cadres. These elites managed to mobilize mass movements that were anti-imperialist by their nature. The national liberation struggles of these peoples solicited international support, including, at least for some time, the sympathy of the Russian intelligentsia.

By replacing Brezhnevites with like-minded leaders, Gorbachev hoped to keep Eastern Europe and the Soviet republics under control and to revamp and preserve the old Soviet empire. Thus, he opted to substitute formal control for informal imperial domination. When matters got out of hand in Eastern Europe, Gorbachev, as Western imperial masters had before him, did not consider the introduction of "formal control" (i.e., reoccupation, as exercised in Hungary in 1956 and Chechoslovakia in 1968 under Brezhnev) as a viable option. When the Soviet republics became restive (as in Karabakh, Tbilisi, Baku, Riga, and Vilnius), Gorbachev hoped (under the paradigm "direct rule only if unavoidable") that he could achieve his goals by imposing military rule. He was wrong. After 1989, formal control no longer applied even within the USSR. After 1990, it did not apply even in Moscow, where Boris Yeltsin's "Russia first" approach won over Gorbachev's "save the Union" slogan. The putsch of 1991 and the following breakup of the empire demonstrated this in a very convincing fashion.

EMPIRE AND EMANCIPATION

To apply Nederveen Pieterse's analysis of metropolitan and peripheral dispositions to the Russian and Soviet cases means to treat the systemic crises of 1917 and 1991 for what they were: the emancipation of non-Russian peoples from Russian domination.[15] In addition, one can see the collapse of communism in 1991 as at least temporary liberation of the Russians from communist oppression.

Nederveen Pieterse, as noted in Chapter One, introduces the concept of ethnic status hierarchy, which is applicable to Russia both in the Romanov period and during the Stalinist and post-Stalinist years. Ethnic Russians were the *imperial people*, similar to Romans in the Roman empire, Englishmen in the British empire, or the Han Chinese in the numerous incarnations of the Chinese empire. In the Soviet period, the Ukrainians and Byelorussians were second highest on the totem pole, followed by the Armenians, Georgians, and Azeris. The list concluded with the Balts, Jews, and Central Asian Turks, all of whom were deemed unreliable. However, at the highest level of the imperial hierarchy, ethnicity played a lesser role than in everyday Soviet life.

According to Nederveen Pieterse's approach, the disintegration of the USSR occurred because of the clash of value systems between the dominant ideology (communist orthodoxy) and the competing value systems that had been temporarily suppressed (nationalism, Western liberalism, and so on). Samizdat, the nationalist and dissident movements of the 1960s and 1970s, religion, and Western broadcasts to the USSR were all of great importance, because they provided an alternative Weltanschauung for the millions involved in these activities.

Nederveen Pieterse stresses the importance of the "imperial minorities" who facilitate the running of the empire for their masters, such as Gurkhas and the Irish for the British. Similarly, in the Soviet case, Chinese and Koreans often served as early Cheka executioners, Central Asian Turks were often posted to guard the primarily European inmates of the Gulag, and the largely Slavic *spetsnaz* was used to quell unrest in the Caucasus and Turkestan.

The Dutch author maintains that the oppressed learn the tools of political and organizational warfare from their oppressors. This may have been the case with anticolonial movements in the Third World, but not in Eastern Europe or in the USSR. On the contrary, in the latter, the oppressors attempted to mimic the demands of emancipation movements and to co-opt them (for example, popular fronts started by CC CPSU functionaries, *perestroika* from above). Liberation movements did not need to emulate the regime to subvert oppression. In what appears to be a sui generis situation, they did not adopt the oppressors' organization and strategy, nor did they appropriate their technology. In Russia and the Baltic states, it was mass movements with extremely undisciplined and unprofessional leaderships, chaotic and nonviolent tactics, that subverted and won over the highly centralized, professional, and bureaucratic machine. In August 1991, the Democratic Russia bloc had an apparatus of seven people![16] This is hardly the "October Revolution in reverse," an armed rebellion of hardened, disciplined anticommunists. Thus, while the analytical tools of emancipation theory are valid, its description of the mechanism of political change needs updating.

SYSTEMIC THEORIES

It was tempting for many political thinkers to create a comprehensive theory of empires. In analyzing an empire, the majority of authors seek to discern the most prevalent forms and the most potent forces of domination. In the case of B. J. Cohen, his theory, advanced in the early 1970s in response to conventional Marxism, was primarily based upon an examination of Western colonial empires as opposed to Eastern contiguous ones. Cohen's theory, as outlined in Chapter One, stresses the inequality between the subject and the object of domination, as well as the forms and forces of dominance. He advances the criterion of the extent to which an imperial power *interrupts* the vital relationships of other nations as a measure of their degree of dependence. It is the power politics of strong, expansionist states, not the interests of private business, that make a critical contribution to the creation of empires.[17]

In the case of Russia and the USSR, domination was enforced most often in the form of direct military conquest, and more rarely via informal rule. It was the victorious march of tsarist troops and the Red Army that made Russia the largest state on earth since the empire of Genghis Khan. It was the onslaught of the Red Army that introduced informal Soviet dominance behind the facades of the local communist regimes in post–World War II Eastern Europe.

According to Cohen and his fellow "power theorists," Russia's great power politics would be perfectly rational. It would be a legitimate response to the uncertainty surrounding the survival of the Russian nation. From the trauma of the Mongol invasion to clashes with Catholic Poland and the Ottoman Porte, Russia had developed the rather unique ideology of a besieged giant, involved in a holy war with the rest of the world.

Since empire building is contingent upon the availability of resources, Russia, rich in both manpower and raw materials, had the advantage of the "disequilibrium of resources" over her poorer neighbors. For centuries, Russians considered the bottom line of the "costs and benefits of empire" calculation to be positive. As global domination would have been an extremely high cost goal to achieve, it did not figure as the stated strategic objective (except in the revolutionary *Sturm und Drang* of the early Comintern). Russia, therefore, according to the power theorists, was not an exception in the international system. Her bid for domination stemmed from the nature and logic of international competition, having its roots in the anarchic organization of the international system of nation-states. But over time, the costs of maintaining the empire became too high. When the imperial calculus broke down, the majority of Russian elites became, at least for a while, anti-imperialist and abandoned the sinking ship of the USSR. The lack of support for the August 1991 coup in the broad public and the elite proves the point. However, the events of the 1990s may indicate that the pendulem is swinging toward imperialism once again.

Another systemic theory was advanced in 1986 by Michael W. Doyle. According to Doyle, the Russian state in its expansion had three options: despoiling conquered states (as pursued by Beria and Malenkov with regard to East Germany after World War II),[18] indirect rule, and direct control. In most cases, the Russians and the Soviets opted for direct control. Doyle, as noted, distinguishes between *imperialism* and hegemony or suzerainty. The Soviet case, with its extremely centralized control from the imperial hub, was an empire almost in its purest form.

The metropole penetrated the periphery through the agency of numerous actors: missionaries (ideological workers), merchants (factory managers), soldiers, secret policemen, and bureaucrats. By controlling the political life of the peripheries through an elaborate system of rewards and punishments,[19] the imperial agents exercised effective sovereignty, thus going beyond conventional dependency. Soviet imperial rulers controlled the lives of their subjects without sharing their values. These actors shaped peripheral norms and tastes, and influenced the contents of domestic factions, classes, coalitions, and parties in the periphery.

The decision-making process was a complex one, with some decisions made in the provinces, while others were formulated in the metropolis. From Lenin on, the majority of decisions were taken in Moscow, with the local communist bosses playing the role of satraps or enforcers of the center. With such a strong emphasis upon centralization, it is understandable why the degree of political and cultural penetration was so high that many USSR-watchers considered it a monolithic, unitary state.

If one applies Doyle's Patrick Henry's rule to the USSR (efficient empires control the political regimes of their peripheries extremely effectively),[20] one finds that the Soviet imperial enterprise satisfied this definition for over seventy years. Doyle's Jefferson's rule stated that an empire is characterized by a "long train of abuses" committed to keep the peripheries in subordination. The Soviet case fully conforms with this rule. The Red Army's storming of the non-Russian areas of the old Romanov empire, the horrors of the Stalinist crimes, including the exile of entire nations, are widely known.

Doyle applies a four-dimensional analysis to the phenomenon of empire. The metropolitan aspect in the case of Russia is quite clear: For centuries there were strong centripetal forces, both before and after the 1917 revolution, which supported a vigorous, centrally controlled unitary state. But in the end, the empire began melting away through the fingers of its leaders. The ineptitude and misunderstanding of the systemic crisis were demonstrated in the Politburo materials discussed in the previous chapter. Even when a large part of the elite perceived the costs as being too high, the Gorbachev administration clung to the failed cause of "indestructible union."

The peripheries that Russia dealt with were militarily and often politically quite weak. For decades, developed nations, such as Poland and Finland, were controlled by the Russian, and later, indirectly, by the Soviet state, without losing their distinct national characters. Even 300 years of imperial subjugation failed to disengage the Ukrainians from the dream of their own state. The Russian and Soviet assimilation efforts failed to transform the various nationalities into one imperial nation. Once the ideological press was stopped and violence as the tool of political control was relinquished, there was not enough centripetal power to hold the empire together. What appeared as the glorious exploits of the forefathers in Kursk seemed more like a colonial expedition in Lviv, Tallinn or Bishkek.

The transnational system (culture, technology, international norms, and fads) for a long time did not interfere with the business of running the empire. Effective border controls kept Western influences at bay. The state decided what was allowed in and what was to be kept out. But with the technological advances of the post–World War II era, such as computers and xerox machines, maintaining these controls became more difficult. As a result, a planetary culture replete with rock 'n roll, blue jeans, and cheap, affordable consumer goods began spreading across the Iron Curtain to points east. Once the new generation of *nomenklatura*, which included Mikhail Gorbachev and his entourage, became "contaminated," the ideological and doctrinal purity of the empire deteriorated rapidly.

In the 1980s, the international system became particularly unfriendly to the USSR. The war in Afghanistan, support of the Sandinista regime in Nicaragua, assistance to a dozen Third World guerilla movements, and aid to economic basket case regimes made running the superpower a very costly venture. In addition, the United States under President Ronald Reagan was ready to challenge the very ideological foundations of the communist Soviet state. An increasing number of nonaligned and socialist countries understood that the way to economic prosperity lay through Washington, Tokyo, and Bonn, not Moscow or Bucharest.

Thus, only one component out of Doyle's four—the metropolitan one—was supportive of the USSR's imperial existence in the 1980s. Three of the others—peripheral, transnational, and international—were directed against continuation of this imperial venture.

THE RISE AND FALL OF EMPIRES

Paul Kennedy, in his *The Rise and Fall of the Great Powers*, concentrates on the international component of imperial existence. The essence of the imperial phenomenon is to maximize power, security, and wealth. Therefore, the long-term economic performance of an imperial power becomes extremely important.[21]

The old Russian empire was shattered in World War I. Lenin, Stalin, and their successors were always aware of the possibility of a major international conflict. After Hitler's attack, Stalin found himself on the side of the coalition that was destined to win. He then expanded the empire, adding to it informally controlled territories the west. However, the USSR was positioning itself for a global showdown with the main enemy (*glavnyi protivnik*)—the United States and its allies, the industrial West, including Japan, and the European Community. In the late 1960s, Washington effectively brought China into the anti-Soviet coalition. To follow Kennedy's methodology, one has to examine the relative performance of a great power vis-à-vis its rivals. To do this, one has to compare the long-term economic achievements of the USSR with those of all its main rivals.

In the 1970s, Soviet military spending as a part of the gross national product, while always a secret,[22] reached up to one-third or more of the GDP—an extremely high level compared with defense spending in the West (generally up from to 5 to 7 percent).

According to Kennedy's "long-term dilemma," when great powers perceive themselves to be in relative decline, they spend more on defense, thus undercutting investment in the civilian economy. While Kennedy's book was intended as a warning to the United States, its analysis is much more relevant to the USSR. As its economy was much smaller to begin with, maintaining military parity with the West was a tall order.

The USSR might have prevented its own collapse if Stalin had not anticipated another world war soon after 1945 and had opted to demobilize more decisively, as did the United States. The Soviet economy, running on a war footing for forty years, finally ran out of steam. The life span of the Soviet Union might have been longer if Khrushchev's attempts to base defense primarily on nuclear missile deterrence had been accepted by the Soviet military top brass, and expensive conventional forces had been drastically reduced. The USSR might still exist if it had not entered into the arms race and international involvement in the Third World of the 1970s during the Brezhnev era, and if the space arms race of the late 1970s and early 1980s had not been undertaken. Finally, if the adventure in Afghanistan had not taken place, the Berlin Wall might still be standing. But these are no more than speculations. Declining powers, according to Paul Kennedy, have a logic and destiny of their own.

Similar to Habsburg Spain, discussed by Kennedy, the USSR demonstrated politico-economic blindness by not allowing for even rudimentary private property and free enterprise. Key technologies, such as information processing and computers, were not widely disseminated in the 1970s and 1980s. Earlier, Stalin had opposed research into supersonic flight and the theory of relativity. Decision making was at the whim of a geriatric coalition in the Brezhnev Politburo, and affairs got out of control under Mikhail Gorbachev. Entrepreneurial ethnic elements, such as Jews, Germans, and Armenians, were emigrating. Young, better educated people were fleeing the Eastern Bloc countries in droves. Despite the boasts of Soviet propaganda to the contrary, by the late 1970s a deep sense of inferiority had overtaken both the Soviet citizenry and the elite.

The Gorbachev reforms were an attempt to trade off some of the USSR's security and superpower status for more systemic viability. Gorbachev attempted to rationalize imperial control and make the realm more manageable. But the Soviet military resisted cuts till the end. The factories continued to manufacture military hardware even after the collapse of the Soviet Union, despite financial cuts (up to 80 percent of the military budget) using strategic stockpiles of raw materials. They incurred multibillion-ruble mutual debts and thus contributed to the "nonpayment crisis" of 1992.[23]

In addition to an obvious case of internal degeneration, the Soviet Union collapsed under the strain of international competition and economic inefficiency.[24] It would be a supreme test of the Russian national leadership of the post-*perestroika* generation to break the 500-year-old vicious circle of military mobilization and expansion and the resulting economic debilitation. Thus far, their achievements have been mediocre at best. While significantly cutting the military budget, long-overdue reforms in the armed forces have not occurred. In the past, periods of economic prosperity in Russia were rare and their lessons remained unlearned. Marxism-Leninism, the empire's ideology and analytical frame of reference failed to provide viable solutions to the game its adherents were seeking to play, which was to create a winning combination of economic, military, and political power needed to achieve world domination.

The only alternative open to the USSR and republican leadership by the end of 1991 was the creation of several nation-states in its stead, possibly united in a federation, a confederation, or a common market.

Will Russia, for the first time in its history since the fifteenth century, abandon attempts to become a universal empire or a dominant state—one that, in various ideological guises, incessantly strives for imperial domination of a known political "universe"? As independence was proclaimed by all members of the union, a new page in East-Central European, Central Asian, and world history could be opened, to include the participation of Russia in a multipolar and hopefully more cooperative international political system. The construction of adequate democratic mechanisms to create legitimate government structures should become a high priority in Russia and the rest of the Newly Independent States. However, the forces nostalgic for the days of yore are still strong, as evidenced by the communist ascendancy in the December 1995 Duma elections and beyond. The glory of past conquests excites politicians and generals in Moscow. The battle for the future of Russia is still in progress.

FINAL OBSERVATIONS

Charles Fairbanks, searching for the reasons to explain why communism collapsed, why Sovietology failed to predict it, and what we can learn from this failure, remarked

It was the specific field of Soviet studies that had the greatest responsibility for grasping the fragility of the Soviet system and which has the most to learn from the reassessment that ought to follow its collapse. For us in Soviet studies the sad reflection must intrude: We were not ready for this. Soviet studies as a discipline did not anticipate, and still cannot easily account for, the changes that emerged from the Soviet system...none of us, until the very eve of the collapse presented such a radical transformation of the system as a serious possibility. To put it bluntly, we were all wrong. Not, of course, about every aspect of Soviet reality, but about important aspects that generated or allowed the unexpected changes since 1985.[25]

Sovietology, in the main, failed to predict the collapse of the USSR by employing the tools it was supposed to apply: comparative history and political science analyses that extend beyond area studies. If these tools had been utilized, it would not have been difficult to discern that the USSR was a contiguous multinational empire. Recognized as such, the experiences of its predecessors, such as Austria-Hungary and the Ottoman Porte, as well as Rome, Han China, and the British empire, may have proved enlightening. Generalizations extracted from imperial experiences might have been applied to the Soviet case with great explanatory and predictive value. However, this largely did not occur. Instead, many academics in the field worked hard to prove the totalitarian model wrong.[26] Few gave a thought to the application of an *imperial* model, which would have at least allowed for an understanding of the ways and possibilities of collapse as these were experienced in other places and epochs. This is not to say that everybody who dealt with the issue of the future of the USSR got it wrong. For example, Zbigniew Brzezinski, Hélène Carrère D'Encausse, Robert Conquest, Paul Henze, Peter Reddaway, and especially Bernard Levin[27] provided major insights into the processes that led to the Soviet disintegration.

When it came to the decision makers, there was even less understanding of the imperial component of Soviet (and post-Soviet) developments. The Bush administration seemed to be uniquely obtuse about the inevitability of the USSR's collapse. Bush's "Chicken Kyiv" speech, calling (in the capital of independence-seeking Ukraine) for the continuation of the Russian-dominated Soviet empire in the summer of 1991, illustrates the point. So do the rebukes dispatched by the administration to independence-seeking Georgia. President Bush and Secretary of State Baker, preoccupied with the survival of "the last emperor," Mikhail Gorbachev, to a great degree missed the boat as far as the quest for freedom was concerned. Even Boris Yeltsin, the gravedigger of the empire, was repeatedly snubbed by Washington, despite his obvious upper hand over the proponents of the Soviet Center.[28]

Little was accomplished by the U.S. government in 1991–1992 in terms of providing aid to the Newly Independent States, especially as far as nation building was concerned. Assistance with market-oriented economic reforms for these nascent nation-states was held off for at least three years, and then implemented in a haphazard fashion.

Washington's policy was at odds with its own historical track record: Almost never were the old colonial powers, Britain and France, supported by the United States against their former colonies as these sought or built independence.

Unfortunately, even today, after the collapse, the imperial roots of the current political chaos in postcommunist Eurasia are often forgotten or misunderstood by analysts and decision makers. There is little comprehension that most of the conflicts under way in the former Soviet Union have erupted due to their "defrosting" as a direct result of imperial collapse. The similarity between these contests and the Graeko-Turkish wars of 1920, the Arab-Israeli conflict of 1948, African tribal warfare, or the Indo-Pakistani wars is too great to be ignored. The issue of the Russians in the "near abroad" and the *pieds noirs* in Algiers have a great deal in common. The new regimes often lack internal legitimacy and a political vacuum exists in the region. In such an environment, state and nonstate actors (militias, clans, warlords, political parties, and so on) with little experience in "civilized" dispute resolution resort to violence to settle scores.

After previous imperial collapses, new international rules of the game and structures were settled upon in a series of international conferences. These often bred dissent, as externally imposed borders without dispute-resolution mechanisms could not satisfy every player.

The Clinton administration thus far has not found an effective way to deal with the postcommunist crises. It has often ignored them altogether, issued statements of sympathy, or proposed U.S. troop participation in peacekeeping operations under United Nations command.

"Moral equivalency" is occasionally proclaimed by some Western analysts between the reformist faction in Moscow (radical reformers, democrats) and the revanchist faction (hard-line nationalists and communists). In the latter group, one can find Communist party leader Gennady Zyuganov; the ultranationalist Vladimir Zhirinovsky; General Alexander Lebed; former Vice President Alexander Rutskoi; and other hard-liners. It must be remembered that any Russian attempt to rebuild the empire will mean the end of democratization. Such an attempt would require the enormous, centrally controlled concentration of resources that is possible only under a dictatorship. It would also badly damage economic reforms, the rule of law, and the creation of civic societies. The "party of war"[29] coming to power in Moscow would not only mean an attempt to rebuild the empire using a vast array of means, from military force to local elite co-optation and manipulation, to currency manipulation and economic blackmail, but might also entail Russia's resumption of an anti-Western, anti-American stance.

It would have never occurred to American policy makers to accept the friendly British empire trying to "put the Raj together again" in India. Anglo-French intervention in the Suez (1956) was met with a sharp American rebuke. The case of Russian imperial renaissance is even more extreme: The proponents of the renewed empire are on record saying that "Atlanticists" and "mondialists" (euphemisms for the United States and the Western alliance) will be the enemy of a future Eurasian community.[30] Scenarios for a Slavic-Turkic alliance,[31] a Slavic-Moslem coalition,[32] and even a Sino-Russian alliance are currently being floated in Moscow. A prosperous, democratic free-market Russia would be a desirable partner for the West, but a rebirth of the Russian/post-Soviet empire would pose a major threat to Western security in the twenty-first century. Even if START II agreements were fully implemented, a hostile Russia would remain the second largest nuclear power in the world. Instead of a century of peace, we may find ourselves facing a neo-imperialist Russia ruled by a revanchist leadership playing the role of bête noire.

Therefore, an understanding of the imperial underpinnings of postcommunist Eurasian politics becomes a crucial aspect of American policy making. And thus, preemption of any potential Russian imperial renaissance, advancement of economic reform and democratization in the NIS, and effective dispute resolution and peacekeeping must become the ultimate Western foreign policy imperative for the remainder of the twentieth century and beyond.[33]

NOTES

1. Jan P. Nederveen Pieterse, *Empire and Emancipation* (New York: Praeger, 1989), p. 245.

2. John Starchey, *The End of Empire* (London: Victor Gollanz, 1959), p. 319.

3. See Chapter One.

4. Ibid.

5. For example, these were Russian miners in the Ukrainian Donbass; Ukrainian peasants in Kazakhstan; Russian, Ukrainian, and Tatar blue-collar industrial workers in the Baltic states; and Russian industrial workers in Tatarstan to mention just a few.

6. Michael W. Doyle, *Empires* (Ithaca, N.Y.: Cornell University Press, 1986), p. 43.

7. George Lichtheim, *Imperialism* (New York: Praeger, 1971), pp. 88–89.

8. Frantisek Silnicky, *Natsional'naya Politika KPSS (1917–1922)*, 3rd ed. (Washington, D.C.: Problems of Eastern Europe, 1990), pp. 70–195.

9. See Chapter One.

10. Justice Boris G. Ebzeev of the Russian Constitutional Court defended a "supreme arbiter" role for the president of Russia, despite the obvious violation this would imply of the principle of the separation of powers, and the creation of a quasi-judiciary function within the executive branch. Personal interview, Moscow, July 1993.

11. See Chapter One.

12. Moreover, parts of the Russian Federation, such as Chechnya, Tatarstan, Sakha, Tuva, and Buryatia demonstrated centrifugal tendencies.

13. J.A. Gallagher and R.E. Robinson, "Imperialism of Free Trade,"*Economic History Review*, 2d series, VI, I, 1953; see also John A. Gallagher, *The Decline, Revival and Fall of the British Empire* (London: Cambridge University Press, 1973). In addition, refer to Chapter One.

14. A notable exception was Soviet Georgia, whose leadership put up a most consistent fight against the creation of the USSR.

15. See Chapter One.

16. Personal interview, Dmitri V. Karaulov, cochairman, St. Petersburg branch, Republican Party of Russia (RPR), July 1993.

17. See Chapter One.

18. See Gavriel Ra'anan, *International Policy Formation in the USSR: Factional Debates during the Zhdanovshchina* (Hamden, Conn.: Archon Books, 1983).

19. Among the rewards was the possibility of receiving state-controlled education, chances to pursue a political or military career, travel abroad, or improving one's housing conditions. Punishments began with denial of one's career advancement and travel abroad, escalating all the way to exile, imprisonment, and execution.

20. See Chapter One.

21. See Chapter One.

22. Figures of from 17 to 40 percent of the GNP are quoted in Western sources.

23. Colonel Vitaly Shlykov, former deputy minister of defense of the Russian Federation, presentation at a conference on Civil-Military Relations in Post-Communist Russia, The Heritage Foundation, Washington, D.C., October 1992.

24. Stephen Sestanovich, "Did the West Undo the East?", *National Interest*, no. 31, Spring 1993, p. 26.

25. Charles H. Fairbanks, Jr., introduction to "The Strange Death of Soviet Communism: An Autopsy", *National Interest*, no. 31, Spring 1993, p. 6.

26. It became unfashionable to treat the USSR as a totalitarian state despite the great explanatory value of that model. Instead, more conventional models, such as the "bureaucratic state," were advanced.

27. Bernard Levin, "One Who Got It Right," *National Interest*, no. 31, Spring 1993, p. 64. Writing in 1977, Levin not only predicted the date of the external empire's collapse—1989—but also the *way* it would happen, starting with reform from above, through nationalist fervor, leading to an unstoppable quest for freedom, but without bloodshed and revolutionary terror.

28. The justification for the Bush-Baker policy favoring the preservation of Gorbachev (and the USSR), shared by many in Europe, was to prevent the hard-line overthrow of the reformist general secretary and to assure Russian withdrawal from Eastern Europe. However, a forceful policy designed to accelerate the breakup of the USSR was in the long-term interests of the West and of the non-Russians seeking independence. A hard-line takeover in Moscow may have accelerated such a breakup.

29. Former Russian foreign minister Andrey Kozyrev's term. However, Kozyrev's own pronouncements, as well as statements from the top echelons of the Yeltsin administration regarding Russian geopolitical interests that took centuries to consolidate, indicate that the internal debate is only on the tactics and pace of an imperial *reconquista*.

30. See Alexander L. Yanov, *Weimar Russia* (forthcoming).

31. An idea advanced by Sergei Stankevich, Yeltsin's former advisor, a former democrat and born-again great power statist (*derzhavnik*).

32. This one is advanced by some ideologists of the National Salvation Front, led by former KGB general Alexander Sterlingov. It stems from the common hatred of the West and the perceived need to fight against a pervasive "Judeo-Masonic conspiracy."

33. For specific policy recommendations, see Ariel Cohen, "Russia and Her Neighbors: Creating U.S. Policy for Eurasia," *Backgrounder*, no. 966, (Washington, D.C.: The Heritage Foundation, November 19, 1993).

Selected Bibliography

BOOKS

Almond, G., and G. Powell. *Comparative Politics: A Developmental Approach*. Boston: Little, Brown, 1966.

Baker, James H. and R.A. French, eds. *Studies in Russian Historical Geography*. London: Academic Press, 1983.

Beazley, Raymond, Nevill Forbes, and G.A. Birkett. *Russia*. Oxford: Oxford University Press, 1918.

Bennigsen, Alexander, and Marie Bruxup. *The Islamic Threat to the Soviet Union*. London: Croom Helm, 1983.

Berdiayev, Nikolay. *Istoki i Smysl Russkogo Kommunizma*. Paris: YMCA Press, 1955 Reprinted Moscow: Izdatel'stvo Nauka, 1990.

Brezhnev, L. I. "Leninskim kursom," *Rechi i statyi*, vol. 5. Moscow: Politicheskaya Literatura, 1976.

Bromlei, Yulii, E. Bagramov, M. Guboglo and M. Kulichenko, eds. *Natzional'nykh otnoshenii v SSSR v svete veshenii XXVI s'yeda KPSS*. Moscow: 1982.

Bruchis, Michael. *The USSR: Language and Realities. Nations, Leaders and Scholars*. Boulder, Colo.: Westview East European Monographs, 1988.

Carrère d'Encausse, Hélène. *Decline of an Empire: Soviet Socialist Republics in Revolt*. New York: Newsweek Books, 1979.

————*Islam and the Russian Empire*. New York: Newsweek Books, 1988.

Cohen, Benjamin J. *The Question of Imperialism*. New York: Basic Books, 1973.

Conquest, Robert. *The Nation Killers: The Soviet Deportation of Nationalities*. New York: MacMillan, 1970.

Deutscher, Isaac. *Stalin*. London: Oxford University Press, 1967.

Doyle, Michael W. *Empires*. Ithaca, N.Y.: Cornell University Press, 1986.

Dunlop, John B. *The New Russian Nationalism*. Washington, D.C.: Washington Papers, Praeger, 1985.

Fieldhouse, David K. *The Colonial Empires*. New York: Macmillan, 1982.

————*Economics and Empire, 1830–1914*. London: Macmillan, 1984.

Gallagher, John A., with preface by Anil Seal. *The Decline, Revival and Fall of the British Empire*. London: Cambridge University Press, 1973.

Geyer, Dietrich. *Russian Imperialism: The Interaction of Domestic and Foreign Policy 1860-1914*. New York: Berg, 1987.

Hajda, Lubomyr, and Mark Beissinger, eds. *The Nationalities Factor in Soviet Politics and Society*. Boulder, Colo.: Westview Press, 1989.

Hauner, Milan. *What is Asia to Us? Russia's Asian Heartland Yesterday and Today*. Boston: Unwin Hyman, 1990.

Kaltakhchian, S.T. *Marksistsko-Leninskaya teoriia natsii i sovremennost'* (The Marxist-Leninist Theory of the Nation and Contemporaneity). Moscow: Izdatel'stvo Politicheskoy Literatury, 1983.

Kennedy, Paul. *The Rise and Fall of the Great Powers*. New York: Vintage Books, 1989.

Kluchevsky, V.O. *Skazaniya inostrantzev o Moskovskom gosudarstve*. Petrograd: Literaturno-Izdatel'skii Otdel Komissariata Narodnogo Prosveshcheniya, 1918.

Kolarz, Walter. *Russia and Her Colonies*. London: George Philip and Son, 1953.

KPSS v rezolutsiayakh i resheniyakh s'yezdov, konferentsii i plenumov TsK, vol. 2. Moscow: Politicheskaya Literatura, 1970.

Kravtzov, B.P., ed. *Torzhestvo Leninskoy natzional'noy politiki*. Moscow: Izdatel'stvo V.P.Sh., 1963.

Lenin, V. I. "The Discussion of Self-Determination Summed Up." In *Marx, Engels, Marxism*. Moscow: Politizdat, 1947.

———.*Imperialism: The Highest Stage of Capitalism*. Moscow: International Publishers, 1988.

———.*On Proletarian Internationalism*. Moscow: Progress Publishers, 1976.

Lewis, Geoffrey. *Turkey*. London: Ernest Benn, 1960.

Librach, Jan. *The Rise of the Soviet Empire*. London: Pall Mall Press, 1964.

Lichtheim, George. *Imperialism*. New York: Praeger, 1971.

Makarova, G. P. *Osushchestvleniye Leninskoy natzional'noy politiki v pervyiye gody sovetskoy vlasti*. Moscow, FSU: Nauka, 1969.

MacKenzie, David and Michael W. Curran. *A History of Russia and the Soviet Union*. Homewood, IL: The Dorsey Press, 1977.

Mamatey, Victor S. *Soviet Russian Imperialism*. Princeton, N.J.: Van Nostrand, 1964.

Mason, John W. *The Dissolution of the Austro-Hungarian Empire 1867–1914*. London: Longman, 1985.

May, Arthur J. *The Habsburg Monarchy, 1867–1914*. Cambridge, Mass.: Harvard University Press, 1951.

Miliukov, Paul, Charles Seignobos, and L. Eisenmann. *Empire of Peter the Great*, vol. 1. New York: Funk and Wagnall, 1968.

Mommsen, Wolfgang J. *Theories of Imperialism*. New York: Random House, 1980.

Mommsen, Wolfgang J., and Jürgen Osterhammel, eds. *Imperialism and After*. Boston: Allen and Unwin, 1986.

Moon, Parker Thomas. *Imperialism and World Politics*. New York: MacMillan, 1926.

Motyl, Alexander J. *Sovietology, Rationality, Nationality*. New York: Columbia University Press, 1991.

Nederveen Pieterse, Jan P. *Empire and Emancipation*. New York: Praeger, 1989.

Nekrich, Aleksandr M. *The Punished Peoples: Deportation and Fate of Soviet Minorities at the End of the Second World War*. New York: W.W. Norton, 1974.

Parker, Geoffrey. *The Geopolitics of Domination*. London: Routlege, 1988.

Pipes, Richard. *The Formation of the Soviet Union*. Cambridge: Harvard University Press, 1954.

Platonov, S.O. Lektzii po Russkoy istorii. 9th ed. Petrograd: Iv. Blinov, 1915.

Programma Kommunisiticheskoy Partii Sovetskogo Soyuza, 1961, any edition.

Pushkarev, S.G. *Rossiya v XIX veke*. New York: Izdatel'stvo imeni Chekhova, 1967.

Ra'anan, Gavriel. *International Policy Formation in the USSR: Factional Debates During the Zhdanovshchina*. Hamden, Conn.: Archon Books, 1983.

Rostow, W.W. *The Stages of Economic Growth*. London: Cambridge University Press, 1971.

Ryzhkov, Nikolay Ivanovich. *Perestroika: Istoriia predatel'stv* (*Perestroika*: History of Betrayals). Moscow: Novosti, 1992.

Sbornik dokumentov i materialov po istorii SSSR sovetskogo perioda. Moscow: Izdatel'stvo Moskovskogo Universiteta, 1966.

Semanov, Sergei. *Serdtse rodiny*. Moscow: Moskovskii Rabochii, 1977.

Shaheen, Samad. *The Communist (Bolshevik) Theory of National Self-Determination*. The Hague: W. Van Hoeve, 1956.

Shturman, Dora. *Gorodu i Miru*. Jerusalem: Tretya Volna, 1988.

Silnicky, Frantisek. *Natsional'naya Politika KPSS (1917–1922)* 3d ed., Washington, D.C.: Problems of Eastern Europe, 1990.

Simon, Gerhard. *Nationalism and Policy toward the Nationalities in the Soviet Union*. Boulder, Colo.: Westview Studies on the Soviet Union and Eastern Europe, Westview Press, 1987.

Spengler, Oswald. *The Decline of the West*. New York: Alfred A. Knopf, 1962.

Starchey, John. *The End of Empire*. London: Victor Gollanz, 1959.

Sudebnyi otchet po delu antisovetskogo "Pravo-Trotskistskogo bloka." Moscow: Yuridicheskoye izdatel'stvo Narodnogo Komissariata Yustitsii, 1938.

Swallow, Charles. *The Sick Man of Europe*. London: Ernest Benn, 1973.

Thompson, Terry L. *Ideology and Policy: The Political Uses of Doctrine in the Soviet Union*. Boulder: Westview Special Studies on the Soviet Union and Eastern Europe, 1989.

Thornton, A. P. *Imperialism in the Twentieth Century*. Minneapolis: University of Minnesota Press, 1977.

Toynbee, Arnold J., and Kenneth P. Kirkwood. *Turkey*. London: Charles Scribner's Sons, 1927.

Usubaliyev, T. U. *Druzhba narodov—nash bestzennoye zavoyevaniye*. Moscow: Izdatel'stvo Politicheskoy Literatury, 1977.

Vernadsky, G.V. *Nachertaniye Russkoy istorii* Part One. Prague: Yevraziyskoye Knigoizdatel'stvo, 1927.

———.*The Tsardom of Moscow, 1547-1682* New Haven: Yale University Press, 1969.

Von Rauch, Georg. *A History of Soviet Russia*. New York: Praeger, 1957.

Vucinich, Wayne S. *The Ottoman Empire, Its Record and Legacy*. New York: Van Nostrand, 1965.

Wesson, Robert. *The Imperial Order*. Los Angeles: University of California Press, 1964.

Wimbush, S. Enders, ed. *Soviet Nationalities in Strategic Perspective*. London: Routledge, 1989.

Winslow, E. M. *The Pattern of Imperialism: A Study in the Theories of Power*. New York: Octagon Books, 1972.

Yakovlev, Alexander N., with a preface by Alexander Tsipko. *Predislovie. Obval. Posleslovie.* (Preface. Collapse. Conclusion.) Moscow: Novosti, 1992.

Yanov, Alexander L. *The Russian Challenge and the Year 2000*. New York: Basil Blackwell, 1987.

———.*Weimar Russia* (forthcoming).

Zeman, Z.A.B. *Twilight of the Habsburgs: The Collapse of the Austro-Hungarian Empire.* New York: American Heritage Press, 1971.

ARTICLES

Abele, Daniel. "Recent Developments in Soviet Georgia." *Newsletter of the American Association for the Advancement of Slavic Studies*, vol. 31, no. 2, March 1991.

Afanasyev, Yurii. "Tekst nesostoyavshegosia vystupleniana sjezde narodnykh deputatov." *Russkaya mysl*, 15 September 1989.

Chalmayev, V. "Inevitability." *Molodaya gvardiya*, no. 9, pp. 271 ff.

Cohen, Ariel. "Russia and Her Neighbors: Creating U.S. Policy for Eurasia." *Backgrounder,* no. 966. The Heritage Foundation, Washington, D.C.: 19 November 1993.

Dunlop, John B. "Crackdown." *The National Interest*, Spring 1991.

Fairbanks, Charles H., Jr. Introduction to "The Strange Death of Soviet Communism: An Autopsy." *National Interest*, no. 31, Spring 1993.

Gafurov, B. "Uspekhi natsional'noi politiki KPSS i nekotoryie voprosy internatsional'nogo vospitaniya." *Kommunist*, no. 11, 1958, pp. 10–24.

Galbraith, John S. "The 'Turbulent Frontier' as a Factor in British Expansion." *Comparative Studies in Society History*, vol. 2, no. 2, January 1960, pp. 150–168.

Gallagher, J. A. and R. E. Robinson. "The Imperialism of Free Trade." *Economic History Review*, 2d series VI, I, 1953.

Goble, Paul. "Ethnic Politics in the USSR." *Problems of Communism*, July–August 1989.

Gorbachev, Mikhail S. "Mir na perelome" (World at a breaking point), *Svobodnaya mysl* (Moscow) no. 16, November 1992, p. 10.

"Gorbachev Yields on Sharing Power and Cuts in Prices." *New York Times*, 25 April 1991, pp. A1, A8.

Lenin, V. I. "The Right of Nations to Self-Determination." *Prosveshcheniye*, nos. 4, 5, 6, 1914.

Levin, Bernard. "One Who Got It Right." *National Interest*, no. 31, Spring 1993.

Lobanov, M. "Educated Shopkeepers." *Molodaya gvardiya*, no. 4, 1968, p. 297.

Machavariani, Vladimir. "Natzia, ee kul'tura, i yazyk." *Literaturnaya gruziya*, no. 7, 1971, p. 79.

Ostrovsky, Daniel. "The Mongol Origin of Muscovite Political Institutions." *Slavic Review*, vol. 49, no. 4. Winter, 1990

Pavlov, Maksim. "Ukraina: Natsional'naya Ideya Tsenoy Territorial'nogo Raspada" (Ukraine: national idea at the cost of territorial disintegration.) *Vek XX i mir*, no. 3, 1991.

Platonov, S.O. *Lektsii po Russkoy istorii*, 9th ed. (Petrograd, Iv. Blinov, 1915), p. 153.

Oskotskii, V. "V bor'be s anti-istorizmom", *Pravda*, 6 May 1984, p. 2.

Rybchuk, Mykola. "Two Ukraines?" *East European Reporter*, July–August 1992.

Sestanovich, Stephen. "Did the West Undo the East?" *National Interest*, no. 31, Spring 1993.

Solchanyk, Roman. "Ukraine and Russia: Before and after the Coup." *Report on the USSR*, vol. 3, 27 September 1991.

———."Ukraine, the (Former) Center, Russia and 'Russia'." *Studies in Comparative Communism*, vol. 25, no. 1, March 1992.

Solzhenitsyn, Alexander. "Kak nam obustroit' Rossiyu" (How we should restructure Russia.)

Komsomolskaya pravda, 18 September 1990.

Stalin, J. "Critical Remarks on the National Question." *Prosveshchniye*, nos. 10–12, November–December 1913.

Stalin, K. "The National Question and Social Democracy." *Prosveshcheniye*, nos. 3–5, 1913. It was also published as a pamphlet, *The National Question and Marxism*, 1914, and in Stalin, *Collections of Articles* (Moscow: Commissariat of Nationalities, 1920) and republished in the English edition of I.V. Stalin, *Marxism and the National and Colonial Question* (London: 1937) and in the subsequent *Works*.

Sturua, Melor. "The Real Coup." *Foreign Policy*, Winter 1991/1992.

Tucker, Robert C. "On the 'Letter of an Old Bolshevik' as an Historical Document." *Slavic Review*, vol. 51, no. 4, Winter 1992, pp. 783–784.

ARCHIVAL MATERIALS AND UNPUBLISHED PAPERS

Cohen, Ariel. "Front Organizations as a Tool of Soviet Power Projection in the Third World." Master's thesis, Fletcher School of Law and Diplomacy, Tufts University, 1989.

"K zapiske otdela natsional'nykh otnoshenii TsK KPSS 'O situatsii vokrug problemy sovetskikh nemtsev'" (On the memorandum of the Department of National Relations of the CC CPSU 'On the Situation around the Problem of Soviet Germans.' No. ST-6/36 g, Moscow, 5 October 1990.

Politburo TsK KPSS "O neotlozhnykh merakh po navedeniyu obshchestvennogo poriadka v Azerbaijanskoy SSR i Armianskoy SSR" (Politburo CC CPSU On urgent measures to install public order in the Azerbaijani SSR and Armenian SSR.) Secret. No. P 141/56, Moscow, 23 November 1988, fond 4, opis 102, d. 1058, ll. 22–26.

————."O pravovom regulirovanii rezhima chrezvychainogo polozheniya, obyavlennogo v otdel'nykh mestnostiakh ili po vsey strane s vremmenym vvedeniyem pri neobkhodimosti osobykh form upravleniya" (On legal regulation of the regime of emergency rule, declared in some areas or countrywide, with temporary introduction if a need arises, of special forms of rule.) Secret. No. 144–35, Moscow, 9 December 1988. Source: materials, declassified for the CPSU trial, available in *Tsentr Khranenia Sovremennykh Documentov*.

————."O pervoocherednykh meropriyatiyakh po uluchsheniyu osveshcheniya voprosov mezhnatsional'nykh otnoshenii v tsentral'noy pechati i mestnykh organov massovoy informatsii Azerbaijanskoy i Armianskoy SSR" (On high-priority measures to improve coverage of inter-nationality relations in the central press and local media.) Top Secret. No. P143/2, Moscow, 2 December 1990, fond 3, opis 102, d. 1065, ll. 120–122.

Sekretariata TsK KPSS. "O neotlozhnykh merakh v sviazi s usilenieyem antiarmeyskhikh proyavleniy v ryade regionov strany" (Resolution of the Secretariat of the CC CPSU. On urgent measures in connection with the increase of anti-military manifestations in a number of regions of the country.) No. St-11/17g, from 15 November 1990, and appendix. The report of the party's military policy commission.

————."O rekommendatsiyakh partiinym komitetam v sviazi s trebovaniyami predstaviteley Demokraticheskoy platformy" (On recommendations to party committees in connection with demands by representatives of democratic platform.) Secret. No. St-4/61g, Moscow, from 27 August 1990.

————."O telegramme Prezidenta Azerbaijanskoy SSR, pervogo sekretarya TsK kompartii

Azerbaijana t. Mutalibova A.N." (On the telegram of the president of the Azerbaijani SSR, First Secretary of the Azerbaijani CC Comrade Mutalibov, A.N.) No. St-15/1g, Moscow, 17 January 1991, p. 3., fond 4, op. 42, d. 55, ll. 2–4, 16.

———."Ob obrazovanii i organizatsii raboty kommisii po ekspertnoy otsenke obyektov sobstvennosti KPSS" (Regarding the creation and organization of commissions on special evaluation of CPSU property objects. Secret. No. St-12/1g, Moscow, 1990.

———."Plan deystvii Secretariata TsK KPSS po realizatsii zadach, vytekayushchikh iz postanovleniya Politburo TsK KPSS "Politicheskiye itogi referenduma SSSR i Zadachi Partiynykh Organizatsii" (Plan of action of the Secretariat CC CPSU on the realization of tasks resulting from the Politburo decision on 'Political Outcomes of the USSR referendum and the tasks of party organizations.') Secret. No. St-21/2, Moscow, 10 April 1991.

Schapiro, Leonard. *International Front Organizations and Peace Campaign*, manuscript.

TsK KPSS Postanovleniye "K voprosu o sozdanii Kommunisticheskoi Partii Rossii" (Resolution of the CC CPSU. On the question of the creation of a communist party of Russia.) Top Secret. Moscow, No. 187–115, 8 June 1990.

———."O fraktzii 'Kommunisty za demokratiyu'" (On the faction 'communists for democracy.'). No. St-0996, Moscow, 15 April 1991.

———."O negativnom aspekte mezhdunrodnykh sviazey nekotorykh samodeyatel'nykh obshchestvennykh obyedineniy" (On the negative aspects of the international connections of some informal social groups.) CC memorandum and Politburo resolution concerning it. Top Secret. No. P147/8, Moscow, 25 January 1989, fond 3, opis 102., d. 1102, ll. 90–98.

———."O nekotorykh merakh protivodeystviya podstrekatel'skoy deyatel'nosti zapadnykh radiostantsii", Zapiska 15 Marta 1991 ("On some measures of counteraction against the inciteful activity of Western radios, Memorandum 15 March 1991.) Authored by A. Degtyarev, head of the Ideological Department, and V. Rykin, deputy head of the International Department, Moscow, 1991, unpublished.

———."O nekotorykh predlozheniyakh po izmeneniyu poryadka naznacheniya prokurorov i predsedateley KGB souyuznykh respublik" (On some suggestions on change of order regarding nominations of procurators and chairmen of the KGB of the Union Republics.) Secret. No. 164-103, Moscow, 16 August 1989, fond 3, opis 102, d. 1226, ll. 56, 57, 59–62.

———."O nekotorykh problemakh, svyazabnnykh s reabilitatsiyey repressirovannykh narodov" (On some problems connected with the rehabilitation of repressed peoples.) Moscow, 13 June 1991. This decree was prepared by the Nationality Policy Department of the CC CPSU, No. St-30/7g.

———."O situatsii v baltiiskikh respublikakh" (On the situation in the Baltic Republics. Secret. No. St-16/3, Moscow, 7 February 1991.

———."Ob itogakh vstrech i besed s pariynym aktivom, kommunistami i trudiashchimisia Litovskoy SSR" (On results of meetings and talks with party *aktiv*, communists and workers of the Lithuanian SSR.) Secret. No. St-4/5, Moscow, 29 August 1990.

———."Ob obshchestvenno-politicheskoy obstanovke v zapadnykh oblastyakh Ukrainy" (On the socio-political situation in the western oblasts of Ukraine.) Moscow, 28 August 1990.

———."Zapis' osnovnogo soderzhaniya besedy A.I. Lukyanova s iyerarkhami Russkoy Pravoslavnoy Tserkvi 1 fevralya 1990 goda" (Transcript of the basic content of talk between Anatoly Ivanovich Lukyanov and hierarchs of the Russian Orthodox Church 1 February 1990.) Iskh. No. 131-AL, Moscow, 1990.

Revolutzia i natzional'nyi vopros. Dokumenty i materialy po istorii natzional'nogo voprosa v Rossii i SSSR v XX veke, vol. 3, Moscow, 1933.

Wyman, Lowry. "Soviet Constitutional Law: Towards a New Federalism." Paper presented the at American Association for the Advancement of Slavic Studies annual convention, Washington, D.C., October 1990.

Index

Aron, Raymond, 20
Abalkin, Leonid, 120
Aganbegyan, Abel, 120
Achalov, Viktor, 135
Akhromeev, Sergei, 142
Alexander I, Tsar, 52
Alexander II, Tsar, 52–53, 54, 55, 57
Alexander III, Tsar, 53
Alexei Mikhailovich I, Tsar, 41, 42, 43
Aliev, Geidar, 134
Andreev, Leonid, 92
Andropov, Yurii, 105, 109, 110, 119, 126
Arbatov, Georgii

Bakatin, Vadim V., 123, 139, 140, 141
Baker, James III, 165
Batu Khan, 29, 30
Bessmertykh, Alexander, 141
Berdiayev, Nikolay, 87 .
Beria, Lavrenti, 7, 8, 86, 92, 97–98, 160
Besancon, Alain, 104
Bezobrazov, A.M., 60
Bogomolov, Oleg, 120
Bondarenko, 86
Braichevsky, Mikhaylo, 106
Brailsford, Henry N., 2
Brazaukas, Algirdas, 128
Brezhnev, Leonid, 7, 19, 98, 100–103,
    105, 107, 109, 110, 118, 140, 154, 158,
    162
Brzezinski, Zbigniew, 164
Bukharin, Nikolay, 8, 72

Bush, George, 164–5

Cardinal Casaroli, 131
Cardinal Willebrands, 131
Catherine II (the Great), Empress, 45,
    48–50, 51, 96, 97
Chicherin, 72
Chernenko, K.U., 109, 110, 117
Chubar, Vlas, 86
Churchill, Winston, 154
Clinton, William J., 165
Cohen, B.J., 1, 20–21, 24, 159
Cohen, Stephen P., 140
Conquest, Robert, 164
Constantine, 8
Court, W.H.B., 20

D'Encausse, Hélène Carrère, 110, 164
Denikin, 76
Disraeli, Benjamin, 1
Donskoy, Prince Dimitrii, 89
Doyle, Michael W., 1, 21–22, 24, 32, 33,
    34, 160–1
Doroshenko, Petro, 43
Dzerzhinsky, Felix, 75, 78, 79, 142
Dzhandildin, 99
Dzuba, Ivan, 106

Enver Pasha, 75

Fairbanks, Charles, 164
Fieldhouse, David K., 5

Franco, Francisco, 18

Gafurov, B., 99
Gailbraith, John S., 17
Gallagher, John A., 15–17, 24, 30, 53, 156–7
Gamsakhurdia, Zviad, 136, 137
Genghis Khan, 29, 44
Girenko, 126
Glazunov, Ilya, 103
Godunov, Boris, Tsar, 40
Gorbachev, Mikhail, 8, 10, 22, 52, 53, 100, 105, 117–143, 157–8, 161, 163, 165
Gorbunovs, Anatoljs, 128
Goryn', Mykola, 132
Grechko, Andrey A., 98
Gromov, Boris, 18, 140
Grozny, *See* Ivan IV (the Terrible)
Gumbaridze, Givi, 136

Henze, Paul B., 142, 164
Hilferding, Rudolf, 2
Hitler, Adolf, 72, 90, 105, 162
Hobson, John A., 2, 24, 152
Hrushevsky, M., 85

Ibragimov, Veli, 84
Ivan III, 34–36, 39, 41
Ivan IV (the Terrible), 8, 36, 37–40, 89, 106, 153
Ivanov, Anatoly, 104
Ivashko, Vladimir, 126
Izrailov, Khasan, 92

Kaganovich, 8, 92, 98
Kalanta, Romas, 108
Kalinin, 92
Kalita, Ivan, 31
Kamenev, L., 78
Kautsky, Karl, 3
Kennedy, Paul, 22–24, 30, 32, 162–3
Kerensky, Alexander, 70, 142
Khasan, Izrailov, 42
Khmelnitsky, Bohdan, 42
Khodzhanov, S., 84
Kluchevsky, V.O., 36, 42, 57
Khrushchev, Nikita, 6, 7, 87, 92, 94, 97–

100, 103, 118, 142, 154, 162
Kiernan, Victor G., 2
Kirov, Sergei, 8
Kolbin, Gennady, 127
Kolchak, A., 74
Kosygin, Alexei, 92, 100, 107
Kravchuk, Leonid, 133, 141
Kriuchkov, Vladimir, 130, 141, 142
Kruchina, Nicolay, 126
Kubilay Khan, 30
Kunayev, Dinmukhammed, 126–127
Kuropatkin, 61
Kutuzov, Mikhail, 89

Landes, David, 20
Landsbergis, Vitautas, 123
Laski, Harold, 2
Lebed, Alexander, 18, 135, 165
Lenin, Vladimir, 2–3, 24, 67–80, 109, 110, 128, 151, 152, 153, 154, 160, 162
Levin, Bernard, 164
Ligachev, Yegor, 119, 127, 136
Likhachev, Dmitrii, 140
Luchinsky, Petr, 126
Lukyanenko, Levko, 107, 131
Lukyanov, Anatoly, 121, 124
Luxemburg, Rosa, 2
Lyubchenko, Panas, 86

Machavariani, Vladimir, 106
Machiavelli, Niccolo, 21
Makashov, Albert, 18, 141
Malenkov, Georgi, 8, 97, 98, 160
Malinovsky, R. Ya., 98
Mannerheim, 75
Medvedev, V.A., 123, 141
Meir, Golda, 96
Miasnikov, 78
Mikhail Feodorovich, Tsar, 41
Miliukov, Paul, 69
Mikoyan, Anastas, 8
Molotov, Vyacheslav, 8, 78, 85, 88, 92, 98
Motyl, Alexander J., 143
Mommsen, Wolfgang, 5, 16–17, 24
Morgenthau, Hans, 20
Mutaboliv, Ayaz N., 124–5, 135

Mzhavanadze, V.P., 98

Napoleon III, 1
Nazarbayev, Nursultan, 127, 141
Nederveen Pieterse, Jan P., 17–19, 53,
    110–11, 158–9
Nevelskoy, 58
Nevsky, Prince Alexander, 30, 89
Nevinson, Christopher R.W., 2
Nicholas I, Tsar, 52, 54, 57, 59, 96
Nicholas II, Tsar, 53, 60–61
Nikonov, A., 104
Novodvorskaya, Valeria, 10

Ordzhonikidze, Sergo, 8, 78, 79
Oskotskii, V., 105
Parker, Geoffrey, 13–15, 155–6
Patiashvili, Dzhumber, 136
Päts, K., 88
Paul I, Tsar, 51
Pavlov, Valentin, 141, 142
Pelshe, Arvidas, 128
Petlura, Simon, 72
Petrakov, Nikolay, 120
Perovsky, 58
Peter I (the Great), 9, 13, 39, 41, 45–
    48, 89, 97
Peter III, 48–49
Platonov, S.O., 34
Podgornyi, Nikolay V., 98
Polozkov, Ivan, 121
Polyansky, Dimitrii S., 98, 102
Pozharsky, Prince Dimitrii, 89
Pugo, Boris, 128, 140, 141, 142
Pyatakov, Grigorii, 72

Quazi Mohammed, 96

Reagan, Ronald, 161
Reddaway, Peter, 164
Richelieu, Armand Jean du Plessis 9
Robbins, Lionel, 21
Robinson, Ronald, 15–17, 30, 156–7
Rodionov, Igor, 136
Roosevelt, Franklin Delano, 95
Rostow, W.W., 4
Rudenko, Mykola, 107
Rutskoi, Alexander, 18, 126, 165

Ryskulov, Turar, 82
Ryzhkov, Nikolay I., 118, 119, 120, 123,
    129, 139, 141
Ryzhov, Yu., 126

Sadvokasov, S., 84
Samoilovich, 43
Scherbitsky, Volodymyr, 131
Schumpeter, Joseph A., 2–3, 24, 152
Seal, Anil, 15
Seleznev, 105
Selim I, 8
Semanov, Sergei, 104
Semichastny, V.E., 98
Serdiuk, Z.T., 98
Shamil, 57
Shelepin, Alexander, 102–103
Shelest, Petro E., 98, 106–107, 131
Shenin, Oleg, 123–4, 126
Shevardnadze, Eduard, 118, 141
Shuisky, Vasiliy, Tsar, 40
Shumsky, A., 85
Smetona, A., 88
Sobchak, Anatoly, 142
Soloukhin, Vladimir, 105
Solzhenitsyn, Alexander, 12, 103
Songaila, Ringaudas-Bronislovas 128
Stalin, Joseph, 6, 7–8, 10, 11, 19, 38,
    67–97, 101, 104, 105, 109, 110, 154,
    162
Starchey, John, 1, 2
Starodubtsev, Vasiliy, 142
Struyev, A.I., 98
Sultan-Galiev, Mir Said, 83–84, 106
Suslov, Mikhail, 104, 105
Suvorov, Alexander, 89

Tiberius, 8
Tiziyakov, Alexander, 142
Thompson, Terry L., 102
Thornton, A.P., 4
Trajan, 9
Trotsky, Leon, 8, 76, 80, 96, 153
Tsipko, Alexander, 117, 133
Tucker, Robert, 21

Ustinov, 105

Vaino, Karl, 108, 128
Vagris, Janis, 128
Valikov, Zeki, 72
Valjas, Vaino, 128
Vasiliy III, 36
Vasilyevich, Vasiliy, Tsar, 32–33
Vernadsky, G.V., 31, 34, 35
Vikulov, Sergei, 104
Viner, J., 21
Vinnichenko, Volodimir, 72
Vlasov, Andrei, 89
Volsky, Arkady I., 135
Von Kaufman, 58
Voroshilov, Kliment, 92
Vorotnikov, Vitaly, 119
Voznesensky, A., 92

Wang An-shih, 9
Wertheim, W.F., 18
Wesson, Robert, 5–13, 30, 153, 155
Wimbush, S. Enders, 138
Winslow, E.M., 3
Willebrands, 131
Witte, Sergei, 19, 59–60

Yakovlev, I.D., 98
Yakovlev, Alexander N., 104, 105, 118,
    119, 120, 123, 141, 142
Yanayev, Gennady, 142
Yanov, Alexander, 24
Yazov, Dimitrii, 130, 141, 142
Yeltsin, Boris, 7, 121, 130, 133, 139, 141,
    142, 156, 158, 165
Yezhov, Nikolai, 8

Zaslavskaya, Tatyana, 120
Zhdanov, Andrei, 8, 92
Zhirinovsky, Vladimir, 55, 101, 139, 141,
    165
Zyuganov, Gennady, 165

About the Author

ARIEL COHEN is Senior Policy Analyst in Russian and Eurasian Studies at the Heritage Foundation. He frequently appears on CNN, C-Span, and other television and radio programs. He is a guest commentator with Voice of America. His feature articles and op-eds on developments in the field often appear in the *Washington Times* and other newspapers, magazines, and journals.

CPSIA information can be obtained
at www.ICGtesting.com
Printed in the USA
BVHW081916270219
541326BV00009B/50/P